FEMINIST MEDIA STUDIES

The Media, Culture & Society Series

Editors: John Corner, Nicholas Garnham, Paddy Scannell, Philip
Schlesinger, Colin Sparks, Nancy Wood

FEMINIST MEDIA STUDIES

Liesbet van Zoonen

SAGE Publications
London • Thousand Oaks • New Delhi

First published 1994
Reprinted 1994, 1996, 1999, 2000, 2002, 2003

SAGE Publications Ltd
6 Bonhill Street
London EC2A 4PU

SAGE Publications Inc
2455 Teller Road
Thousand Oaks, California 91320

SAGE Publications India Pvt Ltd
32, M-Block Market
Greater Kailash – I
New Delhi 110 048

British Library Cataloguing in Publication data

Zoonen, Liesbet Van
  Feminist Media Studies. – (Media,
  Culture & Society Series)
    I. Title II. Series
    302.23082

  ISBN 0–8039–8553–3
  ISBN 0–8039–8554–1 (pbk)

Library of Congress catalog card number 94–065541

Typeset by Photoprint, Torquay, Devon
Printed and bound in Great Britain by Athenaeum Press Ltd., Gateshead

Contents

Acknowledgements

This book is a product of discussions with colleagues, questions from students, readings of literature, suggestions from friends, debates within the women's movement, meetings at conferences and a whole range of other factors. I have appreciated these exchanges tremendously even if it has now become impossible to trace how each of them added to this book. However, there are a few people I would like to mention explicitly for their contribution to my understanding of feminist media studies and to this book in particular. I would like to thank Ien Ang who directed my attention to poststructuralist theory and whose relentless critical spirit provides a stimulating intellectual example. The encouragement of Colin Sparks for this book and for earlier projects has always been a source of support and is also something to look forward to in the future. Being close friends with Joke Hermes for some ten years now, both at work and in private, has greatly enhanced my pleasure in academic life and has helped me through the numerous frustrations of academia. My work wouldn't be the same without her.

To Jaap

1

Introduction

During the time I was working on this book, a Dutch radio journalist called me one day to invite me to take part in a round table discussion on Madonna. Her CD and book *Erotica* had just come out and had incited considerable uproar in the Dutch media, as it did elsewhere. I told the reporter I was a great admirer of Madonna and that I would happily take part. This was not at all what he had in mind. He had been hoping for 'a feminist who would object to Madonna's exploitation of her body and to her ventures into pornography'. The feminist he had in mind would have to confront other cultural critics with a more favourable outlook on Madonna. As I did not want to take up this preordained position, I had to disappoint him. To the dismay of the reporter, most other Dutch feminist cultural critics had done so too and the reporter complained that he could not find one feminist to criticize Madonna. The discussion was eventually cancelled.

Something similar happened to a student of mine who was invited to a TV show to talk about her MA thesis on the increased usage of male nudes in mainstream advertisements and commercials. Apparently, the TV-producers expected a story on the reversal of gender roles in popular culture with men now taking on the formerly female role of pin-ups as a sign of emerging equality. When my student argued that her evidence did not quite point in that direction, the item and her contribution were dismissed for being 'overly subtle and not outspoken enough'.[1]

One encounters correspondingly limited expectations of feminist cultural and media critique in discussions with students and colleagues. According to their logics, a feminist viewpoint on the media implies a univocal, confident and unswerving denunciation of popular culture, both for its sexist and oppressive portrayal of women and for the devastating effects it is supposed to have on women and men. Students, colleagues and journalists alike will then argue against such a position claiming that feminism draws a narrow picture of media and cultural practice, although – as the above examples show – this narrow point is exactly the one most journalists want you to make. To make matters more complicated, it is not only non-feminists that construct feminist cultural critique as rigid and austere. Within the women's movement itself, wholesale and merciless condemnations of media output are commonplace too (for example, Davies et al.,1987).

As a feminist media critic one is commuting between the different

realities, requirements and interests of the women's movement, journalism
and – in my privileged case – the academic world, partly to find and fight
the same kinds of circumscribed interpretations of feminist media critique
everywhere. Apparently, a straightforward, univocal and identifiable
feminist voice is what many feminist and non-feminists alike are looking
for, possibly hoping for some sense and direction in the complicated and
sometimes bewildering issues that make up contemporary debates on the
media.

Although this book does intend to create some order in thinking about
feminism and mass media and although I shall argue from a distinct
position in this field, I neither aspire to reprobate (or celebrate) popular
culture, nor do I intend to offer anything like correct approaches, closing
arguments and final answers. On the contrary, the book is meant to
provide insight into the enormous heterogeneity of feminist media theory
and media research that has been produced in the past decades. As such
the book will, I hope, serve the needs of researchers, teachers and students
both in women's studies and media or communication departments.
However, apart from the desire to describe and explain the diversity in
feminist media theory and research, a less modest and possibly more
debatable objective of the book is to advance the field by using a cultural
studies framework to appraise and integrate feminist research on the
distinctive elements of the mass communication process. Disagreement
may arise over the particular interpretation of cultural studies adopted in
this book and more fundamentally over the issue whether a cultural studies
framework really has the potential to advance the field, not only academically
and intellectually but also politically, for the feminist academic project is
intrinsically political.

> With its substantial project, it is the reciprocal relation between theory, politics
> and activism, the commitment of feminist academics to have their work
> contribute to a larger feminist goal – however defined, the blurred line between
> the feminist as academic and the feminist as activist, that distinguishes feminist
> perspectives on the media from other possible perspectives. (van Zoonen,
> 1991a: 34)

Therefore, the book should also be useful for the numerous pressure
groups working towards a more varied portrayal of women and sexual
minorities in the media.

In order to facilitate an evaluation of the theoretical and political
objectives of the book I shall begin with outlining my position in the two
fields that inform this book, feminism and cultural studies.

Feminism

Feminism nowadays is not easily delineated or defined. As a political
project – at least in the context of continental western Europe – for the
greater part its character has moved from a highly visible, vital and
sometimes spectacular countercultural form to a customary but at times

still controversial component of established institutions such as political parties, unions, universities and local and national administrations. Much contemporary feminism has taken on the form of women's caucuses, women's studies and women's bureaux which often prefer to speak of their activities as 'emancipatory' instead of 'feminist'. A similar reluctance to associate with 'feminism' seems to occur among women in their twenties who feel that feminism was a battle of their mothers or older sisters and claim that their own struggles are of a different kind. Andrea Stuart (1990), for instance, argues that women of her generation do want change but don't want to be associated with a presumably outdated and rigid lifestyle. For many black women and women from developing countries, 'feminism' for much longer tended to represent a discourse that seemed neither very sensitive nor very relevant to their concerns, given its initial white, first world and sometimes neocolonial biases (hooks, 1989; Wallace,1975). Such controversies have generated the insight that 'women' cannot be considered a unified constituency and the challenge for feminism to build a politics that acknowledges, respects and accommodates difference.

The political fragmentation of feminism has been both a cause and a consequence of multitudinous developments in feminist theory. In the past twenty years, 'the founding principles of contemporary western feminism have been dramatically challenged, with previously shared assumptions and unquestioned orthodoxies relegated almost to history', according to Michèle Barrett and Anne Philips (1992). They claim that feminism used to be united in the quest for the *cause* of women's oppression, which was generally assumed to lie at the level of the social structure, whether this structure was conceived as capitalism, patriarchy or sexist society. Socialist, radical and liberal feminism respectively withstood each other as to the crucial source of women's oppression, but shared their assumption of a determining last instance. Black feminism, psychoanalysis, poststructuralism and postmodernism, and the revaluation by some feminists of traditional 'womanly' conceptions of morality and care, all undermined suchlike structuralist analyses of women's oppression in pointing out their ethnocentric proclivity, their untempered belief in rationality and progress and their 'Enlightenment' conception of a universal, unified human subject.

Whereas this fragmentation makes it impossible to think of 'feminist' theory as a consistent and homogeneous field, there are still some common concepts that distinguish feminism from other perspectives in the social sciences and the humanities. Its unconditional focus on analysing *gender* as a mechanism that structures material and symbolic worlds and our experiences of them, is hard to find in other perspectives on humanity and society. This is not to say that such a focus will always result in the conclusion that gender is *the* defining factor in human relations and society. Ethnicity, sexuality, class and a range of other discourses intersect with gender in various and sometimes contradictory ways, to the extent that poststructuralist feminist thinkers will argue that gender need not even be *a* defining factor in some human experiences:

> There is no reason why sexual difference should be pertinent in all social relations. To be sure, today many different practices, discourses and institutions do construct men and women [differentially], and the masculine/feminine distinction exists as a pertinent one in many fields. But this does not imply that it should remain the case, and we can perfectly imagine sexual difference becoming irrelevant in many social relations where it is currently found. (Mouffe, 1992: 377)

Along with gender, *power* is another key element of feminist thought, although also conceptualized in widely diverging ways: as a non-issue, for instance, when it is emphasized that women are a disadvantaged, minority group that needs equal opportunities and rights much more than power; or as something individual actors possess, when the power of men (or groups of men) over women is reproved; as an offspring of material conditions, when the economic power relations of capitalism are seen as the cause of women's oppression. Others, however, most notably poststructuralist feminist thinkers argue that power is not a monolithic 'thing' that some groups (men, capitalists, whites) have and others (women, working class, blacks) have not. Society is not constituted by orderly and dichotomous divisions of oppressors and oppressed. As the experience of black feminists has made perfectly clear, one can be subordinated in one relation (of woman vs man) and dominant in another (of white woman vs black woman). The issue for feminism therefore, is not who is 'in power' and who is not, for this will inevitably lead to a rather cynical contest of who is 'most oppressed in contemporary society'. Rather, the challenge is to 'theorize the multiplicity of relations of subordination' (Mouffe, 1992: 372) and to analyse how in these relations of subordination individual and collective identities, such as gender and ethnicity, are being constituted.

Gender and power then, although both very much in debate, form the constituents of feminist theory. The discussions that I referred to only briefly and abstractly now will be taken up in more detail in the next two chapters, resulting in an understanding of gender and power that conceives of gender as 'a particular discourse, that is, a set of overlapping and often contradictory cultural descriptions and prescriptions referring to sexual difference which arises from and regulates particular economic, social, political, technological and other non-discursive contexts' (Chapter 3, p. 33). The influence of poststructuralism is salient here, although I only hesitantly want to use such a label for my own work. Hesitantly because of all the dispute around the meaning of poststructuralism and its twin sisters postmodernism and deconstruction resulting in widely different and contradictory interpretations (for example, Nicholson, 1990). Hesitantly, because I would not know exactly how and where to position myself in such an 'unruly field' as Judith Butler (1992: 6) has called it, nor have I a desire to do so. Such labels are more often requested by and imposed on one by others – in another instance of a search for stable and recognizable identities – than happily taken on for oneself.

Cultural Studies

Judging from recent international best-seller lists, culture and representation have once again become important battle grounds for feminism. Naomi Wolff's (1990) *The Beauty Myth*, concerned with the onerous cultural messages about women's appearances and bodies, Susan Faludi's (1991) *Backlash* on the return of conservatism and anti-feminism in American media, and Camille Paglia's (1990) rancorous *Sexual Persona*, besmirching the women's movement, testify – with other publications – of the cultural struggles going on in contemporary first world societies on the nature of femininity, masculinity and feminism; what does it mean to be a woman or a man, how are feminine and masculine subjectivities and identities constructed, individually as women and men, and collectively as 'Woman' or as 'Man'; is one either woman or man or can one be both; which interests are being served by particular constructions? Such struggles at present seem to be engaged in by feminists, intellectuals, politicians, artists and 'ordinary' women and men, since they are not only fought in the symbolic realm of the mass media and the arts, but also in that area of human existence which is characterized by routine, inconspicuous and ordinary activities, thoughts and feelings – everyday life. They can take on a variety of forms ranging from spectacle and marvel, irony and satire to downright vicious attacks, either in discursive or in physical form, on women (and some – mainly homosexual – men) who dare to transgress the boundaries of gender as defined by their adversaries. The astonishing and often exasperating publicity surrounding the American lawyer Hillary Rodham Clinton, married to the American president Bill Clinton, epitomizes these struggles just as do the controversies on other highly visible women such as Margaret Thatcher or Madonna. On a more mundane and imponderable level too gender is ceaselessly being contested, both by women (and again some men) deliberately and joyfully undermining prevailing definitions of gender and by those yearning to maintain the old and predictable dichotomies.

It is therefore hardly surprising that 'culture' has gained new importance on the feminist political and academic agenda. Michèle Barrett (1992: 204) has observed a growing interest of feminists in culture which she defines as the processes of symbolization and representation. Apprehending these processes would possibly generate a better understanding of 'subjectivity, the psyche and the self'. According to bell hooks (1990: 31), the engagement with culture enables feminists to do 'intellectual work that connects with habits of being, forms of artistic expression, and aesthetics that inform the daily life of writers and scholars as well as a mass population'.[2] Sara Franklin, Celia Lury and Jackie Stacey also claim an increasing importance of cultural issues for feminism, but use a much wider notion of culture:

> The power relations of pornography, abortion, male violence, technology and science have increasingly come to be seen not only in terms of social institutions and practices, but also in terms of symbolic meanings, the formation of identities and deeply-rooted belief systems. (1991: 11)

As the slightly different emphases of these authors suggest, to say that this book is aimed at developing a *cultural* understanding of the relation between gender, power and mass media still needs clarification. 'Culture' is probably one of the most widely used concepts in the humanities and the social sciences. A conceptualization of culture as having to do with ways of life, is what I will be referring to in this book. To be more precise, 'culture' concerns 'the conditions and the forms in which meaning and value are structured and articulated within a society' (Corner, 1991: 131). These processes take place in institutionalized forms where the production and reception of mass mediated meanings are concerned and in everyday life when it concerns the daily symbolic interactions between human beings, within and between subcultures and other collectivities. Inevitably, gender is a, if not the, crucial component of culture.

Although it would be hard to identify a coherent theoretical and empirical programme to which a majority of feminist communication scholars would adhere, it does seem justified to say that cultural studies approaches have become somewhat dominant in the field. Cultural studies nowadays appears in many different disguises (Grossberg et al., 1992) that share among other things a concern with manifestations of popular culture and issues of representation and collective identities, such as national, ethnic and gender identities. Like feminist or women's studies, cultural studies, having grown out of Marxist theory and left politics, is linked to progressive political movements and concerns outside the academic world. Both have had the ambition to produce a cultural critique that contributes to a better understanding of relations of power and exclusion which may even turn out to be inspirational to undermine them. However deeply although uneasily involved in poststructuralism and postmodernism, feminist and cultural studies alike have abandoned the unmitigated belief in the relevance and potentiality of academic knowledge to feminist and other progressive political projects, leading to a renewed discussion as to what the relation between the two domains could be. In feminist media studies this debate has focused for an important part on the 'politics of pleasure', in particular on the meaning of popular genres like soap opera and melodrama, women's and gossip magazines or romances for the emancipation or liberation of women. As Ien Ang (1985: 118) in her study of *Dallas* succinctly summarizes: 'Is *Dallas* good or bad for women?' In addition to that Ang raises the question whether studying *Dallas* is good or bad for women? Paradoxically, it seems that the growing theoretical and empirical sophistication of feminist studies on, for instance, soap operas has not only jeopardized its relevance for a critical feminist media politics but also diminished its potential as a comprehensive cultural critique. 'For example, as we acknowledge the pleasure women derive from watching soap operas it becomes increasingly difficult to find moral justifications for criticizing their contribution to the hegemonic construction of gender identities' (van Zoonen, 1991a: 35). The uneasy connection between the pleasures of popular culture and the political aims of feminism is by now more or less a classic issue in feminist media theory, emerging from the particular conjunction between cultural and feminist studies.

Notwithstanding the successful and inspiring alliance between feminist and cultural studies, not all feminist studies are cultural studies and not all cultural studies are feminist studies (cf.Franklin et al., 1991). For instance, with some exceptions (d'Acci, 1987), the area of media production has been largely neglected by feminist communication scholars working within a cultural studies paradigm. That sector is well covered by other researchers aiming at producing labour statistics that can inform emancipatory policy measures, the assumption usually being that masculine discourse in media texts can be attributed to the quantitative and qualitative dominance of men in media production. For instance, in the context of journalism, where the problem has been raised often, many feminist communication scholars have claimed that an increase in the number of female journalists would result in a more balanced and less sexist way of reporting. The relation between male dominance among media professionals and masculine discourse in media texts is another enduring issue in feminist media theory, although one that could benefit from a more theoretical approach *per se*, and as I shall elaborate in Chapter 4, from a cultural studies input in particular (cf. van Zoonen, 1988).

Looking at some other perennial themes and issues in feminist media theory and research taken up within and outside a cultural studies paradigm, for example pornography, advertising, the male and the female gaze, effects of media on gender identities, the relation between feminist media critic and female audiences – one sees the challenge to review all this material while at the same time anchoring it satisfactorily in a coherent analytical framework. Being partly an overview of existing research, intending a breadth of coverage, the book will to some extent have an inevitable collage-like quality, moving for example from a discussion of feminist journalists' working experiences in Chapter 4, to psychoanalytical film theory in Chapter 6 and to television audience research in Chapter 7. As said, however, a second purpose of the book is to apply a cultural studies framework to appraise and integrate feminist research on the distinctive elements of the mass communication. Whereas this perspective will be developed fully in Chapters 2 and 3, in order to understand the structure of the book it is necessary first to allude to some central concepts, in particular the 'encoding' and 'decoding' of meaning in media texts (Hall, 1973).

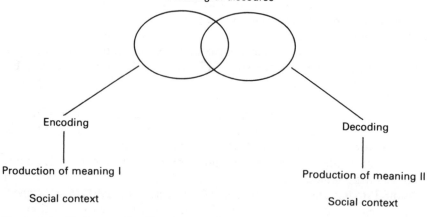

Figure 1.1   *Hall's encoding/decoding model*

Encoding/decoding

A slightly modified version of Stuart Hall's 'Encoding/Decoding' model
(see Figure 1.1) serves as a framework to order the different subjects and
themes covered by feminist media theory and research. The central
problematic of the model involves the construction of meaning in media
discourse which is presupposed to take place at different 'moments' in the
process. In institutionalized processes of media production meaning is
'encoded' in discursive forms that do not constitute a closed ideological
system but in which the contradictions of the production process are
enclosed. The thus encoded structure of meaning serves in another
'moment' of meaning production, the decoding practices of audiences.
Encoding and decoding need not be symmetrical, that is, audiences do not
need to produce meaning similar to that produced by the media institution.
In fact, a certain 'misunderstanding' is likely, because of 'the a-symmetry
between the codes of "source" and "receiver" at the moment of transformation in and out of the discursive form. What are called "distortions"
or "misunderstandings" arise precisely from the *lack of equivalence*
between the two sides of production' (Hall, 1973: 131, italics in original).

A crucial feature of the 'encoding/decoding' model is that media
discourse is supposed to be produced by media institutions and audiences
at the same time, not as an activity of single institutions or individuals but
as a social process embedded in existing power and discursive formations.
Gledhill (1988) identifies this process as 'cultural negotiation' which takes
place at the level of media institutions, texts and audiences. Institutional
negotiation results from conflicting frames of reference within media
organizations, for instance between 'creative' personnel guided mainly by
professional and aesthetic logic and managing directors having commercial
interests in mind. Negotiations at the level of the texts concern the
different meanings available in a text as a result of the contradictions in

...ized production, and as a result of independent and un-
... interactions between contending signs and codes in a text. Such
...egotiations' reverberate in the reception of media discourse, that
...se and interpretation of media texts by audiences producing their
...ited similar or new meanings.

...ough Hall's model has been criticized on various grounds (Morley,
...it does provide a useful framework to review and arrange feminist
... theory and research, suggesting the central question to be: how is
...der discourse negotiated in the 'moments' of the construction of media
meanings – production, text and reception? Evidently, feminist media
theory and research is not part of an orchestrated research programme and
the material available to address that question is widely divergent employing diverse theories and methodologies and focusing on different media
and genres. Feminist research on media production for instance has
concentrated primarily on the work of female and male journalists in
various news media. Analyses of the production of other genres is rare.
Likewise, feminist studies of media reception has dealt with genres popular
among women such as soaps, romances or women's magazines, neglecting
other genres such as news or sports. Clearly the divergence within cultural
studies between the *public knowledge project* focusing on the politics of
information and the viewer as citizen, and the *popular culture project*
concerned with entertainment and the social problematics of taste and
pleasure (Corner, 1991) involves a traditional gender division as well, with
feminist studies seriously underrepresented in the public knowledge
project. It is not my aim nor in my capacity to redress that imbalance in this
book. Inevitably, the book as a whole will reflect the state of the
field. However, the adoption of a leading principle – the negotiation of
gender discourse in media meanings – and an organizing framework (Hall's
encoding/decoding model) may be just enough to keep the diversity
together.

The book then is organized as follows: in Chapter 2 I will present a brief,
to some extent historical overview of feminist thought and debate on the
media, in particular on three central themes: stereotypes, pornography and
ideology. These debates have some issues and problematics in common on
which – in Chapter 3 – I shall build my own perspective on feminist media
theory and research and belabour the negotiation of gender discourse. The
next part of the book covers the different 'moments' of constructing gender
in media meanings. In Chapter 4 I shall review feminist research on media
production and producers and cover the 'encoding' of gender in the
production process. Chapter 5 deals with meanings in media texts, an area
extensively covered – deserving a book of its own – and characterized by a
division between mainly social scientific research on gender roles and
stereotypes in large quantities of media output, and structuralist/semiotic
analysis of feminity in single media texts. To focus the issues concerned I
shall limit the discussion to advertising, a genre in the forefront of feminist
attention. Chapter 6 still deals with media texts and discusses work in

feminist film theory, focusing on the objectification of the female body and the male gaze, female pleasure and on the seemingly reverse problematic of the objectification of the male body and the female gaze. Whereas Chapter 6 is concerned with implied audiences, that is, the audience positions made available by the codes and conventions of the text, in Chapter 7 the interpretation and experience of actual audiences is discussed (the 'decoding moment'), in particular the use and interpretation of 'women's genres' such as soap and romances by female audiences.

The last part of the book is concerned with methodological and 'political' issues: in Chapter 8 I shall suggest how feminist and interpretative research methods can be used in the analysis of the core problematic of this book: the construction of gender in the various 'moments' of media production. Finally, in the concluding chapter the issue of 'politics' returns on the agenda, looking for an articulation of theory, research and politics that would be relevant to the feminist media project.

Notes

1. The representation of the male body will be taken up in detail in Chapter 6.
2. I am indebted to Rosi Braidotti's work (1993) for directing my attention to this particular quote in bell hooks' work.

2
'New' Themes

The media have always been at the centre of feminist critique. In the book that stimulated the revival of the American women's movement in the mid-1960s, the media and in particular women's magazines were scorned for their contribution to 'The Feminine Mystique' – as the book was called – the myth that women could find true fulfilment in being a housewife and a mother. Author Betty Friedan – a former women's magazine editor herself – accused the media and a range of allied experts such as doctors, psychiatrists and sociologists, of installing insecurity, fear and frustration in ordinary women who could not and would not live up to the ideal of the 'happy housewife heroine' (Friedan, 1963). In another feminist classic, *The Female Eunuch*, Germaine Greer (1971) raged against mass produced romantic fiction for conning women into believing in fairy tales of heterosexual romance and happiness.

Obviously, the media had to become important targets of the American women's movement. American communication legislation offered ample opportunity to challenge broadcasters' policies towards the portrayal and employment of women. In the 1970s and 1980s many local television stations saw their legal licence to broadcast challenged by women's groups because of their sexist representation of women and their neglect of women's issues. Media, and television in particular, were supposed to provide women with more positive and liberating role models instead. Although none of these legal complaints ('petitions to deny') was success-ful, they did raise the awareness of broadcasters to the depiction of women, and they triggered academic research to document and support the claims of the women's movement (Cantor, 1988).

In other countries the portrayal of women in the media has aroused similar impassioned feminist critique. For instance, in the mid-1980s, Clare Short, a British Labour Party Member of Parliament, became so infuriated by the display of topless pin-up girls in the tabloid press that she introduced a bill to ban these 'Page Three Girls'. Her campaign received enormous support from ordinary women throughout Britain who finally felt encour-aged to express their frustration about what they saw as a daily insult that had to be endured in public places like subways and workplaces, as well as in the home from husbands or sons. Newspapers and MPs of both parties were extremely critical of Short's campaign and accused her of trying to introduce censorship. Other arguments brought against Short claimed that she represented a prudish morality, an anachronism in a modern, sexually liberated society. Parts of the gay movement and the women's movement feared that, once accepted, Short's bill would legitimize government measures against gay literature and other representations of gay sexuality. There were also feminists who suggested calling for equal treatment by publishing pictures of male pin-ups. Although Short's bill was not passed, the uproar it caused forced one tabloid to move (temporarily) its Page Three Girl to page seven, but more importantly it launched a wider national debate on the representation of women in the media (Short, 1991).

As these examples show, representation has always been an important battleground for contemporary feminism. The women's movement is not only engaged in a material struggle about equal rights and opportunities for women, but also in a symbolic conflict about definitions of femininity (and by omission masculinity). Such a double-edged politics is currently found in other new social movements as well. Alberto Melucci (1988) has characterized new social movements as **new media** that 'publicize' existing conflicts and produce a symbolic challenge to the dominant codes of society. The communication of that challenge exists within a symbolic excess of old and new, strange and familiar, common and exotic signs, and is reconstructed by other communicators, the mass media being definitely among the most powerful (cf. van Zoonen, 1994).

Since the early 1970s a considerable collection of feminist action and thought about the media has accumulated. The purpose of this chapter is to introduce the reader to some salient issues in feminist media theory and research of the past two decades which will lead up to the theoretical framework laid out in Chapter 3. There are several ways of structuring such an overview. A number of authors, myself among them (van Zoonen, 1991a, 1992a), have used typologies of feminist thought. Leslie Steeves (1987) for instance, distinguishes between radical feminism which has a strong interest in pornography, liberal feminism concerned among other things with stereotypes and gender socialization, and Marxist and socialist feminism focusing on the interaction between gender, class and ideology. In Steeves' classification psychoanalysis and cultural studies are discussed in the context of socialist feminism. I use similar distinctions in an article called 'Feminist perspectives on the media' (1991a) seeing cultural studies, however, as a body of thought in itself departing in some fundamental ways from socialist feminism.

The problems with such classifications are manifold. To begin with political and theoretical strands tend to be conjoined in a manner that obscures important differences between and within theories. Liberal feminism, for instance, is much more prominent in the United States than in Britain or continental Europe where the impression is that liberal feminism is a political strategy mainly that has not produced the same elaboration of theory as has arisen from socialist and radical traditions.[1] This is connected with a second point – that liberal, radical and socialist feminism have, over the past twenty years, undergone considerable change and encompass a range of theoretical developments and a huge diversity of positions. Distinctions that used to be meaningful, for instance between liberal and radical feminism, have now become blurred (Eisenstein, 1981) and certainly at odds with the current fragmentation of feminist thought. A diversity, moreover, which is not culturally consistent, in the sense that radical feminism in the Netherlands, for instance, is of a different nature from radical feminism in the United States or in Britain.

Presenting feminism in typologies tends to obscure this change and diversity, and also the ways in which feminist perspectives have developed through debate, critique and countercritique. The existence and importance of black feminism – which is itself diverse and not a monolithic entity – has not been easily recognized in any of these typologies. The same goes for other typologies based on theoretical rather than political differences. Kaplan (1987), for instance, distinguishes between essentialist and non-essentialist feminism; Hermes (1993) differentiates modernist from post-modernist thought; others discern between thinking in terms of gender equality versus thinking in terms of gender difference (Hermsen and van Lenning, 1991). Apart from the explanatory and catalyst value of these juxtapositions, such dichotomies are also bound to elide the variety and intermingledness of feminist theory.

Another problem of many of the typologies mentioned, political and theoretical, is that they are construed out of general feminist thinking (for example, Jaggar, 1983; Tong, 1989) and then applied to feminist media studies imposing a more or less extraneous and not always relevant order on the field. An example of that can be seen in my own typology of liberal, radical and socialist feminist media theory (van Zoonen, 1991a). I suggested that research on stereotypes and socialization belongs typically to liberal feminist media research given its epistemological and political-philosophical premises, therewith overlooking the fact that many feminist communication scholars engaged in that area do not perceive themselves as 'liberal' at all and consider their work misrepresented (for example, Gallagher, 1992).

A typology therefore does not seem to be the most adequate instrument to provide the reader with an introduction to some issues in feminist media critique.[2] I will adopt a different angle, following Brunsdon's observation (1993) that in the past two decades feminist media critique has moved from outside to inside the academic disciplines of communication, media and cultural studies.

> While in 1976 the feminist critic writes a primary address to her movement sisters, in a tone quite hostile to the mass media, yet concerned to justify her attention to television, by the mid-1980s she inhabits a more academic position, tends to address other scholars and is beginning to be anthologized in books used on both Communication and Women's Studies courses. (1993: 309)

Useful questions for this chapter thus may be how and to what extent feminism has acquired a position in these fields, how its themes have been incorporated into the agenda and how it contributed to a paradigm shift.

These particular questions are inspired by Sandra Harding's landmark study on gender and science, *The Science Question in Feminism* (1987).

Feminist critiques on communication studies[3]

Harding identifies several ways in which feminist scholars have criticized traditional science. To begin with feminists have drawn attention to the underrepresentation of women in higher education and as scientists. Formal and informal discrimination have prevented women from gaining access to the academic world. In communication and cultural studies, both in the United States and Europe,[4] the situation is not fundamentally different, with male faculty dominating, despite the high numbers of female students (Schamber, 1989).

Secondly, feminists have pointed to the sexist use of science and shown how disciplines such as biology and the social sciences have contributed to the needs of 'sexist, racist, homophobic and classist social projects' (Harding, 1987: 21). Helen Baehr (1980: 144) claims that the selection of an all-female sample in the by now classic communication study on media and personal influence 'the two-step flow' study of Katz and Lazarsfeld (1955), reflected 'the fact that American women represented an enormously profitable pool of consumers whom it was vital to "persuade" via advertising'. According to Baehr the study obscured the real interests of women in according them relevance as housewives and consumers only.

A third type of critique on traditional science concerns the themes, theories and methodologies which have been shown to be male-biased in the sense that women's problems have been ignored in many research agendas and that the particular experience of men has often been presented as having universal validity, overlooking the particular experiences of women. Apart from the neglect of specific themes, an issue to which I shall return later, communication studies has at least one exceptional case here in the 'two-step flow' study mentioned before. Although based on an all-female sample, it did acquire classic status as the way media *in general* influence people, thus accrediting universal value to the experiences of women, usually perceived as merely particular.

A fourth challenge feminists have presented to science, according to Harding, concerns the tenets of science itself. Feminists have claimed that objectivity, value-freeness and neutrality are offsprings of the hegemony of masculine modes of thinking that cherish dichotomies such as objectivity vs subjectivity, reason vs emotion, expert vs lay knowledge, abstract vs concrete, etc. It is argued that traditional science not only ignores women's themes and experiences, it also denies the validity of women's ways of knowing. Brenda Dervin (1987), discussing the potential contribution of feminist scholarship to the field of communication, argues that feminist scholars bring a 'female' viewpoint to the field, which is 'a new perspective, a new microscope for observation, that is not possible of somebody who is in the system. Women live outside the master's house[5] and therefore cannot use the master's tools for their own articulations' (1987: 113).

Finally, the feminist challenge to traditional science has produced a postmodernist understanding of science as socially constructed, as situated knowledge, grounded in the social experiences of its practitioners which are traversed by the contradictory claims of being a scientist, black, woman, feminist, socialist etc. A notable example in communication studies is Janice Winship's analysis (1987) of women's magazines in which she does not claim to speak for all women or from 'a female experience', but in which she uses her own individually, socially and culturally specific preferences as a starting point to understand the differential meanings of these magazines.

The multifaceted critique of feminist researchers does not seem to have resulted in an acknowledgement of the importance of gender issues in communication studies as a whole.[6] To mention some arbitrary examples: in Denis McQuail's bestselling *Introduction to Mass Communication Theory*, first published in 1983, there is no reference to 'woman', 'gender', 'sexuality' or other feminist concerns. In the revised second edition in 1987 one paragraph on feminist content analysis has been added. In special issues on communication research in western and eastern Europe published by the *European Journal of Communication* (1990) and *Media, Culture & Society* (1990) references to gender or feminism are all but absent. Moreover, there are still various areas in mass communication research that seem relatively untouched by feminist research, such as the study of new information technologies (van Zoonen, 1992a) and (tele)communication policy (Moyal, 1992) or research focusing on media and citizenship, such as political communication and news research (van Zoonen, 1991b, 1994). Although sometimes labelled a little derisorily as the 'add women and stir' approach (cf. Franklin et al., 1991: 2), in such areas it is still necessary to raise the simple question: how about women? In these areas Reinharz's description of the past still holds: 'At first, the very act of discovering sexism in scholarship was revolutionary. . . . it was radical simply to study women' (1992: 11).

In spite of the marginal position of feminist media studies in the discipline as a whole, there are at least two themes taken up and/or revitalized by feminist communication scholars which have gained a more habitual importance: stereotypes and gender socialization, and ideology, the latter of course erstwhile prominent in critical studies. Pornography, a third prominent issue in feminist media theory and research, has not gained similar interest and status within the academic sphere. The observant reader will notice that these are the three themes which some authors say 'belong' to particular currents of feminism, respectively liberal, radical and socialist feminism. However, as said earlier, debate on stereotypes, pornography and ideology has been engaged in by researchers from diverse feminist backgrounds, undermining theoretical or political 'monopolies' on any of these issues.

Feminist themes in communication studies

Stereotypes and socialization

Initially, the new themes that feminist media scholars added to the agenda of communication research were the stereotypical images of women in the media and the effects of these images on the audience. Rakow (1986) identifies two reasons for these particular themes: they were key elements of early feminist texts, such as Betty Friedan's *The Feminine Mystique* (1963), and they fitted well into the empirical research paradigm of communication studies. The latter is supported by an argument of Stacey and Thorne (1985) that a prerequisite for a successful intervention in any discipline is the existence of a tradition or subject matter related to feminist concerns.

The early review articles of images and effect research did not yet address the biases of communication research itself and seemed rather optimistic about the flexibility of the discipline. Busby (1975), for instance, claims that the latest feminist movement may have raised some consciousness within the academic community. Tuchman, however, is much more critical of the communication research community and argues that its scholars have not been very interested in the subject 'woman': 'And why should they? Before the advent of the women's movement these stereotypes seemed natural, "given". Few questioned how they developed, how they were reinforced, or how they were maintained. Certainly the media's role in this process was not questioned' (1978a: 5).

Tuchman was among the first to produce research within a well-developed theoretical framework. In her introductory statement to a collection of articles about women and the media, she says:

> Our society, like any other society, must pass on its social heritage from one generation to the next. The societal need for continuity and transmission of dominant values may be particularly acute in times of rapid social change, such as our own. Then, individuals need some familiarity with the past, if the society is to survive, but they must also be prepared to meet changing conditions. Nowhere is that need as readily identifiable as in the area of sex roles. (1978a: 3)

Drawing from different research data, Tuchman shows that at present the media fail to live up to this function. While an impressive social transformation has taken place with over half of all American women in the labour force, television shows hardly anything of the kind. Television symbolically annihilates women, according to Tuchman, and tells society women are not very important by showing an overwhelming majority of men in almost all kinds of television output. Only in soap operas do women dominate the screen. Not only does television tell us that women don't matter very much except as housewives and mothers, but also it symbolically denigrates them by portraying them as incompetent, inferior and always subservient to men. The symbolic annihilation of women will endanger social development, according to Tuchman, for girls and mature women lack positive images on which to model their behaviour:

Girls exposed to 'television women' may hope to be homemakers when they are adults, but not workers outside the home. Indeed, as adults these girls may resist work outside the home unless necessary for the economic well being of their families. Encouraging such an attitude in our nation's girls can present a problem in the future . . . the active participation of women in the labor force is vital to the maintenance of the American economy. (Tuchman, 1978a: 7)

Tuchman's analysis contains the basic elements of a functionalist feminist media theory: media reflect society's dominant social values and symbolically denigrate women, either by not showing them at all, or by depicting them in stereotypical roles. The models that media offer are restrictive and endanger the development of girls and women into complete human beings and socially valuable workers. Why the media function in such a counterproductive way is not explicitly answered by Tuchman, but other authors working in this paradigm have pointed to the dominance of male broadcasters and journalists whose gender socialization causes them to reproduce society's dominant values (Butler and Paisley, 1980).

An abundance of this type of research has been carried out all over the world, using primarily quantitative content analysis and social experimental methods. Gallagher (1980, 1985) summarized these projects and found depressing similarities between western industrialized, eastern communist and southern developing countries: women are underrepresented in the media, in production as well as in content. Moreover, the women that do appear in media content tend to be young and conventionally pretty, defined in relation to their husband, father, son, boss or another man, and portrayed as passive, indecisive, submissive, dependent etc. Social experimental studies trying to establish the impact of these sex role stereotypes on children in particular have shown contradictory results. Some studies support the socialization hypothesis, while others find too many intervening factors to justify a conclusion about media effects.

Recently, black researchers have raised the question of how black women are portrayed in western mass media. A study by Preethi Manuel (1985) of blacks in British television drama (referring to people from African, Indian, Pakistani and West Indian origin) showed that of the total number of actors involved in more than 600 drama programmes, only 2.25 per cent were black. Mostly they were cast as low-paid workers, students and law breakers, or as background figures. Black women hardly appeared at all. Most worrying to Manuel is the complete absence of black families from British TV drama. She concludes:

In relegating blacks to the 'fringe' and giving them little to say, in portraying them as belonging to a subversive minority, it can only be said that negative attitudes of society towards blacks will be perpetuated. Black children are growing up without positive role models and consequently with a lowered self-image – the effect on white children is potentially as damaging. Inevitably, the pressing need for fair representation is inseparable from the pressing need for a harmonious existence in today's 'multi-cultural society'. (Manuel, 1985: 41–3)

From Melbourne Cummings' (1988) discussion of the changing image of the black family on American television, it appears that television draws from widespread stereotypes about black women. One stereotype of the black woman that is particular to American history is the loud but lovable 'mammy to massa's three little children' (1988: 81). More widespread stereotypes mentioned by Cummings concern the image of the black matriarch, the overpowering black woman and the sexually insatiable black woman. The latter stereotype pervades the European colonial heritage as well. Rana Kabbani's (1986) work on European myths of the Orient shows how racist and sexist illusions of uninhibited black female sexuality abound in the work of British and French writers and painters.[7]

Theory and research on stereotypes has proved particularly valuable for its exhaustive documentation of stereotypes and prejudice which women in many countries have been able to use to raise the awareness of communicators and put pressure on their media to improve the images of women. However, on a theoretical as well as an empirical level this approach is not very satisfactory. I shall briefly mention some points that will be taken up in further detail in Chapter 3. Many analyses tend to generalize about the stereotypical nature of media content being insensitive to the specificities of genres, media and audience experiences. Further, the assumption that media content can be adequately characterized by a reference to the stereotypical *roles* of its population is rather incomplete. The mutual relationships of characters, their contribution to and involvement in the narrative, their visualization and their status in a particular genre, are all equally important. Finally, this type of research assumes an unequivocal meaning and effect of media content, with stereotypical images leading more or less unproblematically to stereotypical effects and traditional socialization patterns. The audience is thus implicitly conceptualized as a rather passive mass, merely consuming media messages.

Pornography

Within academic feminist media research and within communication studies, the study of pornography has not gained the same weight as the analysis of stereotypes or ideology. In an early assessment on the type of research on pornography done in mainstream communication studies, Thelma McCormack (1978) has noted that the majority of studies are seriously biased toward a male perspective, in the sense that they focus on how pornography functions for the male consumer ignoring its degrading portrayal of women. McCormack therefore advances a perspective on pornography from the viewpoint of conflict and inequality: 'Pornography would be seen as an extreme form, almost a travesty, of sexual inequality in which women serve as sex objects to arouse and satisfy men and nothing more' (1978: 578). In McCormack's proposal the feminist debates on pornography resound. Many feminists argue that pornography objectifies women for men's pleasures, that it contributes to the eroticization of power and violence and hence the construction of forms of masculine sexuality which seek pleasure through power and violence. Particularly in the United States considerable theoretical and political work has been done in the area of the representation of women's bodies in pornographic magazines, videos and movies. Radical feminists in particular have initiated most feminist activities against pornography,[8] such as the 'Take back the Night' demonstrations, tours through pornodistricts and assaults on pornoshops (Lederer, 1980). Pornography is considered the ultimate cultural expression of men's hatred against women; it is seen as a form of sexual violence against women, simultaneously a source and a product of a deeply misogynistic society. As one of the key authors in this debate, Andrea Dworkin (1980: 289) says: 'Pornography exists because men despise women, and men despise women because pornography exists.' Pornography cannot be considered as the mere representation of sexual fantasies, or as a potentially liberating depiction of nudity and sexuality, it is rather the glorification of male power over women.

Not all forms of sexual representation are being opposed. Rosemarie Tong (1989: 113) summarizes the distinction made by many feminists between *erotica* (from the Greek word 'eros', love or a creative principle) and *thanatica* (from the Greek word 'thanatos', death or destructive principle). 'Whereas erotic representations show sexual representations between fully consenting, equal partners who identify emotionally with each other, thanatic representations show sexual representations in which full consent, real equality and emotional identification are absent.' According to Tong, thanatic or pornographic representations encourage men to treat women as mere objects, thereby reproducing male dominance. Apart from particular attributes and violent 'narratives' in pornography, various visual codes construct its sexist and misogynistic character: by looking directly and invitingly at the camera lens the pornographic model signifies willingness and readiness to subsume to the male consumer, building on, and reinforcing, the patriarchal ideology of women as available objects; the pornographic convention of fragmenting the female body into close-ups of her sexual organs reduces women to functional, depersonalized body parts for male satisfaction; and finally particular camera angles and body postures construct an image of women as powerless and submissive, as objects of male desire for sexual power and domination (Coward, 1982).

Pornography arouses so much anger among many feminists because they assume it has a serious influence on male behaviour towards women. It is thought to encourage and legitimize violence against women as expressed in the feminist motto: Pornography is the Theory and Rape the Practice. This so-called 'harm principle' used to be a core issue in feminist efforts to ban pornography, however it turned out to be difficult to find compelling empirical evidence to convince legislators of the harmful effects of pornography. Two US presidential committees have studied the effects of pornography extensively and produced contradictory results. In 1970 the Lockhart Commission on Obscenity and Pornography found no evidence that the use of pornography played a role in criminal behaviour among youths or adults. More than a decade later, the Meese Commission concluded that violent pornography did have an effect on male aggressive behaviour. Both commissions were subject to heavy criticism, among other reasons for relying on highly controversial research projects. With such ambiguity over the relationship between pornography and sexual violence, it seemed hard to justify feminist claims to ban pornography. Andrea Dworkin, a radical feminist activist, and Catherine MacKinnon, a radical feminist lawyer, therefore advanced another approach to introduce legislation against pornography. Instead of defining pornography as a criminal act endorsing violence against women, they proposed to see pornography as a civil rights violation against which women, and others who feel offended, should be able to take legal action. In their proposed anti-pornography ordinance they define pornography as:

> Pornography is the sexually explicit subordination of women, graphically depicted, whether in pictures or in words, that also includes one or more of the following: women are presented as dehumanized sexual objects, things or commodities; or women are presented as sexual objects who enjoy pain or humiliation; or women are presented as sexual objects who experience sexual pleasure in being raped; or women are presented as sexual objects tied up or cut up or mutilated or bruised or physically hurt; or women are presented in postures of sexual submission, servility or display; or women's body parts – including but not limited to vaginas, breasts and buttocks – are exhibited, such that women are reduced to those parts; or women are presented as whores by nature; or women are presented being penetrated by objects or animals; or women are presented in scenarios of degradation, injury, abasement, torture, shown as filthy or inferior, bleeding, bruised or hurt in a context that makes these conditions sexual. (in Burstyn, 1985)

It is argued that pornography harms women's opportunities for equal rights, that it creates harassment and private degradation, that it promotes sexual violence and inhibits a just enforcement of the law, and that it significantly restricts women from the full exercise of their citizenship and participation in public life. Therefore, the MacKinnon/Dworkin proposal would enable women to sue the producers, distributors and exhibitors of pornography on the basis of discrimination charges.

The MacKinnon/Dworkin proposal, however, drew mixed support. In the city of Minneapolis many feminists and the liberal city council encouraged the proposal. A similar law was passed in the city of Indianapolis, but here the support came from right wing fundamentalists only. Ultimately, the US Supreme Court declared the ordinances unconstitutional, in contradiction with the First Amendment, which guarantees press freedom in the United States.

MacKinnon and Dworkin's work has incited dramatic and divisive conflicts within the American women's movement. The proposal generated a curious political coalition of feminists and fundamentalist Christians which made many women activists uncomfortable; gay activists saw the representation of gay sexuality in various cultural forms threatened; other feminists argued against the implicit definition in the proposal of female sexuality as friendly, respectful and non-violent and claimed the right of women to enjoy, for instance, S/M practices; liberal feminists defending First Amendment rights were among the most outspoken opponents of the MacKinnon/Dworkin proposal and contributed much to its later defeat (Burstyn, 1985).

The particulars of the feminist debates on pornography and sexuality cannot be rehearsed here (see for example, Vance, 1984), however, one element is of particular relevance to media theory and research. Defining pornography as an act of violence raises a question on the nature of representation and its relation to social reality. Opponents would argue that radical feminists inaccurately collapse representation into social reality and claim that pornography is a representation of something, an image in words and pictures, but that it is not the act itself (cf. Leong, 1991). Such an argument, however, ignores the point that representation is a social practice in which current beliefs and myths about women and sexuality are (re)constructed, and that the act of consuming these representations is more than a private pleasure, but also embedded in gendered social and cultural formations that have defined women's bodies as sexual objects. The latter observation, in its turn, then raises the question why pornography should be treated as a separate phenomenon, given a wider cultural tradition of representing women as objects of the male gaze, present, for instance, in advertising and mainstream Hollywood movies. Such issues of representation, reality and social practices are central to feminist media studies and extend beyond the pornography debate. They will be taken up in detail in Chapter 3.

Ideology

Theories of ideology are part of the 'critical' domain in communication studies and cultural studies. Critical communication scholars used to ignore gender just like mainstream communication scholars did, as the account of the Women's Studies Group of the Centre for Contemporary Cultural Studies (CCCS) at Birmingham confirms: 'We found it extremely difficult to participate in the CCCS groups and felt, without being able to articulate it, that it was a case of the masculine domination of both intellectual work and the environment in which it was being carried out' (*Women Take Issue*, 1978: 11). Feminist interventions in ideology theory have come from radical and Marxist, but in particular from socialist feminism. Because the cultural studies perspectives that will be discussed in the following chapter are in large part grounded in socialist feminist theory, ideology will be discussed more extensively than the previous themes of stereotypes and pornography.

Socialist feminists have shown a profound theoretical and political interest in connecting the capitalist mode of production to the oppression of women. Neo-Marxism, psychoanalysis and ideology theory provide the sources for this theoretical project.

From **Marxism** it takes not only the political economic analysis of capitalism, but also a conception of human nature as constituted in society: 'Specific historical conditions create distinctive human types' (Jaggar, 1983: 125). But whereas Marxists only recognize the capitalist and the worker as human types, socialist feminism acknowledges that human beings are defined by gender, race, ethnicity, age, sexuality and nationality as well. Its theoretical challenge has been to relate these differences, and gender difference in particular, to historical, social and economic conditions.

Among the different **psychoanalytic theories** adopted by socialist feminists the reinterpretation of Freud by the Frenchman Jacques Lacan and the work of the American Nancy Chodorow are of particular importance. Freud located the development of gendered subjectivity in the 'phallic stage' of infancy when children discover their genitals. This phase is characterized by the Oedipus and castration complexes that need to be negotiated in order to develop into 'normal' adults. Freud argued that at the same time a little boy becomes aware of his love for his mother, he recognizes her lack of a penis and becomes afraid that he might lose his penis too. He perceives his father as the powerful figure possessing his mother and capable of castrating the boy for his desire for the mother. To develop a 'normal' masculine subjectivity then, it is necessary that the boy denies his love for his mother, identifies with his father and internalizes his values. In the process he develops a 'superego'; the condensation of the patriarchal social conscience. Were the boy not to emerge from the Oedipal position and were he to remain immersed in maternal plenitude, his 'normal' masculinity would be endangered and indeed he would end up symbolically castrated. Thus, for a boy to become a man he has to separate from his mother and identify with his father. The little girl on the other hand passes these phases differently. As she becomes aware of her own lack of a penis, she develops penis envy and resents the mother for badly equipping her. To take revenge she turns to the father, competing for his love with her mother and desiring his penis. Only if the girl succeeds in substituting her phallic desire by the wish to have a baby – the ultimate penis substitute for women according to Freud – will she develop as an untroubled mature woman.

In Lacan's rewriting of Freud it is not so much the physical penis that is central, but the social and cultural power it represents, the phallus. Lacan argues that the child's separation from the mother takes place through the acquisition of language, or to put it differently, by the child's entry into the symbolic order. Without such a symbolic order which connects human beings to each other and makes sense of human experience, people cannot function and end up as psychotic. The Lacanian symbolic order is inevitably patriarchal, due to the structural position of the father as the intervening third party between mother and child: 'In the imagination, the father's position is the same as that occupied by language, in that language intervenes in the imaginary dyad [between mother and child] as the symbolic words that rupture the threads of phantasy that hold lack at bay and the illusion of union in place' (Brennan, 1989: 3). The patriarchal nature of the symbolic is thus a product of the equivalent structural position of language and the father as interveners in the mother–child bond. Submission to the patriarchal symbolic order – the Law of the father in Lacan's words – is a prerequisite for human autonomy and sanity. However, for boys the process implies access to social power, whereas for girls it involves entry into a patriarchal order in which 'the feminine' has no place and cannot be spoken.

According to the materialist psychoanalysis of Nancy Chodorow, the acquisition of gender identity takes place before the Oedipal phase. In this early period in life the child is completely dependent on the parent, usually the mother and there is a strong mother–child symbiosis in which the child continually wonders whether he or she and the mother are one. This symbiosis is much stronger for mother and daughter since they are of the same sex: daughters develop a personal identification and a more continuous relationship with the mother. Boys have less opportunity for such direct identification because of the relative absence of the father. The boy develops a sense of being not feminine, and identifies with the position of the father rather than with his person. As a result, girls come to think of themselves in relation to others (the mother) while boys perceive themselves as unconnected individuals (the absent father). Penis envy in Chodorow's theory is not the female desire for the physical thing, but represents the desire to separate from the mother and become an autonomous person.

There is a crude resemblance to the developmental ideas of Freud and Lacan, but the major difference is that Chodorow's psychoanalysis is materialistic in that it explains gender difference from the social process of mothering. In Chodorow's theory femininity is not characterized by 'lack' or 'otherness' but by the capacity for meaningful triadic relationships.

Psychoanalysis has been instrumental to socialist feminist thought through locating the reproduction of gender and patriarchal relations at the level of **ideology**, as theorized in particular by neo-Marxists like Althusser and Gramsci. Within Marxist/socialist theory, ideology is the key concept to explain why it is that the conditions necessary for the capitalist mode of production are maintained and, for instance, workers do not revolt against their oppression. More formally ideology has been defined as:

> The means by which ruling economic classes generalize and extend their supremacy across the whole range of social activity, and naturalize it in the process, so that their rule is accepted and natural and inevitable, and therefore legitimate and binding. (O'Sullivan et al., 1989: 109)

While Althusser's and Gramsci's theories ignore the gender issue, the ideological mechanisms they analyse have been a source of inspiration for socialist feminists, who claim that gender is a crucial component of ideology.

Althusser drew from the Lacanian notion of subjectivity as constituted in language for the development of his theory of ideology. According to Althusser people become subjects because of interpellation by ideology. This is to say that we are only able to make sense of ourselves and our social experiences within the limits and possibilities that language and the meaning systems available in a given society set for us. Language is not seen as a transparent medium conveying one's authentic experiences, or what really happened, but as constructing subjectivity and reality. According to the Lacanian dictum: 'we don't speak language, language speaks us'.

Althusser introduced the term **ideological state apparatuses** (ISAs) to refer to institutions such as religion, education, politics, the law, the family, media and culture. Although relatively autonomous from the state and capital and despite their variety and internal contradictions these institutions are said to function as agents of the state and the ruling class. Since ISAs cannot be directly controlled by the ruling class, they are ideological battlegrounds that betray the contradictions within dominant ideology. In the end, however, ISAs will function in favour of dominant ideology, although Althusser fails to explain exactly why and how this is achieved.

In Althusserian theories of ideology the individual is interpellated by dominant ideology; in other words, individuals are inexorably drawn into dominant ideology. Gramsci's notes on 'hegemony' provide an important addition to such a concept of ideology. Gramsci used 'hegemony' to refer to the *process* by which general consent is actively sought for the interpretations of the ruling class. Dominant ideology becomes invisible because it is translated into 'common sense', appearing as the natural, unpolitical state of things accepted by each and everyone. Like Althusser, Gramsci identifies ideological institutions and intermediaries like the priest and the intellectual, who translate the concepts of the ruling class into the ordinary language and experiences of the worker.

Clearly, the media are the contemporary mediators of hegemony, the question being how, and to whose avail, particular ideological constructs of femininity are produced in media content. Much of the research done in this vein consists of ideological analyses of singular media texts using the instrumentarium offered by psychoanalysis, structuralism and semiotics (for example, Coward, 1984). The idiosyncratic nature of these analyses makes any comprehensive and meaningful review impracticable and therefore I shall discuss only one research project, which, although dating from the early 1980s, exemplifies the approach and issues concerned.

A typical ideological analysis of popular culture for women is Angela McRobbie's (1982) examination of the British teenage magazine *Jackie*, aimed at girls in the ten to fourteen age group. McRobbie sets out with a brief description of the publishing house responsible for *Jackie*, D.C. Thompson of Dundee, whose history is characterized by 'a vigorous anti-unionism' and a 'strict code of censorship and content', according to McRobbie. Its annual profit margins rise as high as 20 per cent even in a time of crisis in the publishing industries. Having thus identified D.C.

Thompson as a classic capitalist entrepreneur, McRobbie argues that these companies are not simply pursuing profits, but they are involved in 'an implicit attempt to win consent to the dominant order – in terms of femininity, leisure and consumption, i.e. at the level of culture' (p. 87). Publishing companies are part of the relatively autonomous apparatuses of the social formation that have their own particular operational modes and that cannot be seen as a unified whole. McRobbie acknowledges the internal contradictions of hegemony and argues that the working class, and especially the working class youth, has found ways to subvert hegemony by reappropriating cultural products and incorporating them into oppositional and subcultural styles of their own. However, the possibilities for that reappropriation are much more difficult for girls, says McRobbie, since the cultural forms available to girls are limited and their use – such as reading teenage magazines – is primarily confined to the personal sphere. Thus, while for working class male youth a cultural negotiation of the dominant social order is thought feasible, McRobbie finds resistance much harder to envisage in teenage girls' subcultural practices. In their leisure time, free of any direct coercion from work, school or the family, girls enjoy the illusion of freedom. But capital effectively controls leisure time as well, with magazines like *Jackie* as intermediaries. How does McRobbie think this control is achieved in *Jackie*?

McRobbie uses semiology, the analysis of visual and verbal signs, to examine the 'connotative codes' present in *Jackie*. 'Connotation' here refers to implied or associative meanings of signs whereas 'denotation' refers to their literal meaning (see also Chapter 5). For instance, in *Jackie*'s picture stories brunette girls do not only have brown hair and probably brown eyes , but the brunette is also usually involved in some vicious plot to get the man she wants, her best friend's boyfriend for instance. Brunettes thus mean trouble (connotation). McRobbie distinguishes four codes of connotation in *Jackie*: the code of romance; the code of personal/domestic life; the code of fashion and beauty; the code of pop music. Heterosexual romance is the core theme of *Jackie* and it comes to the reader in picture stories, on the problem page and in 'true life' stories. The picture stories usually feature two or three main characters, who are a little older than the average reader, their social backgrounds are unclear and their surroundings or use of language do not give them away either. The main characters come in easily recognizable stereotypes, according to McRobbie. Boys are irresistible charmers, tousled scatterbrains, sensitive artists or wild but sexy delinquents. Girls are blonde, quiet and timid, unreliable brunettes or plain ordinary. They are a fun loving group whose main occupation is to pursue each other. For girls the main task in life is to get and keep a man and in this respect other women cannot be trusted. 'The girl's life is defined through emotions – jealousy, possessiveness and devotion. Pervading the stories is a fundamental fear, fear of losing your boyfriend or of never getting one' (p. 107). And it is not simply the boy that the girls are after, what they want is romance, a publicly recognized relationship. Girls in *Jackie* see boys as romantic objects not as sexual objects, McRobbie claims. The code of romance in *Jackie* thus constructs hetereosexual romance as the all-pervasive concern of girls' adolescence and solidifies at the same time separate and distinct male and female roles.

In real life these themes are fraught with problems of course and these are indeed discussed on the problem page. Here, the ideological operations of *Jackie* show more openly, encouraging conventional individualism and conformist independence. 'That is: the girl is channelled both toward traditional female (passive) behaviour and to having a mind of her own. She is warned of the dangers of following others blindly and is discouraged from wasting time at work, playing truant from school or gossiping' (p. 115).

Fashion, cosmetics and beauty are signs of another central code in adolescent femininity. Clothing and cosmetics themselves are signs that girls are taught to operate to create a particular and recognizable image for themselves. While fashion and beauty are not central to the magazine, their message is that they are absolutely necessary components of a girl's life. It is taken for granted that the adolescent female body is in need of continuous maintenance and improvement, and *Jackie* provides step-by-step manuals to achieve self-improvement.

Finally, pop music is a central element of *Jackie*; however, it is not the music itself that matters but the star, with each week a single and double page devoted to a pop musician. In fact, the pictures of pop stars enable *Jackie* readers once again to fantasize about romance: 'Instead of being encouraged to develop an interest in this area, or to create their own music, the readers are presented, yet again, with another opportunity to indulge their emotions, but this time on the pop star figure rather than the boyfriend' (p. 126).

All in all, *Jackie* articulates the centrality of personal life for girls. It presents an all-embracing, suffocating totality of romance and emotion, stopping girls from doing or thinking about anything else. Although McRobbie cautions in her conclusion against the idea that readers will swallow the ideological axioms without question, she does consider the discourse of *Jackie* as immensely powerful, 'especially if we consider it being absorbed, in its codified form, each week for several years at a time' (p. 131).

McRobbie's analysis is a good example of an ideological analysis of popular culture. She focuses on the ideological operations of media texts produced within a capitalist context leaving the impression of an all pervasive hegemonic process from which there is no escape. McRobbie later conceded that her textual analysis 'created an image of *Jackie* as a massive ideological block in which readers were implicitly imprisoned' (1991: 141). While McRobbie's project allows for contradictions in the hegemonic process, in the actual analysis of *Jackie*, theoretical sophistication gives way to a rather straightforward interpretation of *Jackie* as a monolithic ideological construction of adolescent femininity. Later research among the readers of *Jackie* showed a multiplicity of interpretations and reactions not necessarily in line with hegemony (Frazer, 1987).

Feminist contributions to a new paradigm?

Aside from adding new themes to the research agenda or transforming old ones, a more fundamental issue concerns the question whether feminist media theory and research has offered new ways of approaching these themes. Did feminist communication scholars develop new frameworks, new designs and new methods, and did these innovations affect the guiding paradigms in the discipline at large? In order to answer that question, it is necessary to take a closer look at the theories of communication behind the three themes discussed – stereotypes and socialization, pornography and ideology. Contrary to the first impression, the work done on these topics shares similar assumptions on the role of the media in the construction of gender. They are perceived as the main instruments in conveying stereotypical, patriarchal and hegemonic values about women and femininity. In research on all three themes media are conceptualized as agents of social control: in research on stereotypes it is said that media pass on society's heritage – which is deeply sexist – in order to secure continuity, integration and the incorporation of change (Tuchman, 1978a); anti-pornography campaigners argue that media serve the needs of patriarchy by representing women as objects and by suppressing women's own experiences (Dworkin, 1981); and in theories of ideology media are viewed as hegemonic institutions that present the capitalist and patriarchal order as 'normal', obscuring its ideological nature and translating it into 'common sense' (*Women Take Issue*, 1978). In all three areas a structural functionalist media theory is employed, following the Lasswellian question: who, says what, to whom, and with what effect? Carey (1989: 15) has labelled this conceptualization as a transmission view of communication: 'The center of this idea is the transmission of signals and messages over distance for the purpose of control.' In feminist terminology media are thought to transmit sexist, patriarchal or capitalist values to contribute to the maintenance of social order. In such models meaning is located primarily in relatively consistent and uncontradictory media texts. The transmission view of communication has become subject to strong criticism, from feminist and other communication scholars, to the extent that several authors now argue that the academic study of mass communication is in the middle of a paradigm shift involving a movement toward perspectives in which meaning is understood as constructed out of the historically and socially situated negotiation between institutional producers of meaning and audiences as producers of meaning.[9] As alluded to in Chapter 1, meaning is no longer conceptualized as a more or less consistent entity, but is seen as contradictory, divided and plural, in other words as polysemic (Morley, 1989). The ample acknowledgement of the importance of Ien

Ang's (1985) and Janice Radway's (1984) work on the interpretative activities of audiences of soaps and romances respectively, shows that feminist media research has certainly played a part in this reconceptualization of meaning and communication. However, it would be hard to isolate the feminist impact and distinguish it from other influences, in particular those of cultural studies. As said in the Introduction of this book, it is precisely at the junction of feminist and cultural studies that the most innovative and inspiring research is carried out. In the next chapter, I shall expand this discussion, laying out the flaws of feminist transmission models of communication in more detail and build from that a cultural studies framework for feminist media theory.

Notes

1. This point was brought to my attention by Stevi Jackson.
2. Originally, this chapter was divided into three sections on liberal, radical and socialist feminism, the latter including psychoanalysis. Instructive and constructive criticism, in particular from Margaret Gallagher, Stevi Jackson, Irene Meijer and my students who did not feel very updated with this tripartition made me decide to use another angle.
3. I use the term 'communication studies' to refer to mass communication, journalism, media studies etc.
4. The observation on the United States is based on Schamber, 1989. The observation on Europe is based on personal communication with faculty of the more than twenty universities from ten countries involved in the Erasmus student and staff exchange network 'European Cultural and Media Studies'.
5. Dervin (1987) includes the following note at this point: 'The term is from Lourde's *Sister Outsider*: 'For the master's tool will never dismantle the master's house.'
6. With the exception of some special issues of journals, such as *Communication* (1986), *Journal of Communication Inquiry* (1987). The tendency seems to be, however, to treat feminism as a separate area rather than incorporating its concepts into mainstream research.
7. The representation of gender and ethnicity will be discussed further in Chapter 5.
8. At least – as it seems – in the United States. In Britain and continental Europe the demonstrations against pornography were engaged in by socialist feminists as well, another example of blurred distinctions.
9. Other authors argue against the idea of a paradigm shift (Curran, 1990).

3

A 'New' Paradigm?

The feminist research themes discussed in the previous chapter assume a rather straightforward 'sender–message–receiver' sequence in which media are conceived as transmitting particular messages about gender (stereotypes, pornography, ideology) to the wider public. The social control function of the media is central to all three themes, although there are some differences as to how social control is achieved. As far as the 'senders' are concerned, it is sometimes said that 'since those who control the media are almost all (rich) men, there is every incentive for them to present the capitalist, patriarchal scheme of things as the most attractive system available – and to convince the less privileged that the oppression and limitations of their lives are inevitable' (Davies et al., 1987: 2). Other authors point to the immediate producers of media content such as journalists and TV producers and claim that their traditional world views are reflected in media output. Ross Muir (1987: 8), for instance, wonders: 'If a film or television company is a mini sexist society, with women congregated in the lower paid service and support jobs, how can we expect the image of women that they produce to be anything but sexist?' According to such views, an increase in the number of female media producers would be instrumental to creating a more balanced media product (for example, Beasly, 1989).

At the 'receiving' end of the model, in research on stereotypes it is thought that children and adults learn their appropriate gender roles by a process of symbolic reinforcement and correction. For anti-pornography campaigners it is not so much learning which is at stake but imitation; men are feared to imitate the violent sexual behaviour presented to them in pornography. In research on ideology a process of familiarization with dominant ideology is assumed leading finally to its internalization and transformation into common sense.

The differences then between functionalist theories of the media refer primarily to the specific elements of the communication process, but not to how communication works, as Figure 3.1 shows.

	Sender	Process	Message	Process	Effect
Stereotypes	men	distortion	stereotype	socialization	sexism
Pornography	patriarchy	distortion	pornography	imitation	oppression
Ideology	capitalism	distortion	hegemony	familiarization	common sense

Figure 3.1 *Models of communication in feminist media theory*

Several elements of these feminist transmission models have become subject to criticism. Media production, for instance, is neither a straightforward derivative of the malicious intents of capitalist male owners, nor is it merely the product of the sexist inclinations of media professionals. It cannot be seen as a simple black box transmitting the patriarchal, sexist or capitalist values of its producers. As will be elaborated in Chapter 4, it is better characterized by tensions and contradictions between individuals with different professional values and personal opinions, and between conflicting organizational demands such as creativity and innovation on the one hand and the commercial need to be popular among a variety of social groups on the other hand.

Two other elements of the model have been fundamentally reconceptualized, namely 'distortion' and 'socialization'. In this chapter I shall discuss the critiques on these concepts which together provide the building blocks of the cultural studies perspective which will inform the remainder of this book.

Distortion

'Distortion' is a key concept in many feminist approaches to the media. It is often said that women are underrepresented in media content when compared to the 50 per cent of the population which they constitute. Alternatively, it is argued that in reality many more women work than we get to see or read about in media content. Another argument deals with the definition of femininity presented to us in media content: submission, availability and compliance are characteristics held up as ideals, and consumption is presented as the road to self-fulfilment. Muriel Cantor (1978: 88) complains that public broadcasting in America presents images of women 'that are not representative of women's position in our highly differentiated and complex society'. Likewise, Linda Lazier-Smith accuses the advertising industry of not keeping up with changes in society: 'Although the demographies (the math) has changed dramatically, the attitude (mentality) has not. . . . We seem to be suffering from a cultural lag – our culture's beliefs and attitudes and opinions on women are lagging behind the reality about women' (1989: 258).

It seems indisputable that many aspects of women's lives and experiences are not properly reflected by the media. Many more women work than the media suggest, very few women resemble the '*femmes fatales*' of movies and TV series, and women's desires extend far beyond the hearth and home of traditional women's magazines. The feminist calls for more realistic images of women and definitions of femininity may therefore seem entirely legitimate. In fact, they are problematic. To begin with, stereotypes are not images in themselves but radicalized expressions of a common social practice of identifying and categorizing events, experiences, objects or persons. Stereotypes often have social counterparts which appear to support and legitimize the stereotype. A common response to the feminist claim that media distort reality by showing women in stereotypical roles of housewives and mother, is that in reality many women are mothers and housewives too, 'and what is so problematic about showing that?'.

Feminist alternatives to gender stereotypes are not as univocal as the claim for more realistic representations suggests. Feminists are divided among themselves over what is the reality of women's social position and nature. Thus before the media could transmit more realistic images of women, it would be necessary to define uncontroversially what the reality about women is, obviously an impossible project. As Brunsdon aptly argues:

> For feminists to call for more realistic images of women is to engage in the struggle to define what is meant by 'realistic', rather than to offer easily available 'alternative' images. Arguing for more realistic images is always an argument for the representation of 'your' version of reality. (1988: 149)

At the heart of the matter is the understanding of the 'reality' of gender, which in these theories is sometimes defined as social position, as in cases of calling for a more realistic reflection of women's social roles, and at other times is defined as a particular subjectivity, as in the claims for a more varied representation of women's psychological features. Apparently, in transmission models of communication, gender is conceived as a more or less stable and easily identifiable distinction between women and men which ought to be represented correctly. Such a conceptualization of gender is utterly problematic for it denies the dynamic nature of gender, its historical and cultural specificity and its contradictory meanings. What to make, for instance, of transgressions of the male/female dichotomy, manifested in the ambiguous appearances of Grace Jones, Prince or Michael Jackson; in lesbian and homosexual subcultures; in the phenomenon of transsexuality; and in daily lives and experiences of women and men whose identities belie the thought of an easily identifiable distinction between women and men?

An acknowledgement of the historical specificity of current dominant beliefs about women and men opens up new ways of thinking about gender as constructed. In such approaches 'distortion' would be an empty concept, since there is no reference point as to what the true human, male or female identity consists of, and hence there is no criterion as to what exactly the media should represent. Human identity and gender are thought to be socially constructed, in other words products of circumstances, opportunities and limitations.

Some views on the meaning of gender

Psychoanalysis is one approach to theorizing the construction of gender. According to Lacanian varieties gender difference is constructed through the acquisition of language in the Oedipal phase, the submission of the self to the phallocentric symbolic order in which the feminine is undefined and cannot be spoken. The Chodorowian approach emphasizes the gender-specific symbiosis between mother and children in the pre-Oedipal phase to account for gender difference (cf. Chapter 2). Such arguments tend to attribute almost exclusive explanatory power to the constitution of the self in early childhood and ignore the social forces that bear on the subjectivity of human beings. In its conceptualization of gender as a property that human beings acquire early in life prior to their entry into social relations, psychoanalysis borders on the essentialistic:

> For if, as some psychoanalytic theories appear to suggest, social subjects are determined, through family relations and language acquisition, prior to the introduction of other considerations, including race, class, personal background or historical moment, the social construct thus described is a closed system unamenable to other subject formations. (Pribram, 1988: 6)

Other interpretations of gender as construction, for instance those inspired by Gail Rubin's influential theory of the 'sex-gender system', give priority to social relations and consider gender to be shaped within ideological frameworks, as socially constructed by cultural and historical processes and acquired by individuals by socialization through family, education, church, media and other agencies. Although in such an appreciation of gender, its particular meaning might vary according to history and culture, the basic 'sex-gender system', ascribing 'femininity' to biological women and 'masculinity' to biological men, is thought to be universal and all-pervasive (Rubin, 1975). Such notions of gender also perceive the concept as a relatively constant and consistent feature of human identity. 'Ungendered' or multiple and divided subjectivities are hard to envisage, and as in the psychoanalytic view the binary and oppositional character of gender remains, constraining 'feminist critical thought within the conceptual frame of a universal sex opposition . . . which makes it very difficult, if not impossible, to articulate the differences . . . among women or, perhaps more exactly the differences *within women*' (de Lauretis, 1987: 2; italics in original).

The notion of gender I want to advance here concerns gender as a discursive construct and is inspired by poststructuralist thought as expressed, among others, in the work of the French philosopher Michel Foucault and the feminist film theory of Theresa de Lauretis. In order to explain this notion properly we need to return to the Lacanian idea that we become subjects through the acquisition of language. In other words, as we are born and raised into this world we learn to think, feel and express ourselves with the linguistic means socially available. Of course we can invent our own words and symbols, but nobody would understand us. Thus language and its historically and culturally specific semantic and thematic combinations in discourses set limits to our experience of ourselves, others and our surroundings: 'language speaks us'. People who have travelled or migrated to foreign countries and have learned to speak foreign languages will recognize this from experience: sometimes words and concepts common to one language do not have an equivalent in another language. As a result the particular experience connected to that concept is hard to express.

Since we are born into societies that have labelled a particular difference between human beings as woman vs man, and a related difference as feminine vs masculine, we come to think of ourselves in these terms: as being and feeling a man, or being and feeling a woman. Gender, however defined, becomes a seemingly 'natural' or inevitable part of our identity and for that matter often a problematic one. According to Lacan, language not only stipulates sexual difference but also male power. In Lacan's univocal phallocentric discourse women have no means of expressing themselves; without language they cannot speak their own authentic experience, unless in ways defined by men. Thus, in Lacanian terms, feminine experience can only be defined negatively and women can only think of themselves as being 'not-men' (see Chapter 2).

In poststructuralist theory discourse is never univocal or total, but ambiguous and contradictory; a site of conflict and contestation (cf. Sawicki, 1991). Moreover, gender discourse is not conceived as the only dimension of human identity. Rather, human beings are constituted by the different social practices and discourses in which they are engaged. This is of course similar to the Marxist claim about human nature, although in Marxist theory class is the primary social condition defining a binary human identity of capitalist or worker, whereas poststructuralists speak of multiple discourses that are contradictory between and within themselves. Gender can thus be thought of as a particular discourse, that is, a set of overlapping and often contradictory cultural descriptions and prescriptions referring to sexual difference, which arises from and regulates particular economic, social, political, technological and other non-discursive contexts. Gender is inscribed in the subject along with other discourses, such as those of ethnicity, class, and sexuality. Following Foucault, de Lauretis claims that:

> the subject [is] constituted in language, to be sure, though not by sexual difference alone, but rather across languages and cultural representations; a subject engendered in the experience of race and class, as well as sexual relations; a subject therefore not unified but rather multiple, and not so much divided as contradicted. (1987: 2)

Gender should thus be conceived, not as a fixed property of individuals, but as part of an ongoing process by which subjects are constituted, often in paradoxical ways. The identity that emerges is therefore fragmented and dynamic; gender does not determine or exhaust identity. In theory, although hard to imagine in current society, it is even conceivable to be outside gender or to engage in a social practice in which gender discourse is relatively unimportant. Defined as such, gender is an intrinsic part of culture – loosely defined as the production of meaning – and is subject to continuous discursive struggle and negotiation. This struggle over meaning is not a mere pluralistic 'debate' between equal but contending frames of reference. It is traversed by existing power relations, and by the fact that 'in virtually all cultures whatever is defined as manly, is more highly valued than whatever is thought of as womanly' (Harding, 1987: 18). However, a poststructuralist notion of discourse as a site of contestation implies that the disciplinary power of discourse, prescribing and restricting identities and experiences, can always be resisted and subverted. Dominant male discourse can therefore never be completely overpowering, since by definition there will be resistance and struggle.

To view the role of the media in the construction of gender as a process of distorting the 'true' meaning of gender, as occurs in feminist transmission models of communication, thus ignores the contradictory and contested nature of gender. Before presenting an alternative perspective, first a discussion of another key problem of transmission models is necessary.

Socialization

'Socialization' can refer to the various ways in which individuals become social subjects, although in functionalist theories of the media it usually applies to cognitive and behavioural processes. McQuail (1987: 280) for instance, defines socialization as the 'teaching of established norms and values by ways of symbolic rewards and punishment for different kinds of behaviour', and as 'the learning process whereby we all learn how to behave in certain situations and learn the expectations which go with a given role or status in society'. Defined as such it would appear that socialization takes place mainly in childhood, but socialization can be seen as an ongoing long-term process affecting adults as well.

Socialization has been studied in various ways. A common way of attempting to establish socialization effects is the experimental social psychological approach, where children or adults are exposed to a particular type of media output and subjected to some kind of measurement procedure, such as questionnaires or physical monitoring. The kind of questions posed are whether children's exposure to sexist media content is related to their perception of appropriate gender behaviour, or whether men's exposure to violent pornography leads to hostile fantasies and real aggression against women. The results of these studies are contradictory but show among other things that media effects are mediated by other variables such as age, gender or education. More fundamentally, the causal relation between media exposure and sexist attitudes is unclear since it appears that even at a very early age children have considerable knowledge of 'appropriate' gender behaviour. As discussed in Chapter 2, the direction of the causal relationship between pornography and sexual violence cannot be easily established either (cf. McCormack, 1978; Steeves, 1987).

Experimental research examines short term cognitive or behavioural effects and does not reveal much about the influence of mass media in the long term. There has been very little research carried out in relation to feminist concerns, but some studies of long-term media effects have produced relevant results, especially in the area of cultivation theory. This theory proposes that media and television in particular present a 'pseudo-reality' that is different from the social reality most people experience. People who watch television for hours on end will tend to replace their own social experience with that of television reality, resulting in a 'television view' of the world. Steeves (1987) discusses some cultivation studies which do seem to indicate that heavy viewing correlates with sexist attitudes in children. In studies focused especially on the cultivation effect of soap operas it is reported that 'exposure to soap operas correlates with the belief by viewers that men and women have affairs, get divorced, have illegitimate children, and undergo serious operations and that women are housewives, have abortions and do not work at all' (Steeves, 1987: 104). Cultivation research suffers from similar problems as experimental research: the media 'effect' turns out to be mediated by intervening variables such as education, gender and class and the direction of the effect is problematic. Perhaps a particular worldview causes heavy viewing, instead of being caused by it. Moreover, cultivation theory seems primarily relevant to the United States where daily viewing times of over six hours are very common. In many areas of the world this is materially impossible since national or local television stations only broadcast a few hours a day.

Both experimental and cultivation research conceptualize the audience as a relatively passive aggregate of individuals affected differently by mass media as exposure and background variables diverge. Many feminist analyses of the media phrase the issue as 'what do media do with women', ignoring the cognitive and emotional activities of audiences in making sense of mass media. Audience reaction is conceptualized as a dichotomous activity of accepting sexist messages or rejecting them. Either audiences can accept media output as true to reality, in which case they are successfully socialized, brainwashed by patriarchy or lured into the idea that what they see and read is 'common sense', or they see through the tricks the mass media play on them and reject the sexist, patriarchal, capitalist representation of the world. Obviously, many feminists consider themselves among the latter 'enlightened' women raising themselves 'to the lofty pedestal of having seen the light' (Winship, 1987: 140). A deep gap is constructed between the feminist media critic and the ordinary female audience. Soap operas, romance novels and women's magazines are found particularly objectionable: they are said to create 'a cult of femininity and heterosexual romance' that – since these media are predominantly consumed by women – set the agenda for the female world (cf. Ferguson, 1983).

Such a strong conviction about the value (or rather lack of it) of these media for women's lives, is remarkably similar to patriarchal attitudes of men who claim to know what is best for women. Dismissing women's genres for their supposedly questionable content carries an implicit rejection of the women who enjoy them. Moreover, it does not allow 'true' feminists to enjoy these genres and condemns them to being 'closet readers', obviously at odds with the feminist mission to acknowledge and gain respect for women's experiences and viewpoints.

More recently, some feminist inquiries have turned the question around and asked 'what do women do with media', allowing for a variety of audience reactions. These studies seem to suggest that women actively and consciously seek particular types of gratification from mass media use. Soap operas, for instance, are said to satisfy the need for emotional release, identification, escape, companionship, information and relaxation (Cantor and Pingree, 1983). Similar gratifications have been found among the readers of women's magazines who derive a feeling of friendship from reading and who are informed, entertained and advised by women's magazines (Wassenaar, 1975). Such a 'uses and gratifications' perspective on media use has advantages over the earlier 'effect models' by raising the question of differential uses and interpretations of media output and in its perception of the audience as active. It is still a somewhat mechanistic functional model, presuming that an individual will recognize her own needs and will seek a rational way to satisfy them. Why it is, for example, that one turns to media instead of other means to satisfy the need for entertainment, information or relaxation remains unclear. More fundamentally, the 'uses and gratifications' approach tends to focus on individual differences, attributing them to differences of personality and psychology and neglecting the social and cultural contexts in which media use takes place (cf. Morley, 1989).

Communication as ritual

Out of the criticism of the feminist transmission model of communication, the contours of an alternative approach emerge. We need first to take a closer look at the epistemological groundwork of the transmission model before we can arrive at a comprehensive understanding of the alternative. As said, 'reality' is a key term, but the concept itself is given little serious thought. The idea that mass media 'distort' the reality of women's lives gives a clue as to how in these models 'reality' is understood. Apparently, a real world of objects, events, situations and processes is assumed to exist independent of and prior to human perception. This real world is waiting to be measured validly and reliably, as scientists try to do; to be represented accurately and truthfully, as media should do; and to be understood and experienced correctly or mistakenly as ordinary people do. 'There is reality and then after the fact, our account of it' (Carey, 1989: 25). Almost inevitably, media performance will thus only be evaluated in terms of the quality of its representation of reality. There are two problems to this account, the first having to do with the role of the media in contemporary society, the second with the concept of reality itself.

The 'bardic' function

In the first place mass media accomplish much more varied activities than only those of representing reality. Film, television, (popular) literature etc. construct an imaginary world that builds on and appeals to individual and social fantasies. Mass media produce and reproduce collective memories, desires, hopes and fears, and thus perform a similar function as myths in earlier centuries. 'The search for the mythical in contemporary society is grounded not only in the plausible expectation that we too perforce must find ways of expressing basic concerns, core values, deep anxieties; and equally we must find ways of expressing publicly and collectively our attempts at resolving them' (Silverstone, 1988: 24). In their presentation of major social events like coronations, sports games or disasters media present the content of myth, and in their familiar and formulaic narratives they resemble mythical story-telling. Whereas myths connect mundane everyday life with the sacred and unreachable words of Gods and ancestors, modern mass media mark the boundary between ordinary daily life and the inaccessible worlds of show business and top sports (cf. Silverstone, 1988). Carey (1989) has labelled such an approach to communication as a ritual view characterized by terms like 'sharing', 'participation', 'fellowship' and 'the possession of a common faith'.

The ritual view on communication borrows its concepts from anthropology and the sociology of religion, and is directed at the way in which a society reproduces its cohesiveness and its shared beliefs. In other words the ritual approach to communication focuses on the construction of a community through rituals, shared histories, beliefs and values. In such a view, media create 'an artificial though none the less real symbolic order that operates to provide not information but confirmation, not to alter attitudes or change minds but to represent an underlying order of things, not to perform functions but to manifest an ongoing and fragile social process' (Carey, 1989: 19). Two concrete examples will clarify the difference between the transmission and ritual models of communication. When investigating church attendance in a particular community, employing a transmission perspective one might inquire about the messages and instructions present in the sermon and the understanding and recollection of the church-goers. From a ritual viewpoint the joint prayer and chant, and of course the ceremony would be more important. Similarly, television news can be construed as a daily presentation of new information that enables people to learn and process new knowledge, while one could also stress its ritual character as a device to structure the evening and as 'the presentation . . . of the familiar and the strange, the reassuring and the threatening' (Silverstone, 1988: 26).

Ritual models may fail to incorporate notions like dominance and oppression – essential to the feminist and any other critical project – suggesting a more or less pluriform and unproblematic construction of social togetherness. Fiske and Hartley's (1978) proposal to think of the mass media as contemporary bards provides a useful integration of a conception of power with the ritual view of communication. The authors claim that the media perform a social role which is similar to that of the bards in medieval societies. Those poets were licensed and paid by the rulers of their time to mediate between them and the society at large, by writing and performing songs and stories. They did not simply reflect the views of the courts nor those of ordinary people, but they reworked 'raw materials' into meaningful narratives, much as television does today: 'So bardic television cannot by definition simply "reflect" any supposed social or cultural reality that already exists elsewhere, since its main business is to make its own particular kind of sense of the fragmented and conflicting raw materials available to it' (O'Sullivan et al., 1989). That particular sense, however, is firmly connected to the dominant social order, for the bards' task is primarily to render the unfamiliar into the already known, or into 'common sense'. Therefore, the bardic function has inherently reactionary tendencies since it needs to rely on familiar meanings and interpretations. What falls outside an already existing consensus is hard to make sense of, except as 'otherness' or 'deviance'.

The social construction of reality

The second fundamental problem of the reflection thesis in feminist transmission models of communication has to do with its limited interpretation of reality, conceptualizing it as an independent world of objects, relations and processes only, and ignoring the social processes of defining reality. In their classic treatise *The Social Construction of Reality* Berger and Luckman (1966) claim that society exists as both objective and subjective reality. While we perceive the world we live in as 'real', as something that exists beyond our own perceptions and beliefs and that will continue to exist when we are not there, we acknowledge at the same time that not everyone perceives reality in the same way. Still, it is not merely that people perceive reality in a particular way, their perception has consequences for their sense of self, relations with others, their mode of conduct and a whole range of other social practices. In these social interactions people produce, reproduce and adjust definitions of reality: 'If men define situations as real, they are real in their consequences' (Thomas, 1928: 584). Reality is not merely something that exists 'out there', but it is also (re)constructed by the social and sense-making activities of human beings. According to Berger and Luckman (1966), the most important vehicle in that process is conversation. Not that all conversation pertains to matters of meanings and definition. On the contrary, it is precisely in the ordinary, taken for granted exchanges that reality is reconstructed since everyday conversation requires shared definitions of the situation in order to make sense at all. Language of course is the key element in this process, as a means of both apprehending and reproducing the world. The biblical dictum 'In the beginning was the word' summarizes aptly that language constitutes the world and ourselves (in Carey, 1989: 25).

In the previous chapter, the prerequisite of language for the development of individual subjectivity and sanity was discussed, taking its inspiration from Foucault and Lacan. We can now expand this notion and appreciate that language constitutes society and reality as well. Thus language is not a means of reflecting reality, but the source of reality itself. 'Reality is brought into existence, is produced, by communication – by, in short, the construction, apprehension, and utilization of symbolic forms' (Carey, 1989: 25). This is not to say that there is nothing out there except the images in our head, as a collision with a moving car will prove, but that we can only define the meaning and make sense of that experience through language.

'Language' should not be conceived in the limited sense of grammar and lexicons. The articulation of language in 'discourse', in specific combinations of themes and symbols is at stake here. It is not language itself that constructs reality and subjectivity, but its expression in particular cultural and individual histories, beliefs and value systems, institutional and official jargon, subcultural expressions etc. Moreover, several non-linguistic symbolic forms contribute to the sense making process as well. Foucault (1976), for instance, has identified the dormitory lay-out of eighteenth century boarding schools as a sign of a discourse of sexuality: the presence of partitions and curtains, control of sleeping hours etc. all refer to the need to control children's sexuality. Likewise, Edelman (1964) has pointed to the use of symbols in American politics, with the American flag and the White House for instance referring to discourses of nationalism and presidential power. Through these symbolic forms societies construct their definitions of reality. It is not something an individual does by her or himself, she or he is participating in a profoundly social process, in the sense that social relations are reflected in definitions of reality as well as definitions of reality influencing social relations. The former is easily explained by referring to the processes of interaction between individuals, groups, institutions etc. that shape reality. It is important to realize, however, that these processes are not equally accessible to everyone. The power to define is intricately linked to other power relations in society, such as economic, ethnic, gender and international relations.

As emphasized earlier, dominant discourse is not monolithic and impervious, but produces its own opposition and is open to negotiation. On the other hand, discourse itself is a form of power, since both the process of discourse (the symbolic interactions) and the product of discourse (a particular set of meanings and narratives) limit the possibilities of interpretation and privilege certain meanings above others. To give an example: before the advent of the second wave of the women's movement, sexual harassment and sexual violence within heterosexual relationships were considered to be excesses of personal idiosyncrasies, and were not seen as criminal acts. The occurrence of sexual violence in the domestic sphere was made invisible by defining it as a problem which some individual women just had to cope with, an unpleasant fact of life. As a result of that definition, there was no possibility for retaliation, nor were there many support facilities. The definition of the issue as a matter of the private sphere prevented its recognition as a social problem and left the women affected without means to talk about and fight against it.

The power of discourse lies not only in its capacity to define what is a social problem, but also in its prescriptions of how an issue should be understood, the legitimate views on it, the legitimacy and deviance of the actors involved, the appropriateness of certain acts etc. This holds not only for dominant discourse, as can be easily appreciated, but also for alternative, insurgent discourse. For instance, Leong (1991) analyses how the moral discourse of radical feminists opposing pornography imposes a 'proper' standard of correct non-violent sexuality on women, and construes women as victims in need of protection.

Given that the whole idea of society, or any other collectivity for that matter, requires discourse (the mapping, description and articulation of situations and processes), which by definition has the effect of excluding, annihilating and delegitimizing certain views and positions, while including others, Foucault's seemingly extreme and hollow dictum that power is everywhere begins to make sense.

Cultural studies

So far, I have argued that feminist transmission views of communication are unsatisfactory because of their limited conceptualization of gender and communication. With regard to gender, the problem lies mainly in the observation that media distort the 'true' nature of gender, assuming a stable and easily identifiable distinction between women and men. Alternatively, I proposed to construe gender as discourse, a set of overlapping and sometimes contradictory cultural descriptions and prescriptions referring to sexual difference. Such a conceptualization of gender does not deny the possibility of fragmented and multiple subjectivities in and among women (or men for that matter), and allows for difference and variety. The difficulties with the conceptualization of communication primarily concern the 'reflection' and 'socialization' hypothesis. The idea of a reality that media pass on more or less truthfully and successfully, fails at several points: media production is not simply a matter of reflection but entails a complex process of negotiation, processing and reconstruction; media audiences do not simply take in or reject media messages, but use and interpret them according to the logic of their own social, cultural and individual circumstances; media are not only assigned to 'reflect' reality, but represent our collective hopes, fears and fantasies and perform a mythical and ritual function as well; finally, reality itself is not only an objective collection of things and processes, but is socially constructed in discourses that reflect and produce power.

How can these elements be combined into a relatively coherent approach to gender and communication? Defining gender as discourse leads to the question of what 'role' the media play in gender discourse and how that role is realized. De Lauretis (1987: 2) proposes that gender should be thought of as 'the product of various social technologies, such as cinema, and of institutionalized discourses, epistemologies and critical practices, as well as practices of daily life'. Media can thus be seen as (social) technologies of gender, accommodating, modifying, reconstructing and producing disciplining and contradictory cultural outlooks of sexual difference. The relation between gender and communication is therefore primarily a cultural one, a negotiation over meanings and values that inform whole ways of life. This is not to deny the various material aspects of the subject, for instance the underpayment of female broadcasters and the restricted access to mass media of poor and third world women. However, at the heart of the matter is the struggle over the meaning of gender.

How do these technologies of gender operate, or to put it differently, what part do the media play in the ongoing construction of gender discourse? Much depends on their location in economic structures (for example, commercial vs public media), on their specific characteristics (for example, print vs broadcast), on the particular genres (for example, news vs soap opera), on the audiences they appeal to, etc. But obviously all media are central sites at which discursive negotiation over gender takes place. The concept of discursive negotiation applies to all instances of (mass) communication and is visualized in Hall's encoding/decoding model (see Chapter 1). Separately, the elements of production, texts and reception of media make no sense; they are intricately linked in the process of meaning production. At all levels discursive negotiation takes place: the production of media texts is replete with tensions and contradictions resulting from conflicting organizational and professional discourses. For instance, creative personnel such as script writers and directors will be guided mainly by aesthetic aims and personal preferences, while managing directors may have economic and public relations interests predominantly in mind. Through the fragmented production structure meaning is constructed and expressed in the variety of media texts. As a result of the tensions in the 'encoding' process, as Hall calls it, media texts do not constitute a closed ideological system, but 'reflect' the contradictions of production. Media texts thus carry multiple meanings and are open to a range of interpretations, in other words they are inherently 'polysemic'. The thus encoded structures of meaning are brought back into the practices of audiences by their similarly contradictory, but reverse 'decoding' process.

While the concept of polysemy thus assumes audiences to be producers of meaning as well – as opposed to being confronted with meaning only, as in a transmission model – the range of meanings a text offers is not infinite, despite its essential ambiguity. 'Encoding will have the effect of constructing some of the limits and parameters within which decodings will operate' (Hall et al., 1980: 135). Thus most texts do offer a 'preferred reading or meaning' which, given the economic and ideological location of most media, will tend to reconstruct dominant values.

In the rest of the book I will add to the elements and outline of the cultural studies approach to gender and communication which I have sketched only loosely in this chapter. Such a perspective suggests to the feminist media critic and researcher the following questions:

How are discourses of gender encoded in media texts?
Which preferred and alternative meanings of gender are available in media texts and from which discourses do they draw?
How do audiences use and interpret gendered media texts?
How does audience reception contribute to the construction of gender at the individual level of identity and subjectivity and at the social level of discourse?
How can these processes be examined and analysed?

I will discuss each of these moments in the production of (mass mediated) meaning separately in the following chapters.

4

Media Production and the Encoding of Gender

It was argued in the previous chapter that media production can be seen as a process of 'encoding' meaning in media texts. In the context of gender and media studies, the relevant question therefore is how gender discourse is encoded in media texts, what contradictions and tensions in the production process give rise to particular discourses and how amenable the production process is to innovation and change. Given the various kinds of media output and the many tensions in the production process, one might argue that the major questions raised in this chapter could only be answered for each particular case in its particular historical and cultural circumstances. In part, it is the aim of this chapter to underscore just that argument, and to counter the view of media institutions as ideological molochs producing univocal sexist, capitalist and patriarchal content. By reviewing and evaluating existing research on women working in the media industries, I shall map the gendered structure of media production at the micro, meso and macro level, expressed in particular positions, tasks, experiences, values, rewards and appreciation of female communicators. The subsequent question is then whether, and how, this gendered structure affects the encoding process, an issue which has often been limited to the question of whether an increase in the number of female journalists (or producers, script writers, editors etc.) would lead to an improvement of media content. I shall finally discuss the inadequacies of phrasing the question like this – ignoring the organization and social context and assuming a universal definition of gender. In order to illustrate and clarify the complexities and tensions involved in media production, I shall begin with a discussion of Julia d'Acci's fascinating analysis of the production of the popular 1980s American police series *Cagney and Lacey*, which dealt with the work and private lives of two female New York cops (d'Acci, 1987).

Production, encoding and negotiation: *Cagney and Lacey*

Originally, *Cagney and Lacey* was meant to be a feature film. Its creators – the writers Barbara Avedon and Barbara Corday, and Barney Rosenzweig, executive producer for an American production company – were inspired by a book about the portrayal of women in Hollywood films from the early days until the present (Haskell, 1987). Never, it seemed had a pair of female buddies like Butch Cassidy and the Sundance Kid featured in a mainstream movie. Avedon, Corday and Rosenzweig came up with an idea for a film, to be called 'Freeze', involving a complete role reversal of both cops and 'robbers'. Two female cops, Chris Cagney and Mary Beth Lacey – whose friendship was unconsciously moulded on the friendship of the two writers – were to uncover the existence of a brothel with male prostitutes visited by women customers, headed by the 'Godmother'. The development of the idea indicates the different factors which contributed to the final proposal: on a social level the emphasis on role reversal can be deduced to the impact of liberal feminism; both writers were personally involved in the women's movement and anxious to incorporate their experience in their work. Moreover, they drew from their personal friendship for character development. Apart from his support for the women's movement, Rosenzweig saw an opportunity to produce a professionally innovative film, since female buddies had never before been seen.

However, not one motion picture studio wanted to put the script into production because the characters were seen as not feminine, soft or sexy enough. Some six years later, in 1980, Rosenzweig tried again with a rewritten script, but this time he went to the television networks. CBS decided to take it as a made-for-TV movie, but demanded that Cagney and Lacey be played by 'two sexy young actresses'. Rosenzweig managed to maintain his original choice for actress Tyne Daly to play the Lacey character who lives in a family situation with two children and her husband Harvey Lacey, an irregularly employed construction worker. The Cagney character, single and independent was to be played by the network's choice Loretta Swit – a major character in the popular series *MASH* – to whom CBS had a commitment for a made-for-TV movie.

Even before it was transmitted in October 1981, Cagney and Lacey attracted considerable attention from the press who recognized the novelty of a TV-movie focusing on women's work in an uncommon job, their mutual friendship and their independence. The feminist magazine *Ms* urged its readers to write to CBS and demand a weekly series, while *Ms* editors themselves lobbied the board of CBS. When the movie scored way above the average CBS programme rating and reached a 42 per cent share of the audience, CBS decided to pursue the series idea. In this second phase, it can be seen how new influences came to bear on the production of *Cagney and Lacey*. The network's choice of 'sexy young actresses' must have been inspired by its own tradition of women's representation and by an unwarranted view of audience preferences. Moreover, CBS had a promise to keep towards Loretta Swit. Rosenzweig's refusal obviously had to do with professional norms of realistic casting, while the feminist lobby seemed to have doubts about the willingness of CBS to pursue a feminist venture, a distrust which proved painfully correct in the years to come.

As it turned out, CBS was not happy after all and decided to cancel the series after only two episodes. Rosenzweig's heavy lobbying kept *Cagney and Lacey* on the air, but its existence was hardly secure. It was the Cagney character which made the network particularly uncomfortable. Being a single, career-minded and tough urban cop, Chris Cagney undermined any traditional notion of femininity. As d'Acci (1987: 214) notes: 'The evidence points to an extreme discomfort on the part of the network with "woman" represented as non-glamourous, feminist, sexually active and working class and single.' Although the early ratings suggested otherwise, CBS was afraid the audience would find the two women too unfeminine, too feminist and too lesbian. Thus the original angle of the series, focusing on women working in a non-traditional job and fighting sexism, was modified by removing overt references to feminism and by representing Cagney and Lacey as women who 'combine competency with an element of sensuality' (d'Acci, 1987: 215).

Other networks caught on to the women-orientated programming and scheduled movies such as *9 to 5* and *Gloria*, featuring independent women, opposite *Cagney and Lacey*, with the result that the potential audience was fragmented and the ratings for *Cagney and Lacey* were reduced. Had it been for the ratings alone, the series would not have survived, but several other factors contributed to its success: the women's movement launched a successful letter-writing campaign to support *Cagney and Lacey*; the series received several television nominations and awards for best series and best actress; it received critical acclaim in the press; and finally, the reruns in the summer did attract considerable audiences.

Throughout its existence *Cagney and Lacey* was subject to conflict and negotiations between writers, actors, producer, network executives and audiences which had obvious effects on the ultimate representations of gender. In this struggle, the network was the most influential actor exercising its power at all levels, for instance in script development, as illustrated by d'Acci's account of an episode in which Cagney (single, no partner) thinks she is pregnant. The writers did not even consider allowing Cagney to have an abortion, anticipating that the network would never permit such a solution. Although a miscarriage was proposed, the network rejected the story anyway, unwilling 'to shine the spotlight on pregnancy and the problems of an unmarried pregnant woman' (d'Acci, 1987: 219). Obviously, the problem at this point concerned the ideological implications of the script. Network executives countered the writers with a proposal for a story in which Cagney (in her late thirties) has to decide whether she will ever have children. This in turn was unacceptable to the writers for its lack of narrative resolution, the problem now being one of professional standards and sound scripts. Finally, the contending claims were reconciled by letting Cagney think she is pregnant although, as becomes clear by the end of the episode, she is not. How she could have become pregnant, and what she meant to do about it, is hardly discussed in the rest of the episode since that would involve such politically and socially explosive issues as birth control and abortion. A rather dim narrative remains upon which each audience member can play her own experience with (un)wanted pregnancies and 'career–children' dilemmas.

Studies of media production

Case studies like d'Acci's, however, have not been carried out often (see for some examples Ettema, 1982; Gitlin, 1983; Saferstein, 1991). As far as research on production is concerned, there is a heavy bias in communication studies towards journalism and factual programming without much attention being paid to gender issues, or to other types of media content. Feminist media studies, on the other hand, have concentrated primarily on the position, experiences and views of individual female communicators ignoring the immediate context in which they carry out their roles. D'Acci's analysis of *Cagney and Lacey* makes clear that it is not much use to study the production and encoding process from the perspective of the individual (woman) communicator. Already at the level of 'personal' ideas for a programme or a story, the influence of external factors is heavily felt: the existence and strength of the women's movement; the anticipation of network censorship or professional standards; the question of whether the creative ideas of individuals will be selected or agreed by whatever production unit; all depend on a complex interplay of personal, organizational, commercial and other factors. Hirsch (1973) proposes that the transformation of a creative individual idea into a collective mass media product should be construed as a process of passing through increasingly narrow 'gates' of production, media and distribution. In the *Cagney and Lacey* case, the ratings of the initial movie were of crucial importance; for other TV programmes the results of audience testing of pilots can be decisive. In journalism, ideas for stories are selected on the basis of other kinds of considerations mostly originating from organizational requirements such as availability and suitability of sources (cf. Gans, 1979).

The collective nature of media production is even more evident if one moves from selection processes to the actual production and construction of media products. For an outsider to the industry, it is hard to make sense of the particular and different contributions to media output of employees with intriguing and obscure titles like continuity girl, vision mixer, floor manager, executive producer, on-line producer, production assistant, editor-in-chief, senior editor, editor, reporter etc. Such a list of functions, which can be extended easily, does make clear that aside from formal hierarchies no individual communicator can be held responsible for the final product. This association of individuals needs to deliberate, consult, compromise, cooperate, reconsider, bargain, adjust and concede. Their negotiation is constrained by the organizational context which is determined among other factors by the organizational goals and constituencies, and by the social/legal context enabling and inhibiting certain kinds of media output.

Several authors have presented analytic frameworks for studying the production process. Dimmick and Coit (1982), for instance, propose to think of media production as a hierarchic system that can be studied at nine interdependent levels. At the lowest level (level 9) is the individual communicator. Her or his decisions are directly influenced by social-demographic features such as gender, ethnicity, education or age, by their cultural and political convictions, by professional features such as role conceptions and ethics, and by organizational features such as available time, space and budget. While individual freedom and autonomy is a constitutive part of the mythology surrounding media professions, decisions that are purely individual seldom occur. Gans (1979: 13), for instance writes about journalism that: 'obviously, journalists are in the end individuals, but news organizations are also sufficiently bureaucratized that very different personalities will act much the same in the same position'. On the other hand, Murdock (1980) contends that those involved in the production of TV drama are less constrained by organizational routines and that therefore knowledge of individual factors like backgrounds, lifestyles and commitments are essential to an understanding of drama production. In any case, a key issue for any study of media production is to find out which decision criteria are individual and which are determined by the communicator's environment (cf. Dimmick and Coit, 1982: 174).

So-called 'dyadic communication', face-to-face contact with other individuals, is, according to Dimmick and Coit, a direct factor influencing communicators (level 8). A more structured and influential form of interaction takes place in formal and informal groups and meetings of communicators, such as editorial meetings, professional organizations, informal socializing, etc. (level 7). Furthermore, communicators' decisions are shaped by organizational factors such as policy, organizational structure, work routines and power relations within the organization. The organizational dimensions of media production (level 6) have been studied extensively with focus on organizational policies, goals, work routines and assignments, division of labour, hierarchies etc. Most of these studies concern the production of news and indicate the routinized character of news work. Tuchman (1978b), for instance, speaks of news production as 'routinizing the unexpected'. The production of fictional content seems to be less routinized, although the production of weekly TV drama series does seem to necessitate a degree of standardization (Gitlin, 1983). The music, film and book publishing industries produce on a more irregular basis, but these organizations too have implemented routine procedures to ensure a steady input and output of creative material (Hirsch, 1973).

Moving higher up Dimmick and Coit's hierarchy the focus shifts from influences exercised upon the individual communicator to the impact of external factors on the media organization. To begin with, there is the location of the media in the community or market it caters for (level 5). The competitive structure of a market operates also at the level of 'supraorganizational' influence (level 4), which focuses on ownership and

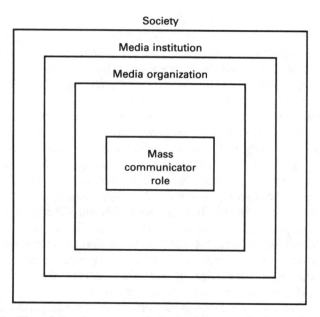

Figure 4.1 The relation between media institution, organization and role (McQuail, 1987)

management structures of media corporations. The next level (level 3) has to do with the organization of the industry as whole, and which vertical alliances (applying to the whole chain of communication from suppliers to retailers) and horizontal alliances (connecting different types of communication conglomerates) are active. Finally, there are the policies of nation states (level 2) and international organizations (level 1) regulating communication industries, communicator behaviour and possibilities, content, advertising etc.

Dimmick and Coit's taxonomy illustrates clearly the range of constitutive influences on communicators and their employers. International and national media policies and regulations place constraints on the actions and courses the media industry can take; whilst the financial-economic organization of the media industry restricts the leeway of media organizations, the latter in turn constitute the direct environment in which the individual communicator has to operate. Seen from the perspective of the individual communicator, media production entails an ever-widening set of circles constraining her or his autonomy. Most of these circles are not directly experienced but are often taken for granted as 'the way things are'. McQuail's (1987) simplified scheme of the various levels of media production demonstrates just how distant are some factors influencing a communicator's autonomy from her or his daily work experience (Figure 4.1).

Models such as that of Dimmick and Coit, McQuail and a number of others (cf. Cantor, 1980; Gallagher, 1977; Hirsch, 1977) should not be understood as adequate descriptions of the production process. They are far too general for such a purpose and suggest too strict and neatly separated hierarchies. Moreover, the basic contradiction of media production between commercial and artistic or social values tends to cut across all levels:

> The dilemma may involve a distinction between high and low culture, between professional or craft standards and commercial judgement, between self-regulation and close bureaucratic control of the work situation, between self-motivation and financial inducement, between self-monitoring and serving an audience, between using one's talents for a purpose and having them used for none except the survival of commercial success of the organization for which the work is done. (Elliott, 1977)

Despite the limitations of such models, however, they do reveal the deeply social and collective nature of media production, in which a range of factors influence the decision making process: there seems to be no such person as the 'individual' communicator. She or he has to cooperate with colleagues, has to take the specific needs, routines and traditions of the organizations into account, and is limited by the social, economic and legal embedding of the media institution. For feminist media research in particular it is important to recognize this, since – as will become clear later in this chapter – too many publications about the role and possibilities of the female journalist or broadcaster assume that women are by themselves capable of changing the media production process. To facilitate the review of research and point to gaps in existing knowledge I follow McQuail's (1987) distinction between the three levels of individuals working together, of organizational requirements and of economic and legal constraints (see Figure 4.1).

The gendered structure of media production

Women as communicators

Employees Reviewing the results of research about gender and media production more than a decade ago, Margaret Gallagher (1980) contended that exact numbers and figures about women working in the media industries were hard to come by. The industries were not particularly disposed to allow access to their organization and to their administrative records. Moreover, the nature of media organizations with their mix of tenured, part-time and freelance staff, and with their idiosyncratic alignments of productional units and facilities, made it hard to collect comparable and verifiable facts about the media workforce. Today, it seems that facts and figures about women working in the media abound, at least in western industrialized countries. The media industries themselves have initiated much research in order to provide a basis for policy measures aimed at increasing the number of women working in the industries. The European Community, for instance, set up a large scale research project on employment and positive action for women in television organizations of the EC member states which resulted in the subsequent issue of EC directives about the employment of women in the television industries (Commission of the European Communities, 1987). However, there are still many fields of communication like the magazine, film and music industry, whose labour force has not been subjected to systematic research. Moreover, we know next to nothing about the position and possibilities of women working in media industries in the developing and former communist countries.

Despite the uneven distribution of knowledge about female communicators, existing research suggests some general tendencies which seem to apply world wide. To begin with, the media industries are dominated by men, and in the western world they are dominated by white men in particular. A Unesco report comparing results from Canada, Ecuador, Egypt, India and Nigeria concludes that 'in every case women are very much a minority presence in . . . the "man's world" of the media' (Unesco, 1987). Stone (1988) contends that while affirmative action programmes stimulated the American news broadcasters to hire women members of minority groups in the 1970s, deregulatory policies of the Reagan administration and increased local competition brought this development to a halt.

Recently, in western countries like the United States, United Kingdom and the Netherlands, the number of women entering schools of journalism or academic training in communication has increased to the extent that some authors speak of a 'gender switch'. Fields like public relations and advertising are said to have become 'velvet' or 'pink collar' ghettos dominated by (white) women (Creedon, 1989). This trend points to the fact that some areas of media production are more easily accessible to women than others. From the few figures which are available, it seems for instance that magazine publishing in industrialized countries has traditionally offered jobs for women at all levels, including senior management (Johnson, 1989). One of the factors explaining why some areas of communication provide more opportunities for women than others is the status of the medium, which can differ from country to country. Radio is a good case in point. In many western countries national radio has lost its audience to television and as a news medium it has been overtaken by television as well. The resulting loss of prestige may have decreased male competition for job openings enabling women to fill the gaps. On the other hand, in many developing countries radio is still the mass electronic medium and dominated by men. For instance, in Ecuadorian radio stations 90 per cent of the total workforce is male (de Camargo, 1987). Another indication of the importance of the medium's status for the employment of women is the fact that local (low prestige) media almost invariably employ more women than national (high prestige) media (for example, Smith, 1980).

The vertical segregation of the media workforce is apparent in other divisions as well. Across the board, men dominate the technical sectors, while women are overrepresented in administration. To a substantial degree women tend to prevail in those areas that can be seen as an extension of their domestic responsibilities: in children's and educational media, programmes or sections; in consumer and domestic programmes; in human interest and feature sections of newspapers; in entertainment programming, etc. Smith (1980) contends that female journalists in Britain work predominantly in 'advertising goal' fields, where the relevance of the sector to the institution is in advertising revenue. Although economically crucial to the media organization, advertising revenue fields are not taken very seriously by media professionals and are seen as 'operating largely in order to finance what is seen as the "real" function of the papers (i.e. providing news, information and comment)' (Smith, 1980: 241). In the "real" fields of, for instance, political, foreign and economic news, and current affair programming, women tend to be a minority.

Like most other employment sectors, the media workforce is also horizontally segregated. It is hard to find women in senior management positions, even in women-dominated areas. Moreover, female managers tend to get paid less than their male counterparts, an inequality most women working in the media industry suffer from. Lafky (1989) studied the salaries of American journalists and found that even after controlling for other variables, like type of job, years of experience, market and editorial size, gender still was a significant determiner of income. For younger journalists the gap seemed to be narrowing, a trend that was also observed by Abrahamson (1990) studying the Swedish Broadcasting Company. In the case of the US journalists, however, the gap was not narrowing because of rises in the salaries of women but through a general decline in the wages of journalists. Creedon (1989: 17) concludes therefore that an increase in the number of women in media production 'does not translate into superior power or influence for women; instead, it has been translated to mean a decline in salaries and status for the field' (cf. Abrahamson, 1990; Baehr, 1981; Butler and Paisley, 1980; de Camargo, 1987; Fahim, 1987; Gallagher, 1980, 1984; Irukwu, 1987; Joshi, 1987; Muir, 1987; Smith, 1976, 1980).

The inequalities faced by women in the media industries have various sources. In many countries, direct sexual discrimination against women is forbidden and many countries and industries have installed some kind of affirmative action policy to facilitate the entrance of women and minorities to the media industries. In other cases, prevailing mores tend to inhibit direct discrimination. However, all kinds of organization procedures and routines can lead to indirect discrimination, which – by being less visible – tends to be more difficult to contest. Muramatsu (1990), for instance, argues that the system of lifetime employment prevailing in the Japanese media prevents the growth of the female workforce because job openings are very rare and thus competition is harsh. Other authors have argued that the informal recruitment procedures of media industries based on personal contacts and ('old boys') networks, tends to exclude women as potential applicants (Gallagher, 1980). Similarly, the lack of formal career structures means that ascent through the hierarchy depends unduly upon personal contacts and acceptance. According to Smith (1980: 243), 'the largely informal occupational socialization . . . tends to act against women in a number of ways by excluding them from informal information grapevines and a number of "key learning situations" which are vital to the development of a wide range of journalistic skills and the acquisition of "relevant occupational knowledge" '.

The most important barrier within the organization comes from the attitudes of male colleagues and decision makers. Gruesome anecdotes of women encountering blatant sexism abound, and can be found in any number of popular press clippings, biographies and research reports. Castro (1988: 42) reports the story of a woman applying for a vacancy at a television station: 'And then the vice president came over and stood so close to me that his nose was nearly touching mine, and said: "We don't have anything right now, but we could probably arrange something. Do you fuck?"' Research from countries as diverse as the Netherlands, the United States, India and Senegal produce strikingly similar results when it investigates the attitudes of male communicators towards their female colleagues. Joshi (1987) carried out a survey among senior level staff of the Indian television company Doordoorshan and found that most men considered women to be incapable of making independent decisions. Moreover, they preferred male colleagues and distrusted women as colleagues, feeling that their workload increased while working with women. Diekerhof et al. (1985) examined the attitudes of male newspaper journalists in the Netherlands. They too expected their female colleagues to be disloyal and some of them considered the women's professional success to be the result of 'feminine wiles'. In a survey conducted by Smith et al. (1989), American television reporters dissented from any form of sex discrimination when asked directly, yet when presented with a particular question on the ability of women to undertake war reporting, male reporters and news directors did express sexist attitudes. Senegalese female journalists experienced discrimination from their male colleagues, who kept the best stories to themselves and doubted the women's capacities (van der Wijngaard, 1990). Whatever particular cultural form they may take, discriminatory attitudes towards women on the workfloor seem to be common practice in media production world wide. Similar examples have been reported at least from Germany (Neverla and Kanzleiter, 1984), Nigeria (Irukwu, 1987), Egypt (Fahim, 1987), Canada (Craen, 1987) and Great Britain (Baehr, 1981; Muir, 1987; Smith, 1980).

A final obstacle for the entrance and advancement of women in media professions has to do with family responsibilities. The domestic and parental responsibilities of working women have proved to be a double burden in all professions. In the media industries, however, the problem seems to be even more acute, since many of its professions are said to require a round-the-clock availability. Part of the professional ideology of journalists for instance is that news happens 24 hours a day, therefore a journalist's work – like a mother's – is never done. Moreover, reporters are expected to be mobile and to travel anywhere at short notice. While the all pervasive nature of journalists' work must be considered a product of professional mythology rather than of organizational necessity, the impact of the myth is considerable. By and large female journalists have considered it impossible to combine career and family, since media organizations do not yet provide many childcare facilities and parental leave arrangements, forcing women to make a choice between a career or children as the age and demographic profile of female journalists and broadcasters testify.[1] The few women remaining in the profession after their thirties usually do not have children, whereas their male colleagues of the same age do (cf. Diekerhof et al. 1985; Neverla and Kanzleiter, 1984; Smith et al., 1989). The lack of childcare facilities and the irregular working hours may be one of the reasons why women seem to prefer public relations and advertising to journalism and broadcasting. Aside from such practical barriers societal norms and values work against the combination of a career with motherhood as well. Irukwu's (1987) study of Nigerian broadcasters suggests that as long as the ideal of the man as 'breadwinner' prevails, a female professional will not be perceived as needing the same kind of payment and rewards. Female journalists in Senegal believe that their fellow country men and women doubt their ability to mother, since they are said to spend so much time away from home (van der Wijngaard, 1990). Dutch female journalists experienced that their employers did not expect female 'career makers' to have a desire for children as well. Moreover, in the immediate surroundings of friends and family, they met with covert hostility for combining work with children (Diekerhof et al., 1985).

While the studies referred to above cover many different countries and different media sectors, the results are similar enough to warrant some rather crude generalizations: press and broadcasting are media industries dominated by men; the higher up the hierarchies, or the more prestigious a particular medium or section is, the less likely is it to find women; women tend to work in areas of communication that can be considered an extension of their domestic responsibilities and their socially assigned qualities of care, nurturance and humanity; regardless of difference in years of experience, education etc., women are paid less for the same work. These inequalities stem from indirect discriminatory recruitment procedures and from discriminatory attitudes among decision makers. Moreover, most women in media professions have experienced sexist behaviour of male colleagues. Finally, media work and motherhood have been made notoriously difficult to combine due to a lack of provisions at the workplace and to social values and beliefs.

Professionals Aside from the question of how women are employed and treated by the media industries, we know very little about their perform-

ance as media professionals. How do women perceive their own professional role and how is this role perceived by their male colleagues?
Research in this area is extremely scarce and limited mainly to journalism.
The discriminatory attitudes women experience in the media industries
seem to indicate that being a woman and being a professional is problematic.
Women are confronted with social and cultural expectations of femininity
and at the same time are expected to meet criteria of professionalism. In
the Netherlands, for instance, many female journalists feel that they are
judged primarily as women being subject to continual comment on their
appearance and 'invitations' from male colleagues. Playing this game
implies losing a great deal of prestige as professional journalists. Women
who ignore it, however – or worse, criticize it – will not be accepted by
their male colleagues as 'real women' (cf. Diekerhof et al., 1985).
Senegalese female journalists experience a different kind of tension
between 'femininity' and professionalism. They are accused of having lost
their femininity since their jobs require them to be away from home and to
'neglect' their husband and children (van der Wijngaard, 1990). Yet
another tension between 'femininity' and professionalism is expressed by
female journalists who believe that 'feminine' values such as compassion,
kindness and humanity are at odds with qualities expected of journalists
such as a certain amount of directness, distrust and toughness (Neverla and
Kanzleiter, 1984).

   While 'femininity' and journalistic professionalism are not inherently at
odds with each other, the current definitions of femininity and the
historically specific requirements of journalism produce tensions which –
while expressed in different forms – are felt by many female journalists.
There is no evidence, however, that they constitute a different group of
professionals from their male colleagues: the results of research examining
women's professional values and performance are too ambiguous to
warrant such a conclusion. For instance, female journalists in the Netherlands were asked on different occasions whether they thought women
contributed in a particular way to journalism. Two-thirds of them believe
that women journalists pay more attention to background information and
are more willing to look for spokeswomen instead of spokesmen. They
perceive a difference in approach, but not in the actual selection of topics
and issues (cf. van Zoonen, 1988).

   On the other hand, American research into journalism which focused on
factors that explain the variety of professional values held by journalists
found no significant difference at all. Johnstone et al. (1976) conclude that
education explains most of the differences of professional values. Women
do seem to hold more explicit, but not fundamentally different views on
journalism. Lafky (1990) analyses the results of a more recent survey
among American journalists and also finds no very significant differences
between women and men in journalism. A study comparing the professional values of British and German journalists suggests that in both
countries female journalists tend to adhere to advocacy or participant

roles, although in Britain this implies a desire to help and advise people, while in Germany it means propagating new ideas (van Zoonen and Donsbach, 1988). Research on actual news selection behaviour shows similar discrepancies. For instance:

Whitlow (1977) submitted to a large number of American journalists hypothetical news items which differed in terms of the traditional and non-traditional roles of women and men. Whitlow found no differences in selection behaviour, with all journalists selecting items mainly on the basis of the presence or absence of conflict.

Merrit and Gross (1978) inferred from a survey among female and male editors of women's pages in the United States that although some women had less traditional purposes in mind for the women's pages than their male colleagues, the majority of women held traditional values.

Jensen (1982) observed and interviewed journalists working in Danish television news. She noticed that women invited more spokeswomen than men.

Muramatsu (1990) conducted several case studies of women working in Japanese broadcasting claiming that women side with underdogs in society and identify with the oppressed. They tend to have a more practical view of everyday life and look at women as individuals rather than judging them by their appearance.

These few examples show that gender itself is not a sufficient factor to explain the professional performance and values of female journalists. Some studies report the absence of difference, while others claim that there is something specific about female journalists, but when examined more closely it seems that what it is exactly that constitutes the difference varies from country to country. These contradictions indicate at least the interaction of gender with the political and cultural environment of the nation state. Moreover, the studies reported have all focused on the individual communicator, ignoring the organizational influences and pressures that bear upon her or him. As was explained in the previous paragraph, the particular location of the individual in the organization might influence his or her performance and values. In order to examine the interaction of gender with political, cultural and organizational variables, we need a higher level of analysis.

Gender and the organization

There exist very few studies that examine the interaction of gender with organizational variables. D'Acci's aforementioned case study of *Cagney and Lacey* is one example, paralleled in journalism by Tuchman's and my own analysis of how the newsmaking process affects coverage of the women's movement (Tuchman,1978b; van Zoonen, 1991c, 1992b). However, these studies focus more on gender related issues than on gender *per se*. With such a dearth of research, it is only possible to give an indication of the kinds of issues and questions relevant at this level of analysis. In doing so, I shall draw mainly from my own research about journalism which addresses a number of different issues concerning gender and news organizations, ranging from the effects of professional socialization, processes and organizational policy, to the influence of national professional cultures.

According to Hirsch (1977: 24) the leading theme in the study of media organizations is the tension and conflict that arises from the necessary subordination of individuals to the organizations they work for. This usually implies a process of adaptation brought about not by repressive force but by a subtle process of rewards and punishments which ensures that communicators newly entering the field become acquainted with unwritten rules, norms and values of journalism and learn to perform accordingly. The continual pressure to produce news, shows, series, books, movies, records etc. usually leaves little room for substantive doubts and debates. A shared set of professional values therefore facilitates decision making, and as such it is instrumental to a media organization's efficiency (van Zoonen, 1989). Some authors argue that professional socialization affects women in a particular way. For instance, Smith (1976) claims that British female journalists tend to be excluded from the 'key learning areas' of hard news experience, sub-editing, night shift working and the informal pub and club culture. As a result they tend to be at a disadvantage with respect to technical, normative and folk knowledge of the organization, which seems to prevent their development as mature professionals. While Smith's argument deals with women's adaptation to the organizational rules and procedures, Neverla (1986) contends that women's disadvantage arises from the requirements of professional socialization and a competitive, assertive and detached style, which are at odds with their socialization as women. Moreover, the specific contribution in the area of sensitivity and humanity that women could make to journalism – following from their socialization as women – is not appreciated by colleagues and editors and is not considered professional. Thus for women to become professionals without forgoing their 'femininity' – the author's ideal – women have to maintain a precarious balance between 'deviance' and adaptation. Putting Smith's and Neverla's argument together suggests an interesting contradiction: Smith's call for equal opportunities accepts the status quo of the news room and implicitly denies the value of 'feminine' qualities; whereas Neverla takes these 'feminine' qualities for granted and criticizes the prevalent norms in the news room. As she herself acknowledges however, a delicate balancing act is necessary between 'femininity' and ('masculine') professionalism in order to be taken seriously as a journalist. In both cases, gender appears as a rather stable feature which journalists bring with them to the news room, remaining unaffected by the daily routines, events and meetings of the profession.

In a study I conducted among young Dutch feminist journalists, I tried to overcome this dilemma by studying how journalistic practices and socialization processes constructed a particular kind of gendered professionalism (van Zoonen, 1989). A central question was how the experience of feminist journalists at the schools of journalism, and subsequently during internships in news and other media, and the beginning of their professional careers as full-time employed journalists, affected their sense of feminism and journalism. Most of them developed their feminist ideas during their education in journalism (in the early 1980s). All three institutes of journalism had been affected by the women's movement and have incorporated a small variety of courses into the curricula which started from the liberal feminist idea that women (and men) suffer from discrimination and sex role stereotyping. The 'individual socialization history' of students was often used as a starting point to discuss the position of women and the media were said to have a responsibility in providing less stereotypical role models for women (and men). The key challenge for feminist journalism then – as expressed by the schools' curricula and my informants – was to find female spokespersons in as many non-traditional areas as possible. 'Where to find her' was the title of regularly offered courses. The way feminist journalism became defined at the institutes implied an individualistic strategy to make women just as visible as men. In their exam papers the feminist journalists all expressed the best intentions for their own professional conduct, but hardly anyone gave any thought to patterns of authority in the news room, organizational routines or the social responsibilities of colleagues and editors.

Despite the attention given by the schools to some feminist issues, the established message spread by precept and example was that feminist journalism was nonsensical and tedious. The courses occupied a marginal and optional place in the curricula; there was no substantial debate among staff and students; students preparing their exam papers about feminist ethic and role conceptions met with a lack of interest on the part of the faculty; and external examiners from newspapers, magazines and broadcasting explicitly rejected feminist concerns. The message students were given was that feminism – even moderately defined – and professional journalism were at odds with each other and this message was reinforced by the experience during internship. Most of my informants adjusted smoothly to in-house norms and values, experiencing an increase in their autonomy along the way. There was hardly any mention of conflict, although the list of issues mentioned that did give rise to tension is conspicuous: a gay demonstration, ethnicity, sexist language and 'locker room' culture in the news room. Some of the women I interviewed were deeply disappointed with journalism as they came to see it during apprenticeship – especially with the chauvinism of male journalists – and decided to pursue another career.

Already at the level of education then, the process of adjusting to professional norms tends to reaffirm a conservative status quo, less by clear cut instruction than by more subtle messages about 'professional journalism' which result in self-censorship among journalists with 'deviant' values. By the time my informants had entered the profession, they knew very well that feminism does not belong to standard operating procedures. Oddly enough though, they all said they have all the autonomy they could possibly ask for and most claim that they have the opportunity to accomplish their ideals. Yet it is strikingly clear from their accounts that a journalist who consciously seeks to make her work contribute to an improvement of the position of women – in whatever modest ways – continually meets almost insuperable obstacles to the realization of her ideals. Little by little these obstacles (attitudes of colleagues, audience conceptions, social-political contexts) take on objective status and become a self-evident part of 'normal' and desirable routines. Feminist journalists tend to accept and internalize these demands of the profession, which leads to the significant paradox that they claim to be autonomous while at the same time they report a considerable number of factors circumscribing their already moderate role conception even further.

From a secondary analysis of data about German and British journalists, another example can be drawn of the way professional and organizational surroundings construct a particular kind of 'gendered' journalism (van Zoonen and Donsbach, 1988). An important difference between German and British journalism lies in their conception of freedom of the press: 'Freedom of the press was interpreted as freedom of social communication from the very beginning in England, while on the continent – including Germany – there was a tendency to view it as a natural right of individuals to develop freely. The latter view encourages subjective evaluation, while the former impedes it' (Köcher, 1986: 49). We therefore assumed that German journalism could be characterized by ample possibilities for personal styles, while the work of British journalists would seem to be less open to individualized routines. We defined gender for the time being as a possible dimension of individuality expecting gender-specific response patterns to questions about professional values and ethics in the German survey, while gender-specific answers should be relatively absent in the British case. Indeed, the conformity among British journalists did appear to be far greater than among the German journalists; but in both countries we found some considerable gender differences. For instance, both German and British female journalists tend to adhere more to advocacy roles than male journalists, implying a desire to help and advise people in Britain, and propagating new ideas in Germany. The question was whether we should attribute these differences to gender itself, or to some other factor. Assuming ample room for individualistic professional performance in Germany we expected that individual factors such as age and political preference would be most likely to explain gender difference. The far more restricted nature of British journalism directed the search for rival explanatory factors towards organizational variables. We observed, for instance, that British female journalists tend to adhere to a conception of journalism in which helping, educating and entertaining the public, and respect for private persons were important mores. These specific role conceptions are very closely linked to traditional definitions of femininity, but they could also be explained by the position of these women in the news organization. British women tend to be overrepresented in those sectors of journalism that serve audience and advertising revenue goals, like education, human interest, women's and consumer pages, fashion and cosmetics. Given the priority which these departments give to attracting readers a role conception that is tuned to audience demands follows simply from organizational logic. Thus existing concepts of femininity are (re)constituted in and by a specific organizational context. For German female journalists the story is slightly different. They opt for an advocacy role in which taking up grievances and propagating new ideas to an audience, perceived predominantly as right wing and opinionated, are important aspects. This specific view can hardly be ascribed to gender, however, since being a woman in German journalism also means being young and on the left side of the political spectrum. Moreover, these role and ethical conceptions may be extreme but they accord with general tendencies in German journalism. Thus in both countries, it is impossible to see gender as an independent variable influencing the ideas and opinions of men and women by itself. The specific organizational context in which journalists work constructs not only whether 'gendered' professionalism can exist, but also how it will be expressed.

As a final example of the interaction of gender and organizational context, I return to my earlier analysis of the position of women reading Dutch TV news (van Zoonen, 1991b). Since the mid-1980s, the majority of news readers on Dutch national TV news have been female. They are all highly acclaimed professionals with a vast experience in other fields of journalism and do not feel that there is anything specifically feminine about their professional performance. Their principals too contend that the women were hired for their superior capacities, not because of affirmative action policy nor because of supposed attractiveness to audiences. The high presence of anchorwomen in Dutch TV news therefore, should definitely be considered a success for the emancipation of women, yet, almost in spite of the news readers themselves, there is also an undeniable gender-specific element in their presence which can be considered a by-product of the organizational goals and editorial policy of the national news. In the mid-1980s the editorial policy and style of the national news was revised. It was thought that the news should offer audiences opportunities to identify with events and personalities. Human interest stories therefore had to be a major ingredient of the news, and news readers were urged to transform their hitherto serious mode of address into a more personal and intimate style. Previously, the rationalistic approach of television news was thought to prevent identification: now the entertainment value and emotional qualities had to be emphasized. As one editor said: 'One tear on TV tells you much more than an ever so well described tear in the newspaper. Television made us communicate and participate in world affairs with tears. TV news without a tear is not good enough and we should adjust to that.'[2] In theory this 'intimization' of television news could have been achieved with an all male anchor team, but that would deny the gendered nature of subjects and the gendered nature of cultural expectations and values. While it is definitely not the case that the anchorwomen were recruited simply because they were women, it does seem that the change in editorial policy opened up a space in which it is more acceptable for women to function. A new women's terrain has been created in which traditional 'feminine' values of intimacy and emotionality are almost coincidentally coupled to women again, that is, the news readers. Writing about the British BBC news, Patricia Holland (1987: 142) has made a similar observation:

> Is there some quality expected of news readers, which, despite the apparent contradictions, is turning this into a suitable role for women to play? . . . Is this role of mediation and management one that can be reconciled with the forms of femininity that have been constructed out of power relations between women and men?

However, while Holland claims that news reading has become a performer's job especially appropriate to women because 'they are easy on the eye', another exploitation of femininity is at stake in the Dutch case. Here the news readers cannot convincingly be described as objects of the audience's gaze. A comparison with the caring and never failing mother who tucks you in after a day of emotional arousal seems more to the point, a characterization which is underlined by the deliberately plain and ordinary appearance of the anchorwomen.

The three studies discussed here are all examples of the way gender interacts with the organizational context. While limited to studies in journalism, the issues addressed – professional socialization, organizational culture and structure, and organizational goals and policy – are relevant to other types of media production as well. In fact, Hirsch (1977: 13) has shown convincingly that in the actual production and distribution of news and entertainment the organizational similarities outweigh the differences. But the three case studies discussed above also warn against too much generalization. The studies have illustrated that gender takes on a specific meaning in particular organizational contexts (although not necessarily a new meaning), but the extent to which this happens or is allowed to happen, and its specific sources, expressions and consequences differ from case to case.

Gender and economic, social and legal contexts

At this level of analysis, the question is how the economic organization of media production, and its social and legal environment, relate to gender, and in particular to the discourses of gender circulated by the media. Apart from rather general political economic analyses of the media, which show that their profit making, commercial interests and their transnational power tend to support consensual and conservative values with regard to gender and many other issues, little detailed and relevant research has been done in this area. This does not mean that the political economic approach has no relevance to matters concerning media and gender; on the contrary, it points to the limits of cultural production set by the prevailing economic and power relations in the industry, and raises the old insuperable issue of the relation between the macro level of the media institution and the micro level of media texts and audiences. This is not an issue I am particularly keen to address here, since it seems that the immediate concerns with gender and media are located at the micro and meso levels of media production discussed earlier, and at the level of media–audience interactions (to be discussed in later chapters). Suffice it to say at this point that the political economic relations of the media industries are an important circumscribing factor inflicting valence on media access and output, that is, a bias towards a particular kind of meaning and social relevance (Bush, 1983). This tendency has been recognized clearly by the women's movement which, by a variety of means, has tried to put pressure on the industries to live up to their social rather than their commercial responsibilities. In Chapter 2, I discussed, for instance, the way the American women's movement challenged the licence renewal of TV stations failing to meet emancipatory demands. While none of the attempts was successful, the action did sensitize broadcasters to the issue of women's liberation. Other minority groups have been in the forefront of criticizing the media as well and have been able to establish themselves as legitimate lobby groups criticizing the media about their representation (Montgomery, 1989). While there are indications that some media organizations will take some minority concerns into some consideration (Gitlin, 1983), the pervasive commercial logic of the media constitutes the overwhelming criterion for decisions and policies. Public broadcasting differs less and less in this respect, since increasingly they have to compete for the same audiences as commercial organizations producing an organizational logic which is remarkably similar (Ang, 1991). As a rule – with the proverbial exception – media organizations will hardly ever bend directly to social pressure from outside, unless it is in their own interest. Thus, when it appeared that women were increasingly taking up paid labour, they were recognized as an important new group of consumers to be addressed by 'modern' advertisements showing women as capable workers, a change much demanded by the women's movement but only realized by the changed market structure (Janus, 1977; Rao, 1992).

Still, the system is not as impervious as it seems. Turow (1982), looking at the conditions under which unconventional innovatory TV shows like *All in the Family* came into being, found that the organizational logic is sometimes superseded by personal ambitions of network executives and producers. A particularly relevant example is given by Marguerite Moritz (1989) in an examination of the possibility of representing gay women on prime time American television. According to Moritz lesbian characters have discretely begun their 'fictional coming out' since a changing institutional context has lifted the former taboo status of the subject. Moritz traces several factors that account for the increased room for lesbian characters and storylines. According to the networks, their policy towards gay and lesbian issues has become more liberal because of the increased social acceptance of homosexuality. There is a less considered reason as well; as a result of budget cuts, standards departments at the networks, which control the standards of morality and decency of programme proposals and scripts, lost up to 40 per cent of their staff, necessitating a less rigid enforcement of rules. Next, the competition of cable and video faced by the networks has undermined their monopoly of the entertainment sector, forcing them to look for new, creative and competitive programmes and approaches. According to Moritz, cable TV and cinema both proved that gay themes can be profitable and appealing to audiences which have been raised on television and are extremely familiar with the usual genres and storylines. Moreover, Moritz contends that American audiences are willing to be entertained and informed about controversial issues. Moritz concludes that the representation of lesbianism relates to white, middle class heterosexuality: 'In this sense what we are getting more of from prime time television is not lesbians coming out, so much as lesbians coming in' (1989: 75). All in all, a change in the social, economic and organizational environment has enabled the incorporation of a particular kind of lesbianism into prime time television programmes.[3]

Encoding

The research presented in the previous sections clearly shows that the gendered structure of media production extends from micro and meso to macro levels. Although in some instances it was clear how this gendered structure affects the encoding of gender discourse in media content, it is difficult, if not impossible, to draw a straightforward connection between the gendered structure of production and the encoding of gender discourse. Nevertheless, the feminist concern with media production is mainly inspired by a desire to influence media content in a more feminist direction, however defined. 'Getting a grip' on media production should theoretically yield strategies for innovation and change, but unfortunately for such aims, the encoding of meaning is a process which escapes simple generalizations, depending rather on particular, historical articulations of the preferences and performance of individual communicators, the organizational context they work in, and the larger social environment of the media institution. As a result it is not easy to hypothesize whether and how in general the gendered production structure affects the encoding of meaning. Case studies like that of d'Acci (1987) presented at the beginning of this chapter are required in all areas of media production in order to get a grasp on the range of encoding practices.

This conclusion is definitely at odds with a premise that underlies much

feminist research on media production, which is that an increased participation of women in the media industries, taking up positions at all levels of
the organization, would be to the benefit of the feminist or emancipatory
project. To a certain extent this is a truism, since as a matter of relatively
straightforward civil rights every profession should be accessible to
women, ethnic minorities and the disabled. Moreover, for isolated women
working in male dominated professions, the arrival of female colleagues
might mean a considerable relief. To this extent, the feminist claim to
stimulate the employment of women in the media industries – journalism
and broadcasting in particular – is entirely legitimate. However, most
authors do not leave it at that, they contend that media content would also
benefit from an increased number of female communicators. One comes
across this argument in different disguises. For example, in a preface to an
equal opportunities guide of the European Community, Vasso Papandreou,
member of the Committee on Employment and Industrial Affairs, notes
that women should obtain equal positions in broadcasting 'in order to
influence and shape the programmes we see'.[4] Miiko Kodama observes
that in Japanese broadcasting there are no women in the positions of
director or producer of news programmes, which means that 'women's
views and volition are totally ignored in the process of news selection'
(Kodama, 1991: 38). Maurine Beasly speculates that 'the nature of
[American] news itself might change, at least somewhat, if women become
the majority in the newsroom', but changes her mind after a disappointing
personal encounter with the press (Beasly, 1989: 189). In the late 1970s,
the Swedish Broadcasting Corporation adopted an equal opportunities
programme, assuming that 'an equal distribution of women and men in as
many occupations as possible is a necessary – if not necessarily sufficient –
condition for equality in the company's programme output' (Abrahamson,
1990: 10).

In spite of its attractive simplicity and apparent utility, there are serious
theoretical fallacies involved in this argument that lead to practical and
political repercussions (cf. van Zoonen, 1988). To begin with, for media
output to change as a result of the presence of women in the profession,
one must be convinced that female communicators share a certain perspective, approach, preference or style that distinguishes them collectively
from their male colleagues. In other words, one must assume 'femininity',
however defined, as a feature of female journalists and 'masculinity' as a
different characteristic of male journalists. Thus, a dichotomous conceptualization of gender emerges, with gender inevitably and consistently
attached to human beings in whatever social context. In the previous
chapter, I argued that gender should not be conceived as a fixed property
of individuals but as part of a continuing process by which subjects 'work'
on a sense of self. Human identity can therefore not be thought of as
stable, but should be seen as fragmented and dynamic, depending among
other things on the particular articulation of various discourses in concrete
historical contexts. If we conceive gender as such, we shall not expect that

female communicators will have enough in common to produce a radically different type of media output. On the contrary, as I tried to show in discussing the articulation of gender and organizational context, the particular position and experience of women in media organizations construct an identity of 'woman and professional' that can take many different forms, mostly traversed by the tension between professionalism and being a woman which dominant culture dictates. Next, it is imperative to realize that gender is not the only relevant dimension when discussing the possibilities of transforming media production. Film and video maker Alile Sharon Larkin, for instance, duly argues that not only white patriarchal culture but white feminists as well, have ignored and framed the experiences of black women:

> I believe that many contemporary Black women artists have been compelled to speak with a voice that is not really our own. . . . As a Black woman I experience all areas of oppression – economic, racial and sexual, I cannot 'pick and choose' a single area of struggle. I believe it is in this way that feminists and other progressive whites pursue their own interests at the expense of those of us subjected to racism. (1988: 158)

Arguing for an increase in the number of women working in the media industries, without incorporating prominent discourses of identity and politics such as race, class, sexuality etc., is an address to the interests of middle class women, mainly from the dominant ethnic groups. In western industrialized countries policies built on this principle are bound to produce improvements, mainly for white middle class women, which is in itself not bad, but certainly extremely limited (see also Baehr, 1981).

Secondly, the call for more women communicators, in order to transform media output, completely ignores the organizational context in which media production takes place. Apart from expecting a particular input from women, it is assumed that the individual communicator is sufficiently autonomous to implement her own preferences without significant modification by colleagues, technical requirements, professional values, organizational routines etc. Admittedly, literary production and film- and video-art, both produced in relatively relaxed organizational settings, have seen the emergence of cultural products labelled 'feminine writing' or '*écriture feminine*' (cf. Showalter, 1989). Others have attempted to develop specific 'feminine' film styles, characterized, according to some, by a disavowal of traditional cinematographic means such as linear narratives, realistic visualization and voyeuristic identification (cf. Mulvey, 1975; Erens, 1990). Cultural products subject to the organizational logic of mass cultural production, as in the press and broadcasting, do not leave much room for individual autonomy. It is tempting therefore to conceive of the organizational logic and routine as a factor inhibiting the expression and impact of women communicators. Apart from the problem of defining the specific nature of these expressions that were discussed earlier, organizational power is not merely restrictive but significantly productive as well. Specific organizational policies, routines, job requirements etc. are intersected by different discourses among which are those of gender, ethnicity, professionalism, to produce an organizational identity reflecting both the individual preferences and styles of the communicator and the productional culture of the media organization.

The argument proposed in this chapter does not lead to straightforward conclusions about the way the gendered production structure affects the encoding process. By demonstrating the complexities, contradictions and tensions involved in the production of the American TV series *Cagney and Lacey*, the concept of negotiation and encoding was made concrete. Then, the different types of possible contradictions were separated analytically by distinguishing micro, meso and macro levels of production. Although existing research on women in media production has been conducted mainly at the micro level of demographic and occupational features and values, the gendered structure of production is visible at meso and macro levels as well. How this gendered structure of production affects the encoding process depends on the particular coupling of 'organizational identities' of communicators – referring to the mixture of discourses of gender, ethnicity, professionalism etc. which constitute the communicator – and organizational routines, requirements and policies. Such a perspective necessitates academic research on concrete cases of media production, such as examining the production histories of particular programmes, the coverage of feminist issues in the news or observing the daily routines and practices of media production units. Strategically, such a perspective does not undermine the call for an increase of the number of women communicators, since that is perfectly legitimated by the consideration of equal opportunities. But to expect that an increase in women communicators will influence media content in a desired feminist direction, is theoretically and strategically unsound. For a feminist cultural politics other strategies are necessary, an issue that I shall return to in the last chapter.

Notes

1. In Dutch journalism, the majority of female journalists are younger than 35, are unmarried and do not have children. Their male colleagues are older on average, married and do have children (Diekerhof et al., 1985).

2. Editor in chief, Peter Brusse, *Elsevier*, 14 May 1988.

3. Moritz' study dates from 1989. Susan Faludi argued in 1991 in her book *Backlash* that the programmes on American TV had rapidly become more conservative as a result of the Reagan decade. It may prove that the spirit of the Clinton administration will inspire networks and producers toward a more liberal style of programming again.

4. Preface to *Gelijke kansen in de Europese Omroep* (Equal Opportunities in European Broadcasting), Commission of the European Communities, no date. My translation from the Dutch.

5

Media Texts and Gender

In an earlier chapter, media were described as technologies of gender, accommodating, modifying, reconstructing and producing, disciplining and contradictory renditions of sexual difference (cf. Chapter 3). One of the sites where we can directly observe how these technologies operate are media 'texts', such as movies, TV programmes, books, newspapers, records etc. When focusing on media output solely, the main task for feminist media research is to unravel both the dominant and alternative meanings of gender encoded in media texts, and their articulation with other discourses such as for instance, ethnicity, class and sexuality. In confronting such issues, feminist media critics have tended to make sweeping statements on media representations of women, femininity and gender. 'According to feminists, the media-created woman is (1) wife, mother and housekeeper for men, (2) a sex object used to sell products to men, (3) a person trying to be beautiful for men' (Hole and Levine, 1971: 249). Franzwa discusses television and claims that

> televised images of women in large measure are false, portraying them less as they really are, more as some might want them to be. . . . Television women are predominantly in their twenties. . . . portrayed primarily as housewives . . . restricted primarily to stereotyped positions such as nurses and secretaries . . . portrayed as weak, vulnerable, dependent, submissive and frequently, as sex objects. (1978: 273–4)

Davies et al. contend that media and women's magazines in particular purvey images that tell women how to be 'a perfect mother, lover, wife, homemaker, glamorous accessory, secretary – whatever best suits the needs of the system' (1987: 4). While mass media do indeed present us with an incessant stream of gender stereotypes that can evoke curious and hilarious as well as indignant or infuriated reactions, general statements such as those above fail to capture the specific nature of media texts. The claim, for instance, that media output underrepresents women has never applied to women's genres such as mass produced romantic fiction, women's magazines, soap operas and such cinematographic expressions of melodrama as the 'women's weepies' (Byars, 1991). Moreover, it seems that television is becoming more and more 'feminized' with the growing popularity of soap operas, talk and game shows (Fiske, 1988). As far as mere numbers are concerned then, inclusive statements about media representations of women are bound to be much too general. Just as we do not speak of the 'content' of speech, books or education, it is impossible to think of mass media content as a unifiable category, 'especially since its volume and internal variety continually increase and the boundaries around "mass media" are increasingly hard to discern' (McQuail, 1987: 176). Research in the area of media output for that matter is vast, and it is inconceivable that a comprehensive review – assuming the possibility – would demonstrate consistent distinctive, gendered features of media texts. Already by 1977 a bibliography about sex stereotypes in media output contained more than a thousand entries (Courtney and Whipple, 1983). Aside from numbers and roles, different media texts are also and often better characterized by their specific narrative and visual conventions which structure the meaning of characters, their mutual relationships and their positions in the 'story'. A range of distinctions such as medium type, genre, formats, target audience etc., differently determine particular representations of gender and make valid generalizations in this area even less feasible. For principal and pragmatic reasons then, this chapter will not offer a general review of the way gender has been encoded in various media texts.[1] Instead, the aim of this chapter is to familiarize the reader with the two basic approaches to the study of media output: content analysis and semiotics. As will become clear later, a semiotic approach fits the theoretical framework of this book best. However, given the frequent occurrence of content analysis of feminist media research and its relevance to specific purposes, its merits and methods will be extensively discussed as well. To facilitate comparison between the two approaches, I shall use a particular genre to illustrate the differences in assumptions, methodology and types of results.

In the context of the representation of gender, a focus on advertising seems a particularly appropriate choice. From its rebirth in the late 1960s, the women's movement has singled out advertising as one of society's most disturbing cultural products. Monitoring projects, consumer boycotts and other means have been employed to put pressure on advertising agencies to come up with more diverse and less traditional portrayals of women. While the accompanying academic research on advertising waned in the mid-1980s, the subject nowadays seems to have attracted the renewed interest of cultural and feminist critics. As a cultural form, advertising displays a preoccupation with gender that is hardly matched in any other genre. 'In modern advertising, gender is probably the social resource that is used most by advertisers. Thousands of images surround us every day of our lives that address us along gender lines. Advertising seems to be obsessed with gender and sexuality' (Jhally, 1987: 135). This obsession is said to spring from the 'signifying power' of gender. Advertisements and commercials need to convey meaning within limited space and time and will therefore exploit symbols that are relevant and salient to society as a whole. As one of the most deeply felt elements of subjectivity and the social structure, gender provides such symbols most effectively: 'Something that can be conveyed fleetingly in any social situation and yet something that strikes at the most basic characteristics of the individual'

(Goffman, 1976: 7).[2] Thus the extremely condensed form of communication in advertising lends itself exceptionally well to an examination of cultural values, beliefs and myths connected to gender.

Just as there is no unity in media output, neither is research about media texts a unified body of work. Nevertheless, according to McQuail (1987: 192) the question of how media output relates to society underlies the majority of analyses of media texts, raising the issue of how mass communication performs its mediating role in society. The feminist transmission models of communications discussed in Chapter 2 assume a rather straightforward relation between media and society, accusing the mass media of conveying a distorted picture of women's lives and experiences and demanding a more realistic reflection instead. Mass media are thought to produce symbols of reality, expressing in an abbreviated form the nature of a particular reality (cf. Carey, 1989). However, symbols have another capacity as well that is often overlooked in transmission models of communication. They function as symbols for reality, (re)constructing reality while simultaneously representing it. The latter view of symbols is central to constructivist views of communication that perceive 'reality' as the product of the social and sense making activities of human beings. Thus, the distinction between transmission and constructivist models of communication discussed in Chapter 3 expresses itself also in a different prioritizing of the dual capacity of symbols to function simultaneously as symbols of reality (transmission models) and as symbols for reality (constructivist models), and in a different conceptualizing of the relation between media output and society. In part, this distinction is reflected in different modes of analysis as well, ranging from content analysis which provides an 'unproblematic' description of media output as consisting of particular social types and categories, to semiotic analyses of the subjective, moral and aesthetic dimensions in media output. Although the interdisciplinary nature of both feminist and cultural studies seems to require at least some convergence between the two methodologies, it is still quite unlikely that one will find both content and semiotic analyses used in the same project, owing to their different disciplinary origins, content analysis being a sociological approach and semiotic analyses rooted in the humanities.

Symbols of reality: content analysis

Assumptions and methodology

Content analysis is often employed to assess the manifest characteristics of large quantities of media output. Typical research problems in this field are for instance: the roles, psychological and physical features of women and men occurring in a variety of genres like country music (Saucier, 1986), advertising (Courtney and Whipple, 1983), television news, commercials and serials (Thoveron, 1986) or films (Haskell, 1987; Rosen, 1973); the incidence of violence in American television programmes (Gerbner et al., 1980). This list gives only an impression of the kinds of questions addressed by content analysis and is by no means exhaustive. In general its aim is to compare features of media output with concomitant features in reality. Thus, a typical conclusion of a content analytic study would be that the occurrence of violence on television grotesquely exaggerates the amount and type of violence one is likely to encounter in real life. In feminist research, the exemplary conclusion is that media output fails to represent the actual numbers of women in the world (51 per cent) and their contribution to the labour force.

Formally, content analysis is defined as 'a research technique for the objective, systematic and quantitative description of the manifest content of communication' (Berelson, 1952). The respective elements in this by now classic dictum require some explanation. To begin with, the focus on manifest media content forms an important limitation of content analysis since the researcher is prevented from reading between the lines of media output, and is expected not to 'dig' below the manifest level of analysis or to descend to the level of latent meanings and associative conclusions. Only the explicit words, sentences, texts, images – the signs that actually appear in the media text – are taken into account. To many this might seem like an unacceptable limitation since so much of what makes media output special, interesting or pleasurable consists precisely of the latent and associative meanings excluded from such an analysis. However, this limitation can also be considered an asset of content analysis, since it enables a methodology that fulfils traditional scientific requirements for 'objectivity' and one that produces results that will be generally accepted as 'true' and 'reliable'. A focus on manifest content ensures that different investigators will reach a level of agreement about the message under study and that a repetition or replication of the same project will produce roughly similar results. The inclusion of latent meanings in the analysis would imply the recognition of individual and cultural-specific interpretations of media texts which would lead to disagreements and contradictions about the material involved, a truly gruesome prospect for most content analysts.

How is a typical content analysis conducted? For instance, suppose we were interested in finding out how women and men are portrayed in television series of the 1990s. While this might seem a stale question, in the past decade such questions have hardly been posed in feminist media research of any significance. One of the reasons for conducting such an analysis therefore, could lie in the desire to have fresh 'hard data' on the portrayal of women. Secondly, one might be interested in assessing whether and how transformations in women's position in society are reflected in television series. Another motivation might be to test the more or less intuitive comments of authors such as Fiske (1988) and Brown (1990a) that television series are typical women's products. Several decisions – whose outcomes depend on the motivation of the research –

Variable	Value	Label
Gender	1	Woman
	2	Man
Race	1	Black
	2	White
Occupation	1	Housewife
	2	Blue collar
	3	White collar
	4	Management
Residence	1	Rural
	2	Urban
Marital status	1	Umarried
	2	Married

Figure 5.1   *Hypothetical coding scheme*

need to be made in order to conduct a successful content analysis (Holsti, 1969; McQuail, 1987). To begin with one needs to decide from which 'universe' or sample of television drama the study will draw: which types of series should be included? Is it necessary to include all series or will a sample suffice? Consequently, is it necessary to analyse all episodes of the selected series or will a second sample do? Is it to be a study of television series that are broadcast in the 1990s, or will the project be limited to those series that were actually *produced* in the 1990s? Should foreign series be included in the sample or is it a study of domestic television only? Decisions like these have important consequences for the extent to which the results of the analysis can be generalized to all series, or domestic series only, police series or soaps only etc.

The next step in the analysis is to construct a coding scheme and decide on units of analysis. The nature of the coding scheme depends on what we actually want to know about the portrayal of women and men in television drama. Possibly, we might be interested in a number of sociological variables like the presence of women and men, race, age, occupation, residence, marital status. The units of analysis could be the individual characters and a hypothetical coding scheme might look like that in Figure 5.1.

While this simplified coding scheme uses the most straightforward categories possible, some of the problems one can run into doing content analysis are already evident. How, for instance, to classify a character's age when we are dealing with a biographical drama in which the main character is followed from birth to burial? Is one not simplifying race by coding it as black or white only? What to do with a double occupation of housewife and reporter for instance? Such problems are exacerbated if one attempts to incorporate more complex features of women and men in TV drama, such as their physical and psychological make-up. Physical characteristics like beauty or strength, for instance, are subject to differences in individual perceptions, while psychological features such as dominance or submissive-

Table 5.1 *Occupation of males and females in American television commercials*

Female (n=230)		Male (n=155)	
Housewife/mother	56	Husband/father	14
Stewardess	8	Professional athlete	12
Model	7	Celebrity	8
Celebrity/singer/dancer	5	Construction worker	7
Cook/maid/servant	3	Salesman	6
Secretary/clerical	3	Businessman	6
		Pilot	6
		Criminal	5
		Mechanic	3
		Lawyer	3
		Interviewer	3
Other jobs	18	Other jobs	27

ness are hardly ever unambiguously distributed among television characters. Whereas the latter kind of information is often more interesting and relevant to the interpretation of television characters than more straightforward sociological characteristics, the reliability of such data is often low due to the ambiguity of such features. Thus there is a trade-off in content analysis between reliability and meaningfulness.

A following step involves matching the coding scheme with the chosen sample of television series. This normally involves a group of coders who have been instructed by the researcher how to employ the coding scheme in such a way that individual variation among coders is eliminated. In fact, tests and figures indicating the reliability of content analyses all stem from statistical procedures which measure the degree of consent among coders (cf. Holsti, 1969; Krippendorf, 1980).

Advertising

The results of content analysis often take the form of frequency tables like the one shown in Table 5.1. These data were collected in 1971 by Dominick and Rauch (1972).[3] From about 1000 commercials shown on New York city network stations, they selected those in which women appeared for three seconds or longer, or in which they had one or more lines of speech. A comparative sample of men was taken too. As Table 5.1 shows, women were depicted in a smaller variety of occupational roles than men, with most of them working as a housewife and/or mother. In addition, 75 per cent of all commercials in which women appeared promoted products used in the kitchen or bathroom. In commercials for cosmetics and personal hygiene women dominated as well, while men on the other hand, held more high status jobs and were seen purchasing high ticket items such as cars. Voice-overs and product representatives were predominantly male.

Courtney and Whipple (1983) report a number of follow-up studies and replications and conclude that trends in TV commercials of the 1970s and 1980s did not change significantly, although there seemed to be a tendency to portray women more often working outside the home, and men more often in domestic settings. Research into changes in the portrayal of men and women in advertisements in American general interest magazines, such as *Time*, *Reader's Digest*, the *New Yorker* and *Newsweek*, roughly corroborates these results. From the late 1950s to the early 1980s women are increasingly shown working outside the home, but this number never exceeds 25 per cent. Working roles of women have changed a little, with more women working in professional and middle level business in recent years. The majority of women are portrayed as non-working, and whereas this meant portrayal in family roles in the early 1960s, in later years the decorative function of women has been exploited more often. As in the TV commercials, the goods which women are seen purchasing in advertisements relate primarily to domestic duties, beauty and cosmetics. Like TV commercials, print advertisements show men less often as workers, but this number is still a considerable 50 per cent. Men's work roles in print advertisements have changed from business to entertainment and sports, and their increasing presence in non-working roles has meant a greater emphasis on their decorative function but not on their role in the family.

The changes in the depiction of women in advertising, especially their increased portrayal as professionals working in high status jobs, have been interpreted by many researchers as a success for women's liberation and as a measure of social and advertiser acceptance of changing sex roles (cf. Courtney and Whipple, 1983: 19). This rather optimistic conclusion would seem to be a direct result of the theoretical assumptions of content analysis and its methodological peculiarities. Advertisements are seen as a reflection of the changing reality of women's social position and of the influence of the women's movement, presenting us with an image of the 'new woman':

> She is independent, confident and assertive, finding satisfaction in the world of work and recreation, seeking excitement, adventure and fulfillment. She is a far cry from the consumer . . . finding her satisfaction within a rather small world and the center of this world is her home. (Cagan, 1978: 8)

There are, however, at least two other stories to be told about the 'new woman'. If we do not conceive of advertising as a reflection of reality, but as an expression of capitalist consumer culture it is clear that the 'new woman' is primarily interesting for her increased purchasing power. Her economic independence supports the capitalist market economy, instead of reforming or even undermining it, as more radical and socialist inclined feminists might have envisaged. Instead of signifying progress, the presence of a 'new woman' in contemporary advertising can thus be perceived as the co-optation of feminist ideals into acceptable fantasies of individual middle class achievement and success. A second problem with the cheerful visions of the 'new woman' is that the image itself is not problematized. The methodology of content analysis only allows a recognition of the social roles which women perform: the evidence of advertisements portraying the 'new woman', however, reveals that she only departs marginally from her older, more traditional sisters.

Take, for example, the slogan used to promote the Jenni Barnes 'Working Style' range of clothing. It proclaims as 'the Jenni Barnes philosophy' that 'A woman should look forward to dressing for the office'. This 'philosophy' constructs the office as another happy occasion for women to dress up and present themselves. And indeed in a photograph used in one of the Jenni Barnes advertisements the woman is portrayed stepping confidently towards the camera in an office environment, observed by a male colleague from behind; but she is not portrayed actually *working*. To focus on her working role would be to ignore completely the dimension of traditional femininity that is exploited in the text of the advertisement.

Content analysis in general suffers from theoretical and methodological problems like this. It gives precedence to manifest content as the bearer of meaning at the expense of latent content and form, and it assumes that frequencies of certain characteristics are valid indicators of meaning. Finally it produces results whose relation to the actual media experience of producers and audiences is unclear:

> This result [of content analysis] is also based on a form of 'reading' of content which no actual 'reader' would ever, under natural circumstances, undertake. In a certain sense, the new 'meaning' is neither that of the original sender, or of the text itself or of the audience, but a fourth construct, which has to be interpreted with care. (McQuail, 1987: 184)

Such objections have made content analysis less and less 'fashionable' in feminist media research. Byars (1991) observes for instance that the 'images of women' approach to gender in film studies has been rejected and ridiculed by most feminist film theorists for its lack of theoretical sophistication. Nevertheless, in certain contexts and for certain purposes content analysis does yield valuable results. When the research in the area of gender and media is scarce, as for instance in most developing countries, content analysis is instrumental in providing a general impression of the representation of women and men. Also, as a resource for policy and programme development – arenas that notoriously prefer 'hard data' – content analysis is an invaluable means of convincing decision and programme makers of the necessity for a diverse portrayal of women and men. Cast within a solid theoretical framework, content analysis can shed light on social and cultural matters of representation. The study of cultural indicators is often mentioned as an example, be it not for its relevance to feminist issues. In this perspective a culture communicates with itself by means of its total mass media output with television being the prime mass medium. Through large scale content analyses carried out over several years, researchers working in this tradition have tried to show that American television as a whole carries consistent messages that devalue

women, blacks and the poor by underrepresenting them and by dispropor-
tionately making them the victims of violence (Gerbner et al., 1980).
Similar patterns have been established by other researchers and for other
genres. It would seem beside the point to deny the relevance of these
findings on the basis of a lack of theoretical sophistication, a neglect of the
specificities of media formats, genres and individual programmes or the
discrepancy with subjective media experiences of audiences (cf. McQuail,
1987). What should be emphasized is that the analysis of such broad and
widespread trends in media output does not produce self-evident meanings, only data upon which to base a substantial discussion of the question:
'So what?' (Cf. Fiske, 1980: 127).

Symbols for reality: semiotics

Semiology or semiotics has become quite popular in feminist media
criticism because of its ability to unravel structures of meaning beyond the
mere presence or absence of women in cultural forms. Drawing on various
disciplines in the humanities, such as philosophy and linguistics, it is not an
easy field to get acquainted with, especially since the relevant authors
differ in their interpretations and often write in an extremely abstract
manner.[4] The purpose of this chapter therefore is not so much to explain
the intricacies of the field as it is to show what semiotics can do in terms of
analysing meanings.

The American philosopher Peirce and the Swiss linguist de Saussure are
considered to have laid the groundwork for semiotics but it was not until
the 1960s that the work of Roland Barthes introduced semiology to wider
audiences applying it to various forms of popular culture, ranging from
toys, hairstyles and chips to cooking, soap powders and the new Citroen
car (Barthes, 1957). As the examples show, almost anything can be considered a sign, but some obvious examples of signs and sign systems are,
for instance, words combined in the sign systems of language or images
combined in the sign systems of art, photography, film, television etc.

Historically, the female body has provided very powerful 'signs'
(cf. Warner, 1985). The French nation, for example, is symbolized by
'Marianne', a virtuous female revolutionary. The Statue of Liberty in
the United States – the first encounter of millions of immigrants with
the American values of freedom and individualism – is a woman. In the
western world Justice is represented in the image of a blindfolded woman
holding a balance. Women have also symbolized less noble ideas, in
Christianity, for instance, beginning with Eve's mistake in tasting the
apple. In mass media output, female characters are often constructed as
archetypes of virtue and vice. Viewers familiar with the codes of Anglo-
American television will 'know' for instance that in cinema and television a
young, blonde girl dressed in white usually signifies innocence and probity,
just as dark haired women tend to signify danger and sexuality. In the

	Symbol	Icon	Index
Signify by	convention	resemblance	connection
Example	words	picture statue	smoke-fire symptom-disease
Process	must learn	can see	can figure out

Figure 5.2   *Three aspects of signs (Berger, 1982: 15)*

American soap opera *Dynasty*, which was extremely popular around the world in the 1980s, this particular set of signs was employed to set up one of the main antagonisms in the series, between blonde virtuous Chrystle (played by Linda Evans), married to business tycoon Blake Carrington and usually dressed modestly in pastel colours, and evil Alexis (Joan Collins), Blake's ex-wife, a brunette often extravagantly dressed in conspicuous colours like red or black. Media output is ridden with such signs and it is up to the semiologist to analyse how particular combinations of signs in sign systems construct particular meanings. In doing so, semiotics approaches every sign system as if it were studying the lexicon and grammar of language, focusing on the choice and particular combination of words (signs). All sign systems are treated as 'texts', which explains the common reference to media output as media texts.

In order to understand how a typical semiotic analysis is conducted, it is necessary to take a closer look at the key concepts involved. According to de Saussure, who looked at language primarily, a sign consists of two elements. Its physical appearance in, for instance, a combination of letters forming the word 'rain' is called the 'signifier', whereas the concept it refers to – a particular type of weather is called the 'signified'. In the case of words the relation between signifier and signified is completely arbitrary and based on convention rather than a self-evident relationship between the four letters *r a i n* and water falling from the sky. Considering other sign systems, however, the relation between signifier and signified is less arbitrary. A statue or a picture, for instance, signify by resemblance between signifier and signified, whereas red spots on a human body may signify a given disease. Peirce, therefore, distinguished between three aspects of signs: iconic, indexical and symbolic (Figure 5.2).

Signs in isolation are hardly ever meaningful, they derive their relevance not only from the particular articulation of signifier–signified, but also from their relation to other signs. Those relations can be syntagmatic, involving the particular combination of signs, or paradigmatic, pertaining to the relation of a sign present within the sign system to its implied absent counterpart. It is in the latter respect that semiotics can be related to the structural analysis of folk and fairy tales (Propp, 1923). Structuralism assumes that binary oppositions like female/male, good/evil, black/white underlie sign systems and broader cultural systems like, for instance, kinship relations (Lévi-Strauss, 1962). For structuralists any particular sign

Signifier	Signified
close up (face only)	intimacy
medium shot (most of body)	personal relationship
long shot (setting and characters)	public distance
full shot (full body of person)	social relationship
pan down (camera looks down)	power, authority
pan up (camera looks up)	smallness, weakness

Figure 5.3   *Camera angles and movements (Berger, 1982: 38)*

thus derives its meaning not only from its relation to other signs within the same system (syntagma) but also from its relation to its absent opposite (paradigma).

In addition to the particular articulation of signs, 'codes' and 'conventions' shared by the members of the culture from which the sign system originates provide clues as to how to understand sign systems. Berger (1982), for instance, gives an example of the way western codes of body language bestow meaning on camera angles and movements (Figure 5.3). Other codes that usually give meaning to the articulation of signs – as we shall see later in this chapter – are codes of femininity, masculinity and heterosexuality.

Sign, syntagma, paradigma, code and convention are the key elements in the different processes of 'signification', the way signs become meaningful within a given culture. Barthes (1957) distinguished between denotation and connotation, or first and second order signification. Denotation is of particular relevance to the semiotics of de Saussure which focuses on language. It concerns the direct relation between signifier and signified and its manifest referent in reality and usually involves a description of what can be seen or read in a text. The denotative meaning of 'black cat', for instance, would be an animal with a certain colour. However, the sign 'black cat' carries important other connotative meanings as well. In some countries, like The Netherlands, it is considered an omen of bad luck, but in other countries it is thought of as a signifier of fortune and happiness. In some feminist circles the black cat is thought of as a signifier of spirituality. Connotation or second order signification thus concerns the latent cultural values and beliefs expressed by a sign or sign system. This can take on the form of associations or of complete narratives, labelled as 'myth' by Barthes. A recognition and understanding of the various codes underlying the particular articulation of signs is necessary for second order signification to work. Consequently, the analysis of connotative meaning requires a thorough knowledge of the culture the sign system originates from. Finally, Fiske and Hartley (1978) distinguish third order signification or ideology, conceiving connotation and myth as the manifest expressions of an underlying structuring principle: the dominant ideology. They summarize the different processes of signification in the scheme shown in Figure 5.4.

While this all may sound rather abstract, semiotic analysis can be seen as a formalization of the interpretative activities ordinary human beings

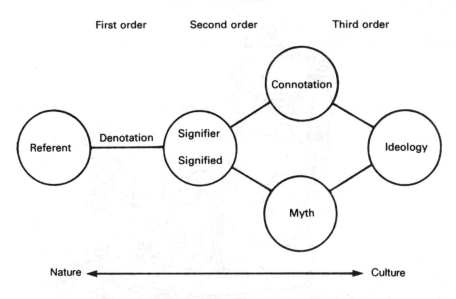

First order   Second order   Third order

Nature ◄─────────────────────────► Culture

Figure 5.4 *Processes of signification (O'Sullivan, 1989: 217)*

undertake incessantly. Imagine, for instance, a women's group monitoring children's books for their portrayal of gender roles. In one book they encounter the drawing shown in Figure 5.5. The women's group finds this drawing sexist and stereotypical for various reasons. They consider dolls and miniature kitchens as toys that are given to girls only, signifying the girls' futures as mothers and housewives. They argue that the picture would be less sexist if a boy was included too and they claim that the drawing would be emancipatory if there was only a boy playing with the doll and the kitchen. Some women in the group claim that the image of the happy housewife conveyed by the drawing, does not fully resemble their own experience, since some of them do not like kitchen work and others are quite happy when the children (doll) are away playing at the neighbours.

In such reasoning, all the elements of a semiotic analysis are present. Let us first isolate the signs in the drawing: a little girl, a doll and a miniature kitchen.[5] These signs all have iconic elements in the sense that the signifiers directly resemble the signifieds. The miniature character of the doll and the kitchen have important indexical elements as well, connecting the world of toys to the real life existence of mothers and housewives. The code of traditional gender roles underlies that connection and is easily recognized by members of many cultures and it is precisely what the women's group objects to. Moreover, the signs are combined in such a way that they convey the image of a girl playing contently, referring to the myth of the 'happy housewife' (second order signification or connotation). Another syntagmatic relation of the signs – the girl for instance destroying the doll and setting fire to the kitchen – would have radically altered the meaning of the drawing. The paradigmatic relation of the signs is

Figure 5.5

important as well and also recognized in the women's group analysis of the drawing. Why is a girl playing with a doll, and not a boy? Or why is the girl playing with a doll and a kitchen and not with a car and a computer? These signs of 'masculinity' are not present in the drawing but they do play a significant role in the analysis of such a drawing as sexist and stereotypical. Underlying the drawing, one may argue, is the dominant ideology of femininity which structures its overall meaning (third order signification).

Ordinarily, the texts subjected to semiotic analysis are much more complex than this drawing and contain elaborate narratives and additional signs systems such as colours, music and editing codes. In such cases a 'lay analysis' will neither be sufficient nor successful, and semiotics provides a means for a systematic assessment of the processes of signification in the text. It is important to realize, that despite the systematic nature of the semiotic approach, there is no clear methodology of semiotics as there is with content analysis. One could, however, translate the different elements of semiotics into systematic 'steps' to carry out the analysis, the first step being the identification of the relevant signs and their dominant aspects (iconic, indexical or symbolic). Then one continues with examining the paradigmatic combination of these signs, for instance by asking what their absent opposites are, and how they relate to each other syntagmatically.

This will also imply an analysis of the codes by which the combination of signs is governed. One thus arrives at an understanding of the different processes of signification in the text: denotation, connotation, myth and ideology.

These 'results' clarify how single discursive expressions, such as a photograph or an advertisement, generate meanings, but they provide no insight into how often that particular process occurs, as would be the concern of traditional content analysis. Also, one should not expect a semiotic analysis to produce the definitive meaning of a text. Since the codes that confer meaning on to the syntagmatic and paradigmatic combination of signs are culturally specific, signification will never be completely unambiguous or univocal. The multi-accentuality of signs, 'consisting in the capacity every sign has to signify more than one meaning, depending on the circumstances of its use' (O'Sullivan et al., 1989: 144) ensures that the meaning of the text is never nor determined only by the features of the text itself. Even though particular syntagmatic and paradigmatic combinations of signs tend to produce 'closure' of meaning, texts are principally 'polysemic', that is, they contain multiple meanings that need to be actualized by audiences, involving the culturally competent application of codes governing the text. Although the acknowledgement of the polysemic nature of texts – inspired by post-structuralism (Seiter, 1992) – has recently undermined the semiotic project and directed researchers to the interpretive activities of actual audiences rather than the processes of signification in the text (Moores, 1990), semiotics remains a powerful tool to understand how sign systems in mass media can evoke emotions, associations, fears, hopes, fantasies and acquiescence.

Advertising

Signification has developed into an art form in advertising, making it probably the most popular object for semiotic analysis. As a concentrated form of communication, advertising needs to present its message in an extremely short time span, and depends heavily on the successful exploitation of the connotative power of signs. An advertisement cannot afford to be cast aside or leafed over; it must stand out in the flow of signs that bombard us daily. For the target group to recognize immediately what is being expressed, it is necessary that advertising draws from relatively common cultural symbols and meanings:

> Advertising is itself a 'multiplexing' form that absorbs and fuses a variety of symbolic practices and discourses. The substance and images woven into advertising messages are appropriated and distilled from an unbounded range of cultural references. Advertising borrows its ideas, its language, and its visual representations from literature and design, from other media content and forms, from history and the future, and from its own experience; then it artfully recombines them around the theme of consumption. (Leiss et al., 1986: 144–5)

The idiosyncratic nature of semiotic analyses prevents any kind of generalization of advertising analysis. In Goffman (1976) and Williamson (1978), for instance, one can find exhaustive analyses of a variety of advertisements that belie any attempt at summarizing. Instead, I shall illustrate the semiotic approach by analysing two advertisements featuring women from particular ethnic backgrounds. The aim of the analysis is to unravel the ideology structuring the specific articulations of gender and ethnicity in these advertisements (third order signification).[6]

The first advertisement (Figure 5.6), for Japan Air Lines, was published in an American news magazine and is aimed at Executive Class business travellers, predominantly men. Essentially we see a young Japanese woman holding an oriental-style teapot in a deferential posture and smiling directly at the camera. The advertisement might seem at first to be just another example of a common representation of women: as the obliging servant attending the needs of (male) passengers. Her plain dress and her friendly smile, which directly addresses the audience, support such a domestic image. However, other signs in the advertisement do not convincingly corroborate that connotation: why is she serving tea – and not for instance coffee or whisky? What is the meaning of the woman we can see in the background, dressed in a kimono and holding a fan, and why is there also a fan featured largely in the lower right corner of the advertisement, next to the text? These are not mere decorative elements but are linked to the central image of the stewardess by the symbol of JAL – a heron – which appears on the fan, the teapot, the stewardess' dress and the fan of the woman in the background, and by the colour red, which appears on the fan and also couples the woman in the background to the stewardess. The slogan of Japan Air Lines, printed at the bottom, controls the meaning of those signs: 'Attentiveness. With us, it's a tradition.' And in the text we find another clue: 'attending to the comfort of guests is a heritage refined over a thousand years'. With this emphasis on tradition, the teapot, the fan and particularly the woman in the background begin to make sense. They are signifiers of tradition, and more specifically of the tradition of the geishas, the famous Japanese companion ladies who received exquisite education and training to provide intellectual and spiritual pleasure to their male customers. For the western male business traveller at whom this advertisement is aimed, the prospect is of a service which to his own culture is both appealing and exotic, especially since the advertisement also opens up space for fantasies about the kind of service the stewardess will offer. The myth of the geisha has always been ambiguous in this respect. While the professional pride of the geisha derives from her intellectual and spiritual capacities, the *métier* has been surrounded by suggestions and fantasies of sexual pleasure as well. The ambiguity of the geisha's image is enlarged by the text: 'And most of all, you appreciate it in the way all JAL attendants seem to anticipate your every need.'

Through the different orders of signification the advertisement articulates a discourse of gender and ethnicity that constructs Japanese femin-

Figure 5.6

inity as geared to everything a man could possibly desire. Attentiveness, forbearance and complaisance are suggested characteristics of the sexuality of Japanese women who know from a thousand-year-old tradition how to serve the needs of men. It has been with them so long that it comes naturally to them, so to speak.

The second advertisement I want to examine (Figure 5.7) was published in a Belgian women's magazine and signifying practices similar to those of the JAL advertisement operate. The first order signification or denotation does not make much sense. As asserted by the text at the bottom of the advertisement, Safari is a sweet liqueur with 'the taste of wild nature' and produced according to an ancient African recipe. There is a bottle and two glasses of Safari ('African drink') in the centre of the picture. Heterosexuality is implied by the two glasses, one a long drink and one on the rocks. An African woman holding a small tiger in her arms is smiling at us from behind a blind. In the background we see zebras moving across a plain and a sunset behind distant hills. Black, white and a variety of browns are the colours that produce coherence in the otherwise dispersed signs of the advertisement. The brownish tints appear in the liquid, the landscape in the background, the tiger and the skin of the woman. Nature, drink and woman are further coupled by the zebra motifs present in the woman's dress, on the label of the bottle and the zebras themselves. Naturalness and wildness – 'the taste of wild nature' – are thus embodied by the woman holding the tiger, the scenes of nature and the zebras. A final element that needs examination is the blind that tries to hide the woman from sight. Why is the woman behind the blind instead of the zebras, for instance? Why is she holding a tiger? What does her smile mean? Is she inviting us or is there danger in her smile as the tiger seems to hint at? The blind prevents us from looking at her directly and symbolically inhibits immediate access to her. A sense of mystery is created. However, the articulation of gender and ethnicity is significantly different from the JAL advertisement. Whereas they share the exotic quality, African femininity is constructed as wild and close to nature while Asian femininity is modest and deferential. Both share, however, a reference to tradition. In the Safari advertisement femininity is linked with an 'ancient African recipe'. The JAL advertisement couples femininity with the age-old heritage of the geishas.

The two advertisements have common characteristics: the emphasis on tradition and mystery produces their exotic spirit. Obviously these signifiers draw from some common frame of reference that is meaningful in the white patriarchal culture they both originate from. This is an issue of third order signification, that is, 'the way that the varied connotations and myths fit together to form a coherent pattern or sense of wholeness, that is, the way they "make sense" is evidence of an underlying invisible, organizing principle – ideology' (O'Sullivan et al., 1989: 217). The ideology underlying the advertisements does not speak for itself, however, and can be approached from different angles. Judith Williamson (1986), for instance, has interpreted exotic advertisements from a neo-Marxist point of view.

De smaak van wilde natuur

Een aloud Afrikaans recept met het verfijnde aroma van mango, papaya, maracuja en wilde limoenen. Safari is altijd lekker: puur, met ijs of als longdrink (1/3 Safari, 2/3 sinaasappelsap of pompelmoes). Of voeg er naar smaak genever, gin, rum of vodka bij. De smaak van wilde natuur.

Figure 5.7

She starts from the assertion that capitalism exploits and controls workers and colonies, suppressing their different interests and value systems. The function of ideology is to contain the resulting antagonism and prevent them undermining the dominant order. This is achieved by creating differences that conceal or transform the true antagonisms: 'The supreme trick of bourgeois ideology is to be able to produce its opposition out of its own hat' (1986: 100). Williamson argues that 'woman' and 'nationality' are the main signifiers in this cover-up, suggesting natural and eternal differences that cut across class. 'Questions of class power frequently hide behind the omnipresent and indisputable gender difference' (1986: 103). Williamson analyses exotic advertisements to show how particular articulations of 'woman' and 'nationality' realize the transformation of structural antagonisms in mere differences of style and preference. She contends that the requirements of the capitalist economy have discarded such human values as sensitivity, care, connectedness and respect for nature as useless for public life. However, the common complaints about western capitalist societies as being cold, unaffectionate and dominated by rationality and considerations of efficiency indicate a dissatisfaction with the system, and a collective need for the lost values. In commodified form these values are still available to us, as the exotic advertisements point out:

> It is as if western capitalism can hold up an image of freedom and fulfillment and say: 'Look our system offers this' . . . Different systems of production which are suppressed by capitalism are then incorporated into its imagery and ideological values: as 'otherness', old-fashioned, charming, exotic, natural, primitive, universal. (1986: 112)

The transformation of a collective aversion to the system into consumer needs and products can be achieved perfectly by the exotic articulation of 'woman' and 'nationality' since – according to Williamson – 'the most likely Other for a white working-class man, is either a woman . . . or a foreigner, in particular somebody black' (1986: 103).

Williamson's analysis duly points to the overall ideological function of exoticism, but tends to overlook the specificities in the phenomenon and the unmistakably sexual undertones in it. The recurring references to black female sexuality as being temperamental and wild – something to be feared and desired at the same time – cannot be explained within Williamson's neo-Marxist framework, but needs rather to be informed by history and psychoanalysis. In Europe, the fascination with black sexuality has been traced to the earliest reports about the crusades and has been a continuous topic in the literature of travellers to Africa and the Orient (Kabbani, 1986). The popular and widespread appeal of the image of the 'wild savage' that feeds western discourses of black female sexuality, is said to have served a double purpose for European colonialism. The image of the 'wild savage' provided a wonderful occasion to fantasize about all that was forbidden, projecting 'upon colonial people the obscurities of their own unconscious' (Mannoni, 1950: 19). At the same time, imagining the

	Semiotics	**Content analysis**
Communication model	construction	transmission
Object	latent content single texts	manifest content large body of texts
Method	qualitative humanities	quantitative social science
Results	signification	occurrence

Figure 5.8   *Differences between content analysis and semiotics*

peoples of the colonies as sexually voracious and insatiable legitimized Europe's colonial enterprise as a project of 'civilization' instead of economic exploitation. Likewise, in the United States the myth of ravenous black sexuality provided an excuse for white slave owners to rape female slaves, and made the lynching and castration of black men possible until long into this century (Nederveen Pieterse, 1990).

Although only exemplary, the analysis above of the two exotic advertisements does illustrate the advantages and disadvantages of a semiotic analysis. Because of the amount of elucidation and detail entailed, it can only focus on single texts or a limited sample at the most. While being close to the 'true' nature of texts and possibly also to actual audience activities and interpretations, the volume of 'findings' resulting from semiotics is usually much larger than the text analysed (cf. McQuail, 1987: 189). Most important, the quality of semiotics depends to a large extent on the researcher's knowledge of cultural codes. The exotic advertisements, for instance, make much more sense when connected to the economic and historical peculiarities of white patriarchal culture and European colonialism, and will possibly gain from a more detailed psychoanalytic angle as well (for example, Doane, 1991). A good semiotic analysis therefore quickly develops into a broad cultural critique.

In this chapter, two approaches to the analysis of gender discourse in media texts were discussed: content analysis and semiotics. Even when limited to the genre of advertising, the overall results of both are hard to summarize. The usefulness and merits of each approach depend on the specific questions being asked. The differences between both approaches have been identified in various ways. Barthes (1957: 120) has claimed that 'semiology is a science of forms, since it studies significations apart from their content'. Likewise, Seiter (1992: 31) claims that 'semiotics first asks *how* meaning is created, rather than *what* the meaning is'. Looking at the differences within feminist media research, it seems that content analysis emphasizes the manifest working and non-working roles women are portrayed in and their visual function as a decorative element while semiotics draws our attention to the power of 'woman' as signifier of almost anything between virtue and vice, desire and fear. Other differences discussed in this chapter are summarized in Figure 5.8.

Some researchers have tried to combine elements of content analysis and semiotics. Jhally (1987), for instance, tried to quantify the occurrence of cultural codes like individuality, romance and friendship in advertisements intended for a female and a male audience. She found that codes of beauty, family and romance occurred more often in advertisements for female audiences, while ruggedness and fraternity dominated in advertisements aimed at men. In general, it seems that in such combined approaches content analysis is used for inventory purposes while semiotics is employed to give depth to and illustrate the overall quantitative results (cf. Leiss, et al. 1986). Within the theoretical framework underlying this book, it might be useful to employ content analysis for inventory purposes. However, conceptualizing gender as a fragmentary discourse that is expressed and reconstructed by technologies of gender such as mass media – a set of 'symbols for reality' – implies a semiotic approach that foregrounds the different signs and contradictory processes of signification in media texts.

Notes

1. The reader with an interest in such review studies is referred to Butler and Paisley, 1980; Ceulemans and Fauconnier, 1979; Gallagher, 1980, 1985. The current impossibility of such a review project is shown by the absence of more recent references in this area.

2. I am indebted to Laura Emmelkamp for these references.

3. Table taken from Fiske, 1980: 122.

4. Useful introductions have been produced by Berger (1982), Fiske (1980) and Hartley (1982).

5. The fact that this is a drawing and not a picture can be considered a sign too.

6. I collected these and other advertisements by making random clippings from magazines over a number of years and have not kept track of the precise information concerning their publication.

6

Spectatorship and the Gaze

A core element of western patriarchal culture is the display of woman as spectacle to be looked at, subjected to the gaze of the (male) audience. Pornography is the most obvious genre built on the exhibition of women's bodies as objects of desire, fantasy and violence, but the 'objectification' of women is not exclusive to pornography. The incorporation of women's bodies as decorative ingredients in advertisements of drinks, tools and – most notoriously – cars is common practice, while in TV game shows the assistant to the quiz master is the predictably attractive, scantily dressed blonde. Fashion and lingerie photography as published in glossy women's magazines has moved beyond the mere presentation of new styles and lines, and has taken over many of the codes formerly restricted to soft core pornography. Hollywood cinema has a long standing tradition of constructing women as a spectacle for voyeuristic pleasure.

This common feature of popular and high culture alike – for in 'art' women's bodies have been exploited in similar ways – suggests that in western society to be looked at is the fate of women, while the act of looking is reserved to men. Even if women do the looking they do not seem to do it through their own eyes. John Berger writes in his classic study *Ways of Seeing*:

> Men act and women appear. Men look at women. Women watch themselves being looked at. This determines not only most relations between men and women but also the relation of women to themselves. The surveyor of woman in herself is male: the surveyed female. Thus she turns herself into an object – and most particularly an object of vision: a sight. (1972: 47)

Many feminist authors have pointed to the devastating effects that this 'to-be-looked-at-ness' might have on ordinary women. Wendy Chapkis (1986), for instance, discusses how cultural messages about beauty and slimness negatively affected her own and other women's sense of well-being in general and of being 'truly feminine' in particular. More recently Naomi Wolff (1990) has made similar arguments in her best selling book *The Beauty Myth*. According to Wolff, the cultural industry's prescriptions for women to be beautiful and slender – a pleasure to look at – has produced a generation of American girls and women who suffer from eating disorders like bulimia and anorexia nervosa.

Obvious as it may seem that for women there is little good or pleasurable in 'looking' as it is structured in western culture, it is an argument that denies the possibilities and historical existence of a positive and pleasur-

able female gaze. Women have been looking at movie stars like Rudolf
Valentino, Clark Gable, Richard Gere, Don Johnson and others, enjoying
not only their narrative characters but their physical appearance as well.
Likewise, adolescent girls have turned male rock stars into objects of
voyeurism and desire. The sight of hysterical girls throwing their under-
wear at the stage has been experienced by groups as diverse as the Rolling
Stones, the Osmond Brothers and the New Kids on the Block, and has
become a normal measure of success.

In this chapter I shall discuss issues like the male and the female gaze and
the construction of women and men as objects of voyeuristic pleasure.
Unlike content analysis and semiotics which concentrate solely on features
of the text, the approaches presented here conceptualize the interaction
between text and audience by analysing the particular subject positions
enabled, suggested or induced by the text. In these approaches the
'spectator' refers to these subject positions, not to actual audiences.

Feminist film studies provide the main angles and examples for this
chapter, however, some arguments may be extended to popular culture in
general.[1] Laura Mulvey's landmark article on classic Hollywood cinema
and the male gaze that inspired many subsequent feminist analyses, forms
the starting point. I shall then review the criticism levelled at such
psychoanalytic approaches focusing on two areas in particular: the possibility and pleasures of female spectatorship and the construction of male
bodies as objects of voyeuristic pleasure.

Men looking at women

Visual pleasure and psychoanalysis

Laura Mulvey's article 'Visual pleasure and narrative cinema' was published in 1975 and has become the most reprinted article in film theory
(Erens, 1990). It has been called 'the founding document of psychoanalytic
feminist film theory' (Modleski, 1990: 53) and it dominated the field in the
1970s and the 1980s in the sense that feminist film studies that were not
psychoanalytic were hard to find (cf. Byars, 1991). The influence of
Mulvey's particular approach has extended to the study of television,
advertising and other forms of visual culture as well (Moores, 1990).
Although apparently abandoned with the renewed interest in actual
audience pleasures, Mulvey's article provides a good starting point to
explore the media construction of women as spectacle, the gender of the
gaze and voyeuristic pleasure.[2]

Mulvey draws on Freudian and Lacanian psychoanalyses to examine the
pleasures of 'scopophilia' and 'narcissistic identification' that the classic
Hollywood cinema offers. In psychoanalytic theory 'scopophilia' is defined
as a basic human sexual drive to look at other human beings, a conscious
and concentrated way of looking that causes particular feelings of lust and
satisfaction that are not directly related to erotogenic zones. In some cases,

this can extend to extreme forms of 'obsessive voyeurism' or 'Peeping Tomism'. Sitting in the darkened auditorium of the cinema, separated from other audience members and exposed to a visual fantasy world that unfolds independently from the spectator – as if she or he were not there – satisfies common human voyeuristic desires and produces scopophilic pleasure: 'Although the film is really being shown, is there to be seen, conditions of screening and narrative conventions give the spectator an illusion of looking in on a private world' (p. 31).[3]

Cinema satisfies a second though seemingly contradictory narcissistic human need to identify with others, in this case with who and what is shown on the screen. Mulvey argues that the identification enabled by cinema is fed by the 'mirror phase' in childhood as described by the French psychoanalyst Jacques Lacan. According to Lacan, at a certain point in its development a child comes to recognize itself in the mirror, but imagines the child in the mirror to be more complete, perfect and powerful. Apart from the direct analogy between watching a movie and looking in the mirror – both framed images – the cinematic experience produces a feeling of omnipotence through identification with the perfect characters on the screen, while at the same time being a reminder of the pre-mirror phase of maternal connectedness by its capacity to make people forget time, place and themselves.

At first sight, these two mechanisms of pleasure – voyeurism and identification – would seem to be at odds with each other and not easily reconciled within a unitary cinematic experience. Cinema, however, is not only a world of fantasy and desire, but is conditioned by the social reality from which it originates. Mulvey contends that the patriarchal definition of looking as a male activity and being looked at as a female 'passivity' allows for a reconciliation of the two contradictory, but constitutive pleasures of narrative cinema. In mainstream Hollywood film, women function simul-taneously as erotic objects for the male audience who can derive scopophilic pleasure from their presence, and as erotic objects for the male protagonists with whom the male audience can identify. Camera angles and movements – the third 'looking party' aside from the protagonist and the audience – are crucial in realizing the double pleasure of scopophilia and identifica-tion. They enable the male audience to look through the eyes of the male protagonist, simultaneously to identify and objectify, or, in more straight-forward terms, to be him and look at her. Thus the conflict between what Freud has called libido (scopophilia) and ego (identification) is resolved by the cinematic display of women as objects of the male gaze.

One might wonder why this process cannot simply be reversed to permit female pleasure as well? Would this not require merely a female protagonist with whom the female audience can identify and a male character displayed as spectacle for both the audience and the female character? Certainly, in the mid-1970s Mulvey found that examples of such reversal – whether in the cinema or other forms of popular culture – were hard to find.[4] Narrative conventions of Hollywood cinema construct the male protagonist as the active agent propelling the story. His actions drive the narrative forward, and since the camera takes his point of view he is given the power of looking as well. While Mulvey did not directly address the issue of female pleasure, the argument developed in her article implies that within patriarchal culture a reversal of the structure of looking – facilitating concurrent female scopophilia and identification – is out of the question. According to Mulvey, cinematic practice is directly related to patriarchy: 'Film reflects, reveals, and even plays on the straight, socially established interpretation of sexual difference which controls images, erotic ways of looking and spectacle' (p. 28).

While female pleasure is inconceivable in Mulvey's psychoanalytic framework, male pleasure is not without its problems either. To the patriarchal unconscious, 'woman' signifies sexual difference and more particularly she connotes the lack of a penis which evokes fear of castration and 'unpleasure' as Mulvey calls it. 'Thus the woman as icon, displayed for the gaze and enjoyment of men, the active controllers of the look, always threatens to evoke the anxiety it originally signified' (p. 35). Male pleasure in looking can only be rendered unproblematic if the unconscious but fundamental castration threat that women signify is eliminated. The scopophilic order of narrative Hollywood cinema allows for two ways of doing this. First, the original trauma of discovering the mother's lack of a penis can be reenacted by 'investigating' the woman and taking visual and narrative control of her body. Voyeurism borders on sadism here and can be recognized in narratives in which women are trouble-makers, guilty of disturbing the peace of mind of the male hero in whatever sense. Second, the castration of the woman can be denied by substituting her lack with a fetish object – high heels, long hair or earrings for instance – or turning her into a fetish object herself, exaggerating, stylizing and fragmenting female beauty into a reassuring object of the gaze. Mulvey mentions the films of Hitchcock and Sternberg who directed many of the early Marlene Dietrich films as typical of respectively sadistic voyeurism and fetishism.

Mulvey's article was part of a political project aimed at destroying the gendered pleasures of mainstream Hollywood cinema; 'to make way for a total negation of the ease and plenitude of the narrative fiction film' (p. 30). Mulvey expanded that project by producing avant-garde films with Peter Wollen in which she illustrated the issues raised in the visual pleasure article, and in which she radically broke with the naturalistic camera movements, angles and frames that facilitate the double satisfaction of libidinous and ego drives in mainstream narrative film.[5] While having educational value in calling attention to the illusory mechanisms of Hollywood cinema, Mulvey's avant-garde project has been accused of being overly successful in destroying the pleasure of looking. It has been criticized by feminist critics and non-feminist women alike of being inaccessible and elitist, relegating feminist film making to the margins of cinematographic practice and experience (cf. Gaines, 1988).

Not only does Mulvey's alternative cinema raise questions, there are also considerable problems in her psychoanalytic arguments. The question why men look at women is sparsely addressed, aside from a rather abstract reference to the way patriarchy has defined the gaze. In such an explanation, the distinction between social and psychoanalytic levels of analysis collapses. While Freud himself acknowledges the co-existence of 'feminine' passivity and 'masculine' activity within single subjects, in many feminist film analyses masculinity and the activity of looking is preserved to biological males and femininity and the passivity of being looked at to biological females. When psychoanalysis is employed in this manner, it appears to offer too narrow a conceptualization of gender which equates masculinity and femininity with being respectively male and female. As discussed in Chapter 3 such a misunderstanding of gender denies the dynamic and contradictory nature of gender discourse and its historic and cultural specificity.

Other authors working from Freudian and Lacanian psychoanalytic frameworks have taken Mulvey's point further and employed a more sophisticated version of psychoanalysis to account for the male gaze. Mary Ann Doane, for instance, draws from French feminist theory to sustain her view that a reversal of the gaze is impossible since it cannot escape the same logic: 'The male striptease, the gigolo – both inevitably signify the mechanism of reversal itself, constituting themselves as aberrations whose acknowledgement simply reinforces the dominant system of aligning sexual difference with a subject/object dichotomy' (1982: 44). Doane's point here is not unambiguous – is she opposed to the system of looking as objectification itself, or does she mean that the exceptions like the gigolo prove the rule of the male gaze? From what follows it is clear, however, that Doane denies the possibility of female subjectivity and voyeurism in current patriarchal society, although she arrives at this conclusion in a different and more subtle manner then Mulvey. While Mulvey sees the opposition between activity and passivity as underlying the exclusiveness of the male gaze, Doane considers the concepts 'proximity' and 'distance' more important. She argues that a precondition for voyeurism is a physical as well as a psychological distance between the bearer and the object of the look. Drawing on Lacan here, Doane contends that the subject's ability to create this distance is located in the appreciation of sexual difference that takes place in childhood. Little boys recognize sexual difference once they become aware of their mother's lack of a penis and are thus forced to dissociate themselves from the mother. Little girls recognize sameness instead and identify with the mother to the extent that separation and distance become problematic or even impossible. According to Doane, female specificity is characterized by proximity and thus women lack the sheer capacity for voyeurism. As a result, the female spectator can only be construed as becoming narcissistically immersed in the cinematic (female) object, or as suffering 'masculinization' by identifying with the (male) hero. While Doane does explain why it is that men look at women, her psychoanalytic framework excludes the possibility that women can look at men, unless they take up a masculine/male spectator position. In a later article published as reaction to the issue of the female gaze, Mulvey (1979) also claims that the female gaze can only be a masochistic adaptation of the male spectator position enforced by the voyeuristic/fetishistic economy of narrative cinema in a patriarchal order. Autonomous, unmediated and pleasurable female spectatorship is thus inconceivable in the psycho-analytic framework employed by Mulvey and many others.

Female spectatorship?

Psychoanalytic feminist film studies have evoked extensive and varied criticisms, some of which are particular to film studies, others to psycho-analytic theory in general. Several authors have claimed that distinguishing two modes of active looking – voyeurism and fetishism – is a poor theorization of the male spectator position. Masochistic male pleasure is said to be engendered by the overwhelming presence of the fetishized women on the screen, being a reminder of the pre-Oedipal phase of maternal plenitude.[6] Other objections concern the understanding, implicit in psychoanalytic film studies, of media texts containing univocal mean-ings. The pleasures of the male/masculine spectators are conceived as the direct result of the way they are positioned by the cinematographic mode of address. The text–spectator relation forms a closed system determined completely by the articulation of visual and narrative means with gendered subjectivities which only permits a dichotomous pleasure of voyeurism or identification, and disregards the ambiguities and tensions present in every text (Stacey, 1987). In that closed system gender is believed to be the key factor to an understanding of the idiosyncrasies of spectatorship and pleasure, at the expense of other considerations such as race, sexuality, class, cultural capital, individual life histories beyond the Oedipal stage etc. (Gamman and Marshment, 1988; Pribram, 1988). Furthermore, psychoanalytic film theory has been criticized, like psychoanalysis in general, for its ahistorical nature and its powerless perspective. It is alleged that by denying the possibilities of female spectatorship, feminist theory itself collaborates in the patriarchal project by silencing and annihilating women's experience of mainstream cinema (Arbuthnot and Senaca, 1982). Moreover if, as psychoanalytic theory would have us believe, gendered identity formation takes place at such an early phase in life, prior to the subject's entry in social relations, we are all 'ideological captives' as Jane Gaines (1987) calls it, and the possibility of change becomes hard to envisage.

Most discussion has been prompted by the psychoanalytic foreclosure of female spectatorship, first by the question of whether women can derive pleasure from looking at women displayed by Hollywood cinematographic codes and conventions. With the growing appeal of popular cultural forms exploring the male body, for instance in films like *American Gigolo* and the Levis 501 commercials, the issue of heterosexual female voyeurism has also come to the fore.

Women looking at women

More psychoanalysis

The psychoanalytic framework employed by authors like Mulvey and Doane allows for very restricted possibilities of female spectatorship only. Since 'woman' signifies sexual difference and castration to the male spectator she needs to be brought under control, either through (sadistic) voyeurism or through excessive fetishism. The female spectatorship allowed for by the violence of such narratives will either entail a masochistic identification with the female object, or a 'transvestite' position – as Mulvey (1979) has called it – of masculinization. Both positions are derived from the active/male/masculine–passive/female/ feminine dichotomy underlying the psychoanalytic approach. As a result female spectatorship that is not cast in patriarchal gender definitions is inconceivable: positive and pleasurable spectatorship can only be masculine and thus 'unfeminine', while the 'feminine' spectator position constructed by the text is problematic and unpleasurable. However, a quest for female spectatorship that is not chained to the restrictions of hegemonic gender definitions does not seem to be without difficulty either. According to Doane (1982) the feminist theorist is confronted with something of a double bind. She can keep pointing out the absence of women in patriarchal discourse, but in doing so she is reconstructing that same discourse. Or she can point out feminine specificity, running the risk of suggesting an essential femininity. While this indeed seems to be the fundamental predicament of feminist theory, the problem actually arises from the dichotomous definition of gender as either masculine and active, or feminine and passive. In assuming sexual difference, or the specificity of female spectatorship, one runs the risk of falling into the trap of (biological) essentialism, while by underlining the invisibility of women in patriarchal culture the hegemony of masculinity is confirmed and reinforced. The only way out of these predicaments is a radical abandonment of dichotomous definitions of gender, which implies in the case of psychoanalytic film theory an escape from the Oedipal prison house of 'normal' heterosexual development.

Psychoanalytic theory itself does suggest some possible routes for this escape which have been exploited by a number of authors in different ways. Whereas for Doane the girl's attachment to her mother forecloses distance and the possibility of female voyeurism and unproblematic spectatorship, others argue that it is precisely the pre-Oedipal bonding of the female child with the mother that facilitates the pleasurable attraction of women to each other. Since girls are never forced to overcome this attachment as boys are, they carry a latent homosexual desire with them that coexists with heterosexual relationships. Therefore, the female spectator looking at women is always involved in a double desire: an active homosexual one which is rooted in the bond with her mother and a passive heterosexual one stemming from her identification with woman as object of the male gaze. The plausibility of such female homosexual desire is underscored by the fact that heterosexually constructed stars like Greta Garbo, Marlene Dietrich and Bette Davis have also featured in lesbian subculture as objects of desire (Becker et al., 1981; de Lauretis, 1984).

Other authors too have referred to the girl's attachment to her mother to account for female pleasure in mainstream narrative cinema (for example, Byars, 1991; Williams, 1984). They differ however in their appreciation of psychoanalysis. Byars (1991) has developed an eclectic approach to film studies, disavowing Lacanian psychoanalysis for its bias towards white masculinity and its appropriation of the feminine as 'different', 'other' or 'lacking'. While Byars agrees that many films are exactly about the threat of female otherness, there are numerous melodramatic films for example, that belie the Lacanian scenario. Instead, Byars exploits Nancy Chodorow's and Carol Gilligan's materialist reworking of psychoanalysis. These authors claim that because girls are raised by a human being of the same gender, they experience themselves as closely related to other human beings and the outside world, while boys identify themselves as different from their mother and in opposition to the outside world. As a result, girls think of themselves in relation to others and boys perceive themselves as unconnected individuals. The main difference here from Lacanian theory is that Chodorow sees the social process of mothering as underlying current gender difference instead of anatomical otherness. Moreover, the specificity of femininity is defined positively as the capacity to engage in meaningful triadic relationships, and not as an absence or lack. Chodorow's theory of female development is particularly convenient for female orientated melodrama and the stories of mothers and daughters that were popular in the 1950s. The central theme of these films concerns the plight of the heroine who wants to reconcile her desire for exclusive heterosexual romance with her wish to maintain significant relations with other women, often family members and in particular her mother.

Even within the confines of psychoanalytic theory, female spectatorship appears to involve more complex mechanisms than masochistic identification or transsexual voyeurism. The never completely ending attachment to the mother underlies a variety of desires and recognitions evoked by the women on the screen producing spectator pleasure that can be considered as a particular form of female gratification constructed out of the capitalist and patriarchal organization of the western nuclear family. Needless to say, such pleasure cannot be considered a universal female response to mainstream Hollywood cinema. Black female authors have wondered whether the debate is relevant to their concerns at all (Roach and Felix, 1988), and recently some of the leading theorists in the field have incorporated issues of race in their work (Modleski, 1991). Mary Ann Doane (1991) argues, for instance, that both women and blacks constitute an enigma and a threat to the patriarchal unconscious that can only be contained by violent repression. Doane's psychoanalytic account of the collective unconscious offers a powerful explanation of the persistent nature of sexism and racism. However, it also produces a somewhat 'egocentric' discourse that is preoccupied with the pathological character of white patriarchal society and that can only define blacks and women as 'different', 'other' and 'deviant'. The potential and realizations of these 'other' subjectivities and cultures in the context of white patriarchy are issues that psychoanalysis leaves undiscussed.

Beyond psychoanalysis

Female pleasure and spectatorship have been theorized outside the psychoanalytic frame as well. Instead of analysing the entire cinema–spectator relation as a re-enactment of pre-Oedipal attachments and Oedipal severance, several authors have examined the pleasures evoked by particular genres and single films. Byars' (1991) analysis of 1950s melo-drama mentioned above, demonstrated that narrative, *mise-en-scène* and characters of the 'women's weepies' can hardly be said to position the spectator in a masculine, voyeuristic or fetishistic engagement, but engender an entirely different text–spectator relation based on maternal bonds. Likewise, analyses of films featuring strong women characters involved in friendships and/or affairs with other women show the possibili-ties these texts offer for female gazing or pleasure. Such examinations focus on the way narrative and visual devices enable different 'readings' of the texts. Whether and how these 'readings' will be actualized by real audiences depends on their particular characteristics and viewing contexts, and is not determined by the psychoanalytic drama inscribed in the text. Two examples of such approaches are often mentioned: Lucie Arbuthnot and Gail Seneca's (1982) analysis of *Gentlemen Prefer Blondes*, a 1953 Hollywood film starring Marilyn Monroe and Jane Russell as showgirls, and Jackey Stacey's (1987) analysis of *Desperately Seeking Susan*, a 1984 mainstream movie featuring Madonna (Susan) as the object of curiosity and longing by a suburban housewife.

Arbuthnot and Seneca reject the dominance of psychoanalytic theory in film studies for its preoccupation with male spectatorship: 'We suggest that it is time to move beyond the analysis of male pleasure in viewing classical narrative films, in order to destroy it, to an exploration of female pleasure, in order to enhance it' (1982: 123). While being a product of popular culture which usually does not allow enjoyment to feminists, *Gentlemen Prefer Blondes* can be seen as a feminist text, according to Arbuthnot and Seneca. The two actresses Monroe and Russell portray strong, indepen-dent women who have ventured on a boat trip jointly to seek a husband. The heterosexual quest for romance might be the manifest narrative of the film, but underneath it is a story of resistance to male objectification and female love and friendship. There is a continuous tension between the romantic text and the feminist 'subtext'. Monroe and Russell are con-structed as objects for the male gaze but they always return the look, scanning their surroundings for appropriate husband material. In their dress and stature they resist sexual objectification which is furthermore prevented by particular camera angles and lighting. The more important source of feminist pleasure for Arbuthnot and Seneca however, involves the friendship of the two women entailing a genuine affection for each other in which feelings of competition and jealousy are absent. They defend each other in the face of criticism, give priority to their friendship over male courting, look at each other lovingly and frequently touch and caress one another. When they have finally succeeded in finding a husband, in their double wedding scene Arbuthnot and Seneca observe a superficial matrimonial commitment only and the endurance of their friendship. The authors conclude that: 'It is the tension between male objectification and women's resistance to that objectification that opens *Gentlemen Prefer Blondes* to a feminist reading. It is the clear and celebrated connection between Marilyn Monroe and Jane Russell which, for us, transforms *Gentlemen Prefer Blondes* into a profoundly feminist text' (p. 123).

In a similar vein, Jackey Stacey analysed *Desperately Seeking Susan*, a film about the obsession of a suburban housewife with a more adventurous cosmopolitan woman played by Madonna. As in most narrative Hollywood cinema, the central object of desire is an attractive, glamourous woman; an image that is reinforced by Madonna's real life spectacular exploitation of her sexuality. But we come to look at Madonna (Susan) through the eyes of Roberta, not a strong male hero, but a timid housewife who becomes so fascinated that she thinks she is Susan after a 'coincidental' concussion which causes memory loss. From that moment, the narrative is moved by the confusion that arises from the existence of two Susans who are a little alike and very different at the same time. Susan/Roberta is desperately trying to find out who she is, an exaggerated expression of an identity crisis which was already suggested in the beginning of the film when she was presented as the traditional unhappy housewife trapped in a dull and unfulfilling marriage. Susan/Madonna on the other hand wants to find out who her substitute is and bursts into Roberta's private life, taking over house, husband, clothes and swimming pool and – the ultimate investigation of her replacement – reading her diary. After a typical sequence of mistaken identities, Roberta, who has regained her memory by the end of the film, and Susan finally come to meet each other and the film ends with the two happily celebrating their new friendship. According to Stacey there is no way in which traditional psychoanalytic film theory can account for the fascination both female protagonists express for each other. The film is not about sexual difference but about difference between women, for which Lacanian psychoanalytic theory provides no angles. The narrative and visual codes do not allow pure identification or erotic desire with either one or the other. It is far more a desire to know about other women and to become – in the case of Roberta – an idealized feminine other, that lies at the heart of the film inviting the female audience to come along on this pursuit.

These two examples of pleasurable and unmediated female spectator-ship inscribed in particular cinematographic texts can be easily extended with analysis of other less well-known films (for example, Byars, 1991; Ellsworth, 1986; Williams, 1984). The common ground in all these analyses is an attempt to rescue from oblivion female pleasure in popular cultural forms. Byars favours 'an approach that enables us to hear the strong, feminine, resisting voices even within mainstream cultural artifacts' (1991: 20) and intends to examine 1950s melodrama with a so-called recuperative eye, revealing the textual struggles that enable female resistance and pleasure. Without denying the continuing, almost casual narrative and visual violence against women in many mainstream films, the evidence of the patriarchal nature of Hollywood cinema has annihilated the enjoy-ment, and even the resistance which women have constructed out of the inbuilt contradictions in patriarchal popular culture. As more authors have recognized this, Mulvey's dark and suffocating analysis of patriarchal cinema has lost ground to a more confident and empowering approach which foregrounds the possibilities of 'subversive', that is, non-patriarchal modes of female spectatorship. It is interesting to notice that in this shift of attention the level of analysis has changed as well. Whereas Mulvey and others talked of masculine spectator positions inscribed in narrative cinema, predominantly, but not necessarily coupled to the male viewer, the 'recuperative' feminist film critics increasingly discuss the possible pleasures offered by the narrative and visual contradictions of cinema-tographic texts to audiences of real women. Inevitably this development has led to an upsurge of studies that have moved away from 'textual' audiences (the audience position as constructed by the text) toward the examination of the pleasures of actual audiences instead. These will be discussed in the next chapter.

Women looking at men

In popular culture and art alike, it is quite rare to see the male body displayed in ways similar to the exhibition of women's bodies. To be sure, we see more then enough images of men but seldom are they subjected to the gaze of the female or male viewer, and it is even more uncommon to see them undressed. This invisibility is a relatively new phenomenon. In her book *The Male Nude* Margaret Walters traces the changes in rep-resentations of naked men.[7] For the ancient Greeks male nudity was unproblematic. The male body was a normal image in art which personi-fied the Gods, and the erect penis was openly on view in the image of satyrs or as an image in its own right, symbolizing patriarchal power and fertility. People used representations and sculptures of erect penises as tokens of good luck, as scarecrows or as guards to their estates. The phallus was there for everyone to see, man and woman, and was considered an object of desire for both women and men. According to Easthope (1986), in Greek culture masculinity was defined through homosexual and hetero-

sexual desire. Christianity changed all that, banishing the erect penis from
the public eye and relegating homosexuality to the realm of deviancy.
From the Renaissance onwards, the representation of the male nude body
became exceptional, always causing uproar and prohibitions. Easthope
(1986) argues that the disappearance of the erect penis as a public symbol
of power has not undermined patriarchy, far from it. Its invisibility is
precisely what makes the phallic order appear natural, not worth mention-
ing or representing: 'Masculinity has stayed pretty well concealed. This has
always been its ruse to hold on to its power' (Easthope, 1986: 1).

Not only does the patriarchal will to maintain power underlie the taboo
on looking at the male body. In an article on the phenomenon of male
strippers like The Chippendales and the London Knights, the ironic outcry
of an editor of the Dutch edition of *Playboy* magazine gives away his
unconscious fears: 'My God! Do I fear the gaze of the girls. I am less
frightened of being destroyed by the wide gap in the ozone layer, than by
the stares of the thronging "cockwatchers"'.[8] The comparison with the
wide gap in the ozone layer is significant here and gives a strong clue to the
castration fear evoked by the female gaze. Who knows what might
disappear under the desiring looks of women? Several authors have argued
however that the female gaze at the male body is infinitely less threatening
than the homosexual desire the male body might provoke in the male
spectator.

> [The male body] is not to be looked at with the eye of desire. This is precisely the
> look the masculine body positively denies as though it were saying, 'Whatever
> else, not that.' The hardness and tension of the body strives to present it as
> wholly masculine, to exclude all curves and hollows and be only straight lines and
> flat planes. It would really like to be a cubist painting. Or whatever. But above
> all not desirable to other men because it is so definitely not soft and feminine;
> hairy if need be, but not smooth; bone and muscle, not flesh and blood. The
> masculine body seeks to be Rambo, not Rimbaud. (Easthope, 1986: 54)

In a society which has defined masculinity as strong, active, in possession of
the gaze, and femininity as weak, passive and to be looked at, it is of course
utterly problematic if not impossible for the male body to submit itself to
the control of the gaze – by definition masculine – and to go over to the
other 'feminine' side, and surrender itself to masculine power. In western
patriarchal society, such a homosexual scenario is inherent to the eroticization of the male body, even if it is constructed for the pleasure of women
only. *Playgirl* magazine – the American female counterpart of *Playboy* –
has, for instance, a large following of homosexual men as well. The
inevitable homosexual scenario has rendered the display of male bodies in
popular culture fraught with complications and contradictions. Steve Neale
(1983) has argued that in all-male Hollywood movies like Westerns, the
fear of any eroticism in the act of looking at other men – on the part of
either the protagonist or the spectator – has produced narratives that are
characterized by sadomasochism. The gaze of the male spectator is never
direct but always mediated by the looks of the protagonists 'and these

looks are marked not by desire, but rather by fear, or hatred, or aggression' (1983: 14). Discussing the films of Anthony Mann, Neale contends that: 'The mutilation and sadism so often involved in Mann's films are marks both of the repression involved and of a means by which the male body may be disqualified, so to speak, as an object of erotic contemplation and desire' (1983: 8). Neale's comment has a more general significance as well, given the repression of homosexuality in western patriarchal culture and the common violence against it.

Despite the patriarchal inhibitions against the eroticization of the male body, historically popular culture has nevertheless provided possibilities for women to look at men, be it in a rather secret and unobtrusive way, for private rather than for public consumption. At the beginning of this chapter I referred to the erotic appeal of rock stars whose pictures cover the walls of the bedrooms of teenage girls, who can look at them and fantasize in the privacy of their own space. In melodrama and soap operas it is also not uncommon to see the male body constructed as an object of desire. Byars for instance reviews a number of melodramas from the 1950s and concludes that camera manipulations and point of view structures enable a 'positive and unabashed expression of feminine desire' (1991: 178). More recent examples can be found on a regular basis in soap operas.

In these cases the context of reception – an all-female audience – reduces the dangers of exhibiting the male body. Textual devices can also modify a full-blown subordination of the male body to the gaze of the spectator, sports photography being exemplary. Easthope (1986) contends that nowadays the male body is mainly celebrated in sports photography, where the frozen image of male physical activity and strength permits a look at the male body as an object of visual pleasure.

According to Ien Ang (1983: 421), sports photography demonstrates the prevailing patriarchal limits for visualizing the male body: 'These pictures are a compromise between activity and passivity; the male body tolerates the transformation into an object of visual desire only when it is in motion.' In the more straightforward pictures of male pin-ups, currently increasingly popular as postcards, these limits are drawn in various ways. Richard Dyer (1982) has observed that the visualization of male pin-ups differs from the female pin-up in at least three ways. To begin with, if men look directly into the camera, the meaning of their look is far removed from the inviting smiles of female pin-ups. 'The male pin-up, even at his most benign, still stares at the viewer' (1982: 66). By his direct and unfriendly return of the look, the male pin-up denies that he is the one being looked at. Such a penetrating gaze prevents undisturbed voyeurism of the female spectator and attempts to restore some of the traditional balance of power in the visual economy. In Figure 6.1, masculinity as activity is further underscored by the muscular structure of the upper body, tautened and certainly not at ease.

The patriarchal tension between masculine activity and feminine passivity responsible for the instabilities of the male pin-up shows also in the way

Figure 6.1 *Shaving (photography by Salvatore, published as a greetings card by Athena International)*

male pin-ups do not look at their spectators. Whereas women often avert their eyes in modesty and submission to the gaze of the male audience, men tend to look up, suggesting spirituality, or away from the camera, expressing a complete lack of interest in the viewer. Again, his presence as a pin-up, existing for the pleasure of the viewers, is denied. Instead he is presented as a man who just happens to be looked at. Not surprisingly, washing, bathing, showering etc. function as excellent excuses for the male body to be displayed. The character in such pictures is certainly not exhibiting himself to the female audience, but is merely caught in the perfectly legitimate masculine act of for instance, shaving.

The male pin-up's lack of passivity is one of his important features. If he is not actually doing something, the picture presents the female spectators with various signs of activity. Sports and muscular structure have already been mentioned, other signs often refer to work.

The male body thus seems to resist straightforward visual eroticization, confining female voyeurism to the incidental bits and pieces offered in patriarchal culture. In an interesting analysis of *Playgirl*, Ien Ang (1983) shows that even there, the explicit attempts to construct the male body as an object of female desire do not escape the conventions of the patriarchal visual economy. The pictures of the *Playgirl* pin-ups display most of the signs of male activity discussed above, like tautened muscles, physical activity or the suggestion of labour. The ultimate difference between *Playgirl* and *Playboy* pornography, however, is realized by the construction of the *Playgirl* man as a romantic object rather than a sexual one. According to Ang, this transformation is achieved in various ways. Contradictory to the penetrating stares of other male pin-ups, *Playgirl* men look at us as if we know them intimately. They are smiling, friendly and reassuring, as if to tell us that we are looking at a close friend and not at a body. The blunt sexuality associated with pornography is further suppressed by aesthetic compositions and lighting, 'effects that draw our attention to the active intervention of photography' (Ang, 1983: 427). Finally, the denial of the sexual qualities of the naked *Playgirl* men is achieved through the text that accompanies the pictures. Attention is focused on the particular personality we are looking at and his diverse qualities as a human being. These men are always presented with their first and last name, signifying that we are watching a person, not just a body. *Playgirl* Man of the Month for March 1992 for instance was introduced as:

> Handsome prince personified. Looking as though he'd been plucked from the pages of a fairy tale, Robert Johnston undoubtedly qualifies for the role of Prince Charming. . . . Bobby is a marine biologist whose fascination with ocean depths often send him into the far reaches of the deep blue sea [sic!]. . . . Single, but always looking, Bob says he never enters a relationship with any 'expectations about how it's going to be. Each experience is always new and rewarding.' Indeed, this taut 26-year-old proves wise beyond his years. 'I am a big believer in the notion that love can cure society's travails', he declares.

In that same March issue, the picture series of that month's 'Mr. Big' –

'proportions like these get noticed' – displayed other mechanisms to 're-personify' the objectified male body. The same picture of subject Tom Marinelli was printed three times with different shades of pastel colours. This man's body showed the evidence of intensive workouts, and also the presence of his motor bike in the picture signified that this was a 'guy on the move'. The accompanying text read:

> At 23, Tom Marinelli has the confidence it takes most people several decades to acquire. But then, this is no ordinary guy. You're looking at someone who actually wakes up every morning feeling good – in fact rarin' to go! . . . Tom the Triumphant credits his parents with instilling in him such old-fashioned values as the work ethic. 'Besides building my pride, doing a good job helps to get the bills paid', he notes pragmatically. Those close family ties may also account for the way he guards his private life – fiercely. Not one to blather about his special lady, Tom just smiles when *Playgirl* scribes attempt to pry.

Ang contends that the manifest display of male bodies in *Playgirl* supports a fantasy of heterosexual romance, rather than of female heterosexual desire. The *Playgirl* men's sex appeal depends on their charming, romantic, mature or whatever personalities, much less on the sexual qualities of their bodies. Even in a soft-porn magazine like *Playgirl* the objectification of the male body is in no way comparable to the objectification of female bodies in *Playboy* and its competitors.

The case of *Playgirl* suggests that within the patriarchal structure of looking, a straightforward reversal of the gaze does not offer much pleasure to the female spectator. Obviously, one-dimensional voyeurism in the masculine tradition does not satisfy female desires. The additional codes of heterosexual romance exploited by *Playgirl* seem just one means to enhance female pleasure. For instance, the popularity among women of film and television stars like Rudolf Valentino and Tom Selleck is said to derive from the articulation of 'masculine' and 'feminine' positions within one and the same character. These 'multi-faceted' characters offer various sources of pleasure, an important one being the polysemic construction of masculinity that encourages the female audience to negotiate its meaning. Sally Flitterman (1985: 46) writes about Magnum P.I., the main character in an American television series played by Tom Selleck:

> Magnum is partly transformed from a dashing macho-mythical figure with which a largely male audience can identify, into a desired and desirable object whom mostly female viewers can long to possess. This psychic collusion of being and having within a single potent figure at once collapses the distinction between traditionally gendered subjectivity and objectivity, identification and desire, and blurs the boundaries between erotic identity and object choice as a form of visual pleasure. (1985: 46)

Miriam Hansen (1986) has argued similarly of Rudolf Valentino films that: 'Valentino's appeal depends, to a large degree, on the manner in which he combines masculine control of the look with the feminine quality of to-be-looked-at-ness.' It thus seems as if a pleasurable heterosexual female gaze depends on the denial and disruption of traditional gender identities.

Ambivalence, contradictions and negotiations can stimulate female voyeurism rather than frustrating it. Although patriarchy has long offered only a few exceptional instances of gender ambivalence, more and more popular culture is beginning to explore the contradictions of gender. In *Miami Vice*, an American police series that was enormously popular around the world in the mid-1980s, one of the attractive male heroes (Sonny, played by Don Johnson) exhibits traditional 'feminine' qualities such as physical attractiveness and a caring and sensitive nature, as well as the hard-boiled masculine qualities expected of a tough policeman. King (1990) even argues that the visual and narrative codes in *Miami Vice* construct Sonny as predominantly 'feminine' and thinks that much male criticism of the series can be explained as fear of the 'effeminate' man.

Advertising is another genre which, while still a stronghold of straightforward objectification of female bodies, has begun to explore the ambivalence of gender, in particular by exploiting the erotic heterosexual appeal of men. According to Wernick (1991: 62), the conventions of advertising have become flexible enough 'to allow men and women to be positioned at either end of the objectified/objectifying sexual continuum'. He contends that the ultimate consequence of this interchangeability is that sex and gender have become arbitrary signs in advertising without any direct relations to their referents in real life. While that conclusion seems more than a little out of touch with most realities of contemporary advertising, images of women and men in popular culture are increasingly hard to interpret in traditional object/subject–active/passive–masculine/feminine dichotomies; a promising prospect for female voyeuristic pleasure.

Despite the contradictions in patriarchal culture and the opportunities these offer for alternative ways of looking, the dominant visual economy is still organized along traditional gender lines: men look at women, women watch themselves being looked at. The reasons for the persistence of the traditional structure of looking have been located by various authors in the patriarchal will to maintain power, and in the anxiety 'woman' produces in the patriarchal unconscious.

While such an analysis may offer a relatively satisfactory explanation of the workings of dominant culture, it denies the experiences of women as spectators and forestalls the examination and development of female pleasure. For that reason, the greater part of this chapter has focused on the 'recuperation' of the experiences of female spectators looking at women as well as at men. To be more precise: in this chapter the visual and narrative codes that construct the female and male body as spectacle to be looked at, have been questioned together with the viewing pleasures they enable. Authors working within a psychoanalytic paradigm have argued that women can derive pleasure from looking at other women, due to a homosexual inclination resulting from the pre-Oedipal attachment to the mother. Other authors have claimed however, that the active/passive dichotomy underlying most discussions about gender and spectatorship is much too simplistic to capture the variety of female viewing pleasures evoked by looking at other women. The analysis of the unstable way in which the male body presents itself to the female spectator supports that argument. 'Masculine' voyeurism of the male body is prevented by visual and narrative codes that signify activity and control by the male pin-up. It shows that within patriarchy a simple reversal of the masculine structure of looking which is based on identification and voyeurism does not produce an equivalent female voyeurism. Female pleasures seem to have their own specific logic, evoked by traditional patriarchal codes of romance – as in the *Playgirl* case, – and by the more subversive codes present in some expressions of popular culture, like *Magnum* and *Miami Vice*, which undermine hegemonic definitions of gender.

Finally, one needs to bear in mind that 'the female spectator' as discussed here is principally an imaginary concept without a direct referent in reality. What is examined in analyses like these are the textual constructions of 'subject positions' to be taken up by actual audiences. In contemporary patriarchal culture, many of these subject positions have a gendered character, like voyeurism and masculinity, and romantic desire and femininity. Moreover, visual and narrative codes are often employed to realize an ideological 'closure' of the text, 'enforcing' a traditional gendered subject position. This does not mean, however, that female spectatorship can only be moulded in the traditional patriarchal framework, nor male spectatorship either for that matter. Texts themselves are seen to offer ample opportunities for cross-gender identification and voyeuristic pleasure, and in the eyes of some the demise of gender as a mechanism for structuring looking pleasure seems likely, turning it into a 'floating signifier . . . free to swirl around and substitute for its paired opposite at will' (Wernick, 1991: 63). Given such developments, the concepts of a 'male' or 'female' spectator position become problematic and too essentialist in character. However, we are still far away from such a situation, since society is permeated with successful discourses of identity that constitute human beings, and of which gender is not the least important.

Notes

1. Flitterman-Lewis (1992) argues that technical, textual and social aspects of film and television are so different that television needs a psychoanalytic theory of its own.

2. This chapter builds on a review essay of recent publications on gender and film published in the *Journal of Communication* (van Zoonen, 1992c).

3. Page numbers refer to the reprint of Mulvey's article in Erens, 1990.

4. Byars (1991) on the other hand points out numerous examples.

5. These films are titled *The Bad Sister*; *Riddles of the Sphynx*.

6. Reported in Modleski, 1990.

7. As referred to in Easthope, 1986.

8. Dutch *Playboy*, August 1992.

7

Gender and Media Reception

In the past decade a new interest in the audiences of the media has emerged, within feminist media studies and within media and cultural studies in general. A variety of media, technologies and genres have been subject to inquiry: popular music, women's magazines, communication technologies such as the telephone, the video cassette recorder (VCR) and the home computer, television and in particular soap operas.[1] A major reason for the increased popularity of studying media audiences lies in the shortcomings of the 'textual determinism' implicit in the content, semiotic and psychoanalytic approaches to media content that were discussed in the previous chapters. There is a strange mismatch between the textual focus of these feminist analyses and the concern of their authors with the cultural and political meaning of media content. In Chapter 2, for instance, the work of Tuchman (1978a) was referred to, who claimed on the basis of content analysis that the lack of positive female images on television would endanger the participation of women in the labour force. Likewise, psychoanalytic film theories, such as that of Mulvey (1975), contend that textual mechanisms place the audience of mainstream Hollywood movies and many other cultural products in the inexorable position of a 'male' voyeur of the female objectified body. While semiology posits less definitive effects, its scope remains restricted to the different meanings embedded in the text itself. However, the rather strong claims feminist media studies have made about the cultural and political meaning of media content seem hard to validate on the basis of textual analysis only: 'If we are concerned with the meaning and significance of popular culture in contemporary society, with how cultural forms work ideologically or politically, then we need to understand cultural products (or "texts") *as they are understood by audiences*' (Lewis, 1991: 47, italics in original). Indeed, if we look again at the central questions about media, as put by various feminist theories, we recognize that audiences are actually at the core of their projects. To sum up briefly: some feminists charge media with maintaining sex role stereotypes, assuming that audiences will be affected by sexist media content. Other feminists add that media and pornographic media in particular instigate men into aggressive and violent acts against women. And again others incorporate insights from psychoanalysis and theories of ideology to support their claim that media contribute to the overall acceptance of the dominant ideology. In the typical research project such claims would be substantiated by a textual analysis of 'sex roles', the 'construction of femininity', or the 'interpellation of the feminine subject' and other theoretical assumptions about the audience reaction and interpretation of the text. From such assumptions a view of the (female) audience would emerge as of passive individuals completely immersed in, incapable of and prevented from recognizing the ideological workings of patriarchal and capitalist hegemony.

Such analyses, however, do not explain much about the popularity and the meaning of popular genres to their audiences. Why are cultural forms like women's magazines, soaps and romances so immensely popular among women? Does their popularity also imply an acceptance of the dominant ideology embedded in the texts? How are they consumed in everyday life? What do they mean to women who enjoy them? Can the popularity of popular culture be reconciled with feminist concerns? What is the relation between audience pleasures and feminist politics? Such questions have neither been addressed nor answered by textual analysis while they are becoming increasingly pressing. A variety of new women's magazines have entered the market successfully adapting to the fragmentation of a formerly unified female readership: girls, young women, older women, career women, rich housewives, the avid cook or gardener, working women, secretaries, travelling women and the traditional housewife all happily subscribe to their own kind of women's magazine; romance novels have introduced new heroines profoundly touched by the feminist calls for independence, but still longing for and always rewarded with everlasting heterosexual romance;[2] soap operas like *Dallas*, *Dynasty* and their successors attract a predominantly female audience in spite of their 'sexist', 'patriarchal' and 'capitalist' content; and feminist media struggle to reach larger audiences, to attract advertisers and even to maintain their old readership (cf. Hermes and van Zoonen, 1988). On top of that, femininists themselves are 'coming out' in large numbers, admitting that they too are hooked on romances, soaps and women's magazines (Ang, 1985; Winship, 1987).

One of the reasons for the popularity of audience research is that these developments seem impossible to explain by textual analysis only. The new audience research assumes that the meaning of popular culture could be understood better if one would only ask the audience about their interpretations, use and experience.[3] Another important reason for the popularity of audience research has to do with the unsatisfactory politics hidden in the textual project. Feminist researchers analysing gender discourse in media texts implicitly claim to have access to the definitive ideological meaning of the text. They recognize the hegemonic thrust of media output and are able to resist its devastating effects, while the audience is still lured by its attractions and temptations. The aim of such research is, among other things, to raise the awareness of ordinary audiences to the extent that they too will recognize the patriarchal nature of media output and overcome their ill-informed preference for it. Dominant ideology expressed by mass media keeps women in their subordinated position, so it is in women's own interest to identify the ideologies embedded in popular culture, and to refrain from their own consumption of it. Thus audience pleasures are not taken seriously as worthwhile in themselves, but are seen as a form of false consciousness. In a way, the feminist critic puts herself in the position of the benign teacher who is able to tell other women what is best for them. As said in Chapter 3, a deep gap is constructed between feminist media critics and other women, whose preferences and pleasures are neither taken very seriously, nor treated very respectfully.

Self-evident, straightforward and long overdue as the movement towards audience analysis may seem then, it is not simply a question of staking out a new terrain of analysis. It reflects a more fundamental paradigmatic shift that has taken place in feminist studies in general, from determinist explanations of women's subordination by, among other factors, mass media, as in the approaches referred to above, to a focus on processes of symbolization and representation which are central to this book, for example. Barrett (1992) claims that feminism has made a turn to 'culture' in the past decade, moving away from models of the social structure – be it capitalism or patriarchy – accounting for current gender relations, to questions of meaning, sexuality and political agency. Theoretically, this implies a change from social science disciplines to philosophy, psychoanalysis and linguistics. Empirically, the focus of attention moves from an analysis of social and economic structures, to the way people engage with these structures, how they make meaning of them, how they adapt to them and through which tactics they try to subvert them; 'making do' in the words of the French sociologist de Certeau (1984). Daily life is seen as the site where the concrete articulation of structures takes place and has become a major concern in contemporary cultural and feminist theory. In feminist media research this paradigmatic shift into 'poststructuralism' has produced new questions that can only be addressed by turning to the audience. A memory from the childhood of the black feminist critic bell hooks tellingly illustrates what one is looking for:

> When we sat in our living rooms in the fifties and early sixties watching those few black folks who appeared on television screens, we talked about their performance, but we always talked about the way white folks were treating them. I have vivid memories of watching the Ed Sullivan show on Sunday nights, of seeing on that show the great Louis Armstrong. Daddy, who was usually silent, would talk about the music, the way Armstrong was treated and the political implications of his appearance. Watching television in the fifties and sixties, and listening to adult conversation, was one of the primary ways many young black folks learned about race politics. . . . The screen was not a place of escape. It was a place of confrontation and encounter. (hooks, 1990: 3)

hooks' recollections show how hegemonic norms and values expressed in popular culture can be negotiated by ordinary people on a day-to-day basis. While the lack of black characters on the screen does not seem to have disturbed altogether the pleasures of watching TV, it nevertheless reinforced a social experience of being excluded and marginalized. hooks' account suggests that television thereby contributed in some way to the family's construction of its black identity. Furthermore, her memories indicate that watching television was not an isolated individual experience but thoroughly intertwined with family life, generating conversation, interaction and critique that expanded to the church, barber shops, beauty parlours, bars and other places of social gathering.

In the theoretical framework developed in this book, the importance of audience experience is also paramount. Media are construed as 'technologies of gender', expressing and incorporating gender discourse that arises from and regulates social, political and other contexts. The questions to be answered by audience research concern the use and interpretation of gendered media texts by gendered audiences. How does audience reception interact with the construction of gender at the level of identity formation, subjectivity and discourse? How do media as 'technologies of gender' regulate and discipline various social contexts? And how does this process relate to a feminist concern, however defined? In this chapter I shall review the kind of research that has emerged around these issues and which is known under a variety of labels: qualitative audience research (Jensen, 1986); reception analysis (Morley, 1991); new audience research (Curran, 1990); critical audience research (Carragee, 1990); empirical reception research (Livingstone, 1991); ethnography (Radway, 1989); interpretative media studies (Carragee, 1990). I shall adhere to one concept throughout this chapter, reception analysis, claiming that processes of use, negotiation, interpretation and accommodation are central to the socially anchored interaction of audiences with media texts. Audiences should be understood as producers of meaning instead of as mere consumers of meaning taking up prescribed textual audience positionings. This production of meaning can only be understood in its everyday context which is, in its turn, located within social and power relations that circumscribe the potential of audiences to make meaning.

To begin with a concrete example of reception analysis, I shall extensively review Janice Radway's study on romance readers, which is by now a classic work, both in feminist and cultural studies. Then I shall review reception analysis in two areas that are of crucial importance for theories of gender and mass media: the uses of television within a domestic context, and the gender-specific pleasures of soap operas. Finally, I shall discuss the contribution of the research discussed to the understanding of mass media as 'technologies of gender'.

Reading the romance

In 1984 Janice Radway published her classic study *Reading the Romance*, in which she presented the results of a combination of textual and audience research into the meaning of popular romance novels. In order to examine how women interpret Harlequin, Silhouette, Mills & Boon and other brands of mass produced romance novels, Radway sent questionnaires to about thirty women and interviewed some twenty women, living somewhere in the American midwest in a town Radway calls 'Smithton'. The majority of them were married and had children of school age. Some of them worked part time, though full time jobs were rare. The overwhelming majority of women Radway talked to read at least one romance a day. Radway's main informant was a Smithton bookseller who was an avid romance reader herself and who published a newsletter in which new publications were rated for their quality. 'Dot' as she was called by her customers advised women on good buys and introduced Radway to her respondents.

For the Smithton women, the quality of a romance appears to depend on the development of the relation between the heroine and the hero, and on their particular characters. The story should focus on a woman with whom the female reader can identify. The ideal storyline entails the slow development of a romance, with the heroine and hero only gradually becoming aware of their feelings and finally overcoming their mutual distrust. Explicit descriptions of sexuality are appreciated only within the confines of the romantic affair. The ultimate pleasure is to see how the hero's masculine defence mechanisms crumble beneath the love of the heroine. The transformation of the reserved and indifferent male into a warm and loving human being signifies a victory of female values of care and nurture. However, the hero is not a weak man, although strength and independence rank low in the ideal qualities the Smithton women ascribe to him. He should be a man confident in public life and ideally he is portrayed as intelligent, wealthy and acknowledged. He is unmistakably masculine, in his looks and his behaviour, but his capacity for tenderness is always betrayed by small hints at the beginning of the story such as the love for an old friend, the look in his eyes or the friendly wrinkle around his mouth. His transformation into a tender and loving husband therefore comes as no surprise. While the ideal hero of the Smithton women shows few signs of independence, the heroine on the contrary should be depicted as an independent, modern individual. She is an extraordinary person who does not live up to the traditional ideals of femininity. She has an unusual job, is sexually innocent and unaware of her own irresistible beauty. The Smithton women's evaluation of the heroine seems curious in the light of the many feminist accusations that romance novels only depict passive and vulnerable women in need of male protection. According to Radway, the readers judge the heroine's capacities on the basis of assertions that she is special and independent, ignoring the events and actions in the narrative that demonstrate otherwise. Radway sees this paradox as a hidden feminist fantasy: 'With a few simple statements rather than with truly threatening action on the part of the heroine, the romance author demonstrates for the typical reader the compatibility of a changed sense of the female self and an unchanged social arrangement' (p. 79).

The Smithton women also have very outspoken ideas about what constitutes bad romances. Unhappy endings are obviously ruled out; they remove the romance from the genre since the Smithton women consider the happy ending as constitutive of romance novels. A male hero who is aggressive and takes to violence in order to convince the heroine of his love is despised. There is a thin line between the male hero's acceptable 'force' which originates in his inability to restrain himself in the face of the heroine's irresistible attractiveness, and unacceptable male violence. In the former case his persistence allows the heroine to give in to her own sexual desires without taking responsibility for it. When the 'hero' resorts to violence however, then the heroine is simply raped, something the Smithton women who identify intensely with the heroine obviously do not enjoy reading. As one woman said: 'That's why I avoid these books that are so depressing. All these terrible things that are happening to the heroine are happening to me – and I hold these emotions over' (p. 159). In bad romances the transformation of a cool and detached hero into a warm and loving partner becomes unconvincing given his previous record of aggression and violence. The romantic love between hero and heroine is then seen to subsist in a very unstable and threatening history. Promiscuous behaviour on the part of the heroine is also considered characteristic of a bad romance. Such 'bed-hopping' implies the adoption of male standards.

The Smithton women can hardly be considered the ignorant, dulled and misguided audience that feminist critics have usually associated with fans of mass culture. On the contrary, the readers demonstrate an intricate knowledge of the genre and their reading cannot be characterized as simply 'absorbing' romances on a daily basis. In some cases their expertise and involvement leads them to write their own romances. What are the particular pleasures reading romances offer? According to the Smithton women, romances provide them with escape or relaxation, and instruction. They experience their daily life as an unending sequence of looking after their husbands and children, in a material as well as an emotional sense. Radway's interviews made clear that the act of reading is at least as important in escaping from this burden as the stories themselves. Taking up a novel creates time and space in which women can be entirely on their own, temporarily released from the never-ending calls for attention of the family members. The Smithton women therefore always try to arrange their reading in such a way that they are unlikely to be disturbed by their family. It is a claim to leisure time otherwise denied to the ordinary housewife. As the discussion about the quality of the romances made clear, not just any book or genre will satisfy this need. The romances are expected to open up a world for the reader in which everything is different from their own everyday life. The romances are often located in exotic settings and promise to be all-fulfilling. Most important, however, is that the hero turns out to be a loving man who is capable of caring for and nurturing the heroine. Not only is the burden of taking care of others released by reading, the readers can also enjoy the experience of being nurtured themselves, albeit that this is only a vicarious pleasure. Radway therefore thinks of romances as compensatory reading, providing women with the care and nurturance they miss in everyday life.

Reading in this sense connotes a free space where they feel liberated from the need to perform duties that they otherwise willingly accept as their own. At the same time, by carefully choosing stories that make them feel particularly happy, they escape figuratively into a fairy tale where a heroine's similar needs are adequately met. As a result, they vicariously attend to their own requirements as independent individuals who require emotional sustenance and solicitude. (p. 93)

Radway uses Chodorow's psychoanalytic theory to account for the particular desires satisfied by romance reading.[3] The hero provides the all-embracing, unconditional love and care which children expect to receive from the mother. Under patriarchy women are the main providers of that care but have no one to be nurtured by, unless vicariously by the romance hero. The therapeutic value of reading only lasts as long as the romance itself, which might explain the almost addictive reading patterns, according to Radway.

A second pleasurable factor of reading which the Smithton women mention is the educational value of the romances. They have a particular preference for historical romances which usually provide well-researched and accurate historical detail. Radway's respondents feel that reading romances expands their horizon and enables them to gather knowledge of other times and places. Many of them surprise their husbands and children with facts and figures from the story and therewith gain a feeling of self-worth and approval. Others feel that the bits of information about exotic locations they find in romance novels are a good substitute for the travel they would like to undertake. The Smithton women's appreciation of the instructional value of the romances is expressed also in their hope that their own passion for reading will generate a love for reading in their children too. Reading is thus framed in a modernist ideology of self-improvement, progress and effort which enables the Smithton women to construct a self-image of intelligence and responsibility. Radway however interprets the emphasis on the instructional value of the romances as a legitimating practice to circumvent the feelings of guilt which the readers experience because of the time and money they spend on their books. Their families need to be convinced that reading romances is worth while, so they claim that there is a lot to be learned from them.

Radway's analysis of the pleasures of reading romances definitely undermines any conception of readers and audiences of popular culture as burdened by a 'false consciousness', so common in many feminist views. The Smithton women have very outspoken thoughts about each separate romance and have developed reading practices that meet the needs and preferences originating in their particular social situation. While the appeals and pleasures of romance reading are convincingly explained, Radway's approach to another key issue of feminist audience research – the 'politics' of pleasure – is much more problematic. Since the readers themselves do not perceive their romance habits in political terms, Radway needs to concoct an interpretation of their reading practices as 'political' activities. Her claim that the love of romance can be seen as a hidden protest against patriarchal culture has much in common with the work of authors like Angela McRobbie, Dorothy Hobson, Mary Ellen Brown and John Fiske, who examine how women use traditionally female forms to resist their situation under patriarchy.[4] In the case of romance reading, this means a claim to leisure time otherwise denied to the ordinary housewife and a possibility of withdrawing from the caring and self-sacrificing role expected of them. Furthermore, the texts offer fantasies of a utopia in which women are nurtured by men, compensating for the lack of nurture they experience themselves. According to Radway 'critical power . . . lies buried in the romances as one of the few widely shared womanly commentaries on the contradictions and costs of patriarchy' (p. 18).

Left by itself, however, that critical power will not develop into conscious resistance against patriarchy, Radway fears, since the overall ideological effect of reading romance is to reconcile women with their unfortunate fate. She claims that several narrative and linguistic techniques render the romance itself a source of learning, as a description of reality. The fact that the romance is a story constructed by an author is denied by employing devices that position readers as if they were reading narratives of real events: historical accuracy and descriptive detail; realistic characters; temporal and spatial specificity; direct referential language and a limited vocabulary. Given that the readers take the historical and descriptive detail as true, teaching them about life beyond their horizon, it is likely – according to Radway – that they will take the romance's assertion that men can fulfil women's need as true also.

> It is precisely because the romance's surrounding universe is always portrayed so convincingly that romance readers might well be persuaded to believe that the romantic action itself is not only plausible but . . . inevitable. Repetitive engagement in it would enable a reader to tell herself again and again that a love like the heroine's might indeed occur in a world such as hers. (p. 207)

For Radway to argue convincingly that the hegemonic power of the romance will be more powerful than the hidden protest she sees embodied in its reading, she needs to deny that the readers will be capable of distinguishing between the different levels of the text: that of historical description and that of romantic fantasy. A collapse of the two would enable the ideological effect Radway fears and would deprive the hidden protest of its potential. The task of the feminist critic therefore is to exploit the threads of dissatisfaction expressed in reading romances and help the readers understand that a better world is possible in which 'the vicarious pleasure supplied by . . . reading would be unnecessary' (p. 222).

While Radway's attempt to understand women's pleasures under patriarchy has been widely acclaimed, her political recommendations and conclusions have been subject to considerable criticism (for example, Ang, 1988; Modleski, 1991). Being the feminist expert, knowing the true nature of the romance and thus rejecting it, she constructs a considerable distance between herself and the ordinary romance fan who still enjoys romances and does not recognize her own dissatisfaction with patriarchy. Otherwise the fan would have found a lifestyle (or a husband) in which she does not need the compensatory literature. Radway puts the feminist critic in a position where it is neither possible nor necessary to resort to the vicarious fulfilment of romantic desires. Popular pleasures and feminist politics are constructed as mutually exclusive; being a feminist and still enjoying romance novels is seen as utterly inconsistent and undesirable. It is on such a conclusion that Radway's book has often been criticized, the critics raising the issue of how 'pleasure' and 'politics' can be related, rather than claiming that they cannot exist alongside each other. Ang (1985), for instance, proposes to consider the fantasies and pleasures involved in consuming popular culture as independent and relatively isolated dimensions of subjectivity that make daily life enjoyable in expectation of feminist utopias, but which do not relate directly to forms of feminist politics. Brown (1990a) on the other hand collapses the distinction between pleasure and politics by appreciating the gendered reception of popular culture as a form of 'feminine discourse' that resists hegemonic definitions of femininity and masculinity by privately making fun of it. The discussion on the (lack of) political or feminist potential of popular cultural forms has also informed research about soap operas, women's magazines and other popular genres, and is – as said earlier – one of the key issues in feminist media research. It will be taken up in more detail and depth in the final chapter.

Radway's analysis is an early sign of the changed focus in feminist media studies, now directed at the meaning of media in the context of everyday life. Radway showed how women use popular cultural forms to make do with their social situation, how they actively react to and shape their own pleasures and desires. Although the question of the subversive or repressive impact of these reading practices remains unresolved, Radway's analysis makes quite clear that the earlier feminist conceptions of the audience as 'mass', implying a composition of isolated individuals easily manipulated by media messages, needs revision.

Television and the family

In many societies the common social context in which individuals watch television is the family (or any other social arrangement that has replaced it). Of course, in student dormitories, kindergartens, schools and bars, television is important as well, but the home is the place where TV is watched most often and which is assumed in programme policies (Leman, 1987).

Increasingly therefore, researchers choose the family as the appropriate unit of analysis for the study of TV audiences. James Lull (1990), for instance, has examined the way in which interpersonal communication in the family is structured by television and other media. Jan-Uwe Rogge (1989) claims that the media, and television in particular, form a part of the family system that define the interpersonal relationships and the emotional and communicative climate in a family. Both authors, however, ignore how power and gender relations within the family intervene in the interaction of the family with its media, in other words they neglect the gender politics of the living room. According to Brunsdon (1986), Gray (1987), Hobson (1980) and Morley (1986) it is crucial to acknowledge the different social positions that women and men have in the traditional nuclear family. Whereas for men the home is a site of leisure, clearly marked by a temporal and spatial distance from the workplace, for women it is a place of work inhabited by husband and children who require continual emotional and material care. It would seem inevitable therefore, that gender differences will occur in the use and appreciation of the family's media. Furthermore, contrary to the image of the family as a 'haven in a heartless world', it is the site where gender conflicts and power differences are directly and incessantly experienced, fought out, modified and accommodated, in an often tacit and inconspicuous process (Komter, 1985). Inevitably, the resulting gendered balance of power will be articulated in the use of the family's mass media too.

Informed by this perspective on gender and the family, David Morley examined how working class and lower middle class families in Britain actually watch television, and how this is linked with the family's particular biography, habits and rituals. He concludes that 'the one structural principle working across all the families interviewed is that of gender' (1986: p. 146), affecting among other things programme choice and preferences, style and amount of viewing, and the operation of the video recorder. It appeared that the men and women whom Morley interviewed have distinct programme and channel preferences which could be a potential source of conflict within the family. From Morley's data an almost caricatured gender difference emerges with women preferring fictional programmes, romances, local news over national news and ITV programmes (Britain's premier commercial channel), and men favouring factual programmes, sport, realistic fiction and BBC output. A similar picture comes from Dorothy Hobson's analysis (1980) of the media preferences of housewives and from Ann Gray's research (1987, 1992) on domestic uses of the VCR.

Both Morley and Gray warn against taking these gender differences too rigidly. In Morley's research, for instance, the few families in which the woman held a dominant position in terms of cultural capital did not follow the usual gendered pattern. He therefore claims that it is the confluence of gender and social position that accounts for particular viewing habits. On the other hand, Gray's respondents were drawn from various social positions, but still showed remarkable similarities in the way they spoke about their viewing practices. Against the backdrop of rating figures, which generally show a less extreme gendered pattern of viewing preferences, Morley wonders how to interpret the data from his own research. The difference can be explained partly by the distinction between 'viewing' as measured in the ratings, and 'viewing attentively and with pleasure' as examined in Morley's research. More interesting however, is Morley's assumption that the way wives and husbands report their viewing preferences might be misleading because of their tendency to live up to their socially expected roles:

> The fact that the respondents were interviewed *en famille* may have predisposed them to adopt stereotyped familial roles in the interviews which, if interviewed separately, they would not adhere to – thus again leading to a tendency towards misleading forms of classical gender stereotyping. (1986: 166)

This misleading representation of the self is not only a methodological problem, but points to a more fundamental issue that Morley unfortunately only touches upon briefly. What might be involved is not so much a false and misleading account but a construction of an appropriate gender identity within the context of family relations. In that case, the relation of gender and media consumption would need to be conceptualized in a radically different manner. To (over)simplify: it is not the fact of being woman or man that explains programme preferences, but programme preferences that construct a particular and appropriate gendered identity. Such an interpretation is more in line with the overall theoretical position taken up in this book and will be developed in the conclusion of this chapter.

Despite the major differences in programme preferences among the members of the family, none of the families in Morley's and Gray's research reported excessive conflicts over watching television. In general, the husband (or the eldest son) decides what will be watched, a decision that is not so much the result of an open discussion but already taken for granted, being an extension of male power in the family. The use of the remote control is almost exclusively reserved to the men, making the device 'a highly visible symbol of condensed power relations'. This pattern is only slightly disrupted in the few families that have female breadwinners. Given such a division of power, it is not surprising that women do not often consult the TV guide, nor do they take much initiative in watching television. They do not seem to care very much about what is on, with the exception of their favourite serials. Still, they watch as much as their husbands and children do, only in a completely different way. While the husbands watch attentively, in silence and without interrupting the flow, their wives perform a host of domestic duties and leisure activities like ironing, sewing, crocheting, knitting or reading a book. Obviously, it is difficult for housewives to step out of their working day while still being in the home. From the many comments quoted in Morley's and Gray's research, it appears they consider 'just watching television' a waste of time. Another aspect of their particular style of viewing also testifies to their particular position in the family. Most women tend to talk while the set is on, commenting on what they see and grabbing the occasion to divert into the family's daily life. Herman Bausinger (1984) has interpreted this kind of behaviour as an extension of the social and psychological tasks women are responsible for in the family, as an attempt to make and maintain contact between family members. Morley concludes in a similar vein that women maintain their role as domestic managers while watching television.

All in all, from the research on television and the family it appears clearly that within the context of the traditional western nuclear family, watching television is a leisure activity for husbands, but an extension of domestic labour for wives. To enjoy television as a leisure activity, women must take special measures which they occasionally do, although often troubled by feelings of guilt. A prerequisite for enjoyable viewing seems to be the absence of family members whose presence exerts claims on them as housewives and mothers, or who in many cases will ridicule their particular preference for romance and weepies. Many of Morley's female respondents say they enjoy watching television on Sunday mornings while the rest of the family are sleeping in. Others arrange to watch taped programmes or rented videos with female friends during the afternoon. Gray, for instance, reports that some of her interviewees living in the same neighbourhood come together weekly to watch videos. They also like soap operas and record episodes for each other. According to Gray, 'these popular texts form an important part of their friendship and association in their everyday lives and give a focus to an almost separate female culture which they can share together within the constraints of their positions as wives and mothers' (1987: 49). However, the experienced pleasures are not totally uncomplicated but are constrained by feelings of guilt and obligation. Taking time out to indulge in their own choices undermines their sense of being a good wife and mother, defined as the ever-available, self-sacrificing and happy housewife/mother. Furthermore, their particular programme preferences are often downgraded by their husbands, many of whom think their wives watch silly or 'badly acted' programmes. Clearly, domestic power relations also includes the definition of bad taste and forces women to watch their favourite programmes secretly. In this respect watching favourite television programmes bears the same feelings of guilt that Radway found among the romance readers.

Most of this kind of research has been carried out within traditional, white, nuclear families. It should be emphasized again that the observed gender differences are a product of the particular social positions that women and men occupy in such families. It is quite likely that other patterns will emerge in families from other ethnic and class backgrounds, and in less traditional 'family' arrangements such as working couples, single parent families, homosexual couples etc. Such research has not yet been widely conducted, although Frissen and Meier (1988) partially replicated Morley's research in the Netherlands and asked traditional housewives and single working women about the role of television in their lives. The experience of the housewives was much the same as that of Morley's and Gray's respondents. They have similar programme preferences which most of their husbands despise and ridicule. They often find themselves watching programmes they do not particularly like, and perform a variety of domestic tasks while watching TV. Television appears to be much less significant in the lives of the working women. They watch only occasionally and prefer to fill their leisure time with social activities such as going to the movies, to the sports club or to the pub with friends. Thus television for them was found to be a second choice, a too solitary activity. Once in a while they would deliberately watch television for a 'good cry'. As one of them said: 'Then, I am totally absorbed by the programme, It is as if I inhabit the space they show. I become totally intoxicated. I take my handkerchief and cry. Wonderful!' (Frissen and Meier, 1988: 88).

Women and soap operas

The research on women and soaps is primarily cast in terms of the articulation of pleasure and politics. As Ien Ang wonders in *Watching Dallas*: 'The widespread and continuing popularity of soap operas among women has attracted a lot of attention from feminists. How must the fact that so many women obviously get pleasure from watching soap operas be judged politically from a femininist perspective? Is *Dallas* good or bad for women?' (1985: 118). The issue therefore is not only why and how women watch and interpret soaps but also whether and how the construction of meaning through the interaction between text and audience contributes to the subversion, negotiation or maintenance of hegemonic gender discourse.The answers to such questions vary as widely as do the ways in which they are arrived at. Tania Modleski contends that a certain critical distance from mass cultural products and their audiences is necessary to formulate a comprehensive cultural critique. According to Modleski audience researchers run the risk of falling in love with their subjects. 'As a result they may unwittingly wind up writing apologias for mass culture and embracing its ideology' (1986: xi). She therefore consistently employs textual analysis to explore the meanings of popular culture (for example, Modleski, 1991).

Many other authors, however, try to combine an empirical finding of audience pleasure with a critical feminist viewpoint. The first concern in these projects is to examine the particular viewing experience engendered by soap operas. Ang (1985), for instance, found that Dutch fans of the American soap *Dallas* experienced the series as realistic drama, in spite of the critics' claims that *Dallas* offers only fantasy and escape. While her respondents acknowledged the unrealistic nature of the complicated family relations and the excessive richness of the environment, they recognized the emotional predicaments of the characters, and found the tragic sequence of rows, intrigues, happiness and misery 'realistic'. Ang therefore calls the realism of *Dallas* emotional realism: 'what is recognized as real is not knowledge of the world, but a subjective experience of the world: a "structure of feeling" ' (1985: 45). Ang's research on *Dallas* has been followed up by numerous other inquiries into the gendered pleasures of soap, to the extent that it has now become a dominant area in feminist media research. A common theme in these projects is the mixed positions of soap opera viewers, who alternate between a critical mode of reception and an involved way of viewing. Dorothy Hobson (1989, 1990) interviewed British working women and examined how watching soaps contributes to the interpersonal relations and the culture of the workplace. In several groups of women working together soaps appear to be a daily subject of conversation. Hobson observes two ways of talking about soap operas between which individual audience members easily 'commute'. First, there is a more or less detached way of looking that acknowledges the constructedness of the story. The women she interviewed tended to speculate about narrative development, and the future feelings of characters based on their own opinions about realistic plots and stories. They tried to 'co-author' the soaps, so to speak, exploiting bits of information about actors from gossip magazines, other media and talks with colleagues, which shows that other texts than the soaps themselves play a part in their reception. Such comments underscore the importance of the 'intertextual' reception of popular culture: 'any one text is necessarily read in relationship to others and . . . a range of textual knowledge is brought to bear upon it' (Fiske, 1988: 108). This detached way of looking has also been observed by Katz and Liebes (1990) in their research on cross-cultural variations in the reception of soaps. They refer to this detachment as a critical mode of reception, characterized by comments such as 'they cannot be happy otherwise we would not have a story next week', or, 'she will die because I have read that the actress wants to leave the series'. Secondly, there is a much more emotional and involved way of relating to soaps. In Hobson's research among working women, it turns out that they use soaps to think and talk about their own lives. This has been coined as a referential mode by Katz and Liebes (1990) and involves comments such as 'I would never behave like Pamela', or 'that man is very much like my own boss'. According to Hobson such referential comments may invoke discussions about personal problems and emotions that might have been too painful to talk about in any other way. Hobson's respondents easily alternate between the two modes of reception, both engaging critically and being involved with the narrative and the characters. In their discussions in the workplace they will catch up with the storyline, speculate about what will happen next and discuss what they would do if they were in the same circumstances. Hobson concludes that 'these accounts disprove the theory that watching television is a mindless, passive event in the lives of viewers. On the contrary, the events and subjects covered in television programmes often act as a catalyst for wide-ranging and open discussions. The communication was extended far beyond the moment of viewing' (Hobson, 1989: 66).

Ellen Seiter found similar patterns among American working class housewives, who frequently criticized their favourite shows and expressed a sophisticated knowledge of the codes and conventions that rule the genre (Seiter et al., 1989). At the same time, however, these women extrapolated the events on television on to their own lives, feeling intimately connected to the characters on the screen. Seiter's team therefore conclude that the appeal of soaps lies in their capacity simultaneously to engage and disengage the viewer, to allow critical comment and psychological investment at the same time, providing at once a sensation of analytical competence and a feeling of emotional involvement. An extensive textual analysis of American and British soaps carried out by Christine Geraghty (1990) shows how the particular organization of time and space, and the contradictory aesthetics of light entertainment, melodrama and realism construct a spectator position which is characterized by the ambiguity of distance and involvement.

Still, the conclusion that soap pleasures basically consist of alternating between critical and involved ways of watching is premature. Katz and Liebes' research (1990) on the cross-cultural reception of the American soap *Dallas* points out that there is considerable variety of viewing practices among ethnic groups. Russian immigrants now living in Israel mainly commented critically on the series, seeing it as an extension of American capitalism, while Israelis of Moroccan descent predominantly used the series to reflect on their own circumstances. Press' analysis (1992) of class differences involved in watching soap operas seems to suggest that middle class women more often adopt a critical viewing style, whereas working class women tend to project the series on to their own lives.

One might argue that the double pleasure of involvement and detachment does not need to be gender-specific. In fact, many soap analyses give little attention to the particular enjoyments of female and male audiences, and ignore the obvious articulation of gender and genre present in the soap experience (Gripsrud, 1990; Katz and Liebes, 1990; Schröder, 1988). Why do soaps attract female audiences specifically, and which pleasures can be considered as distinct to gender? A rather straightforward answer is suggested by the particular scheduling of soaps. Whereas the audiences of prime time soaps consist of men as well – although not in equal numbers – women are the main viewers of soaps broadcast during the daytime, a time at which more women than men are available as viewers. Seiter's research among American working class housewives shows that daytime soaps tend to function as an integral part of a housewife's working day. Some women have managed to organize their working day like a well-run business with rigid schedules, and for them daytime soaps signify the lunchbreak:

People know not to call me between 12.30 and 3.00 unless it's a dire emergency. If it is really something they can call me at 1.30, 'cause *Capitol* is on and I don't really watch it. . . . All of my friends know, do not call at that time. My husband . . . if he comes in he's very quiet and just goes right on out. (Seiter et al., 1989: 230)

These women use soaps to divide work from leisure, a division much more clearly marked for women and men working outside the home. For housewives with a more chaotic routine, for instance because they have small children at home, TV soaps are more like radio soaps and are watched only at the really important moments: 'I listen to them, honest to God, I never sit!' Obviously, one needs to be highly selective and very well informed about the genre and the particular soap in order not to lose touch with the complicated narratives. Friends and family are indispensable sources for help. In fact, many women in Seiter's research were introduced to soaps by their mother or another expert.

Informed by a textual analysis of soaps, Modleski (1984) claims that it is not only the scheduling of soaps that is particularly appealing to house-wives, but the narrative structure of the genre as well. She describes women's work in the home as a sequence of incoherent, widely divergent and boundless activities characterized by repetition, interruption and distraction. They will easily recognize and be able to relate to the fragmented and cyclical narrative patterns of soaps. 'The formal properties of daytime television thus accord closely with the rhythms of women's work in the home' (Modleski, 1984: 102). Modleski's arguments can partly be refuted by referring to the numerous women who are not housewives and yet still enjoy soap operas. Other authors have used essentialist arguments to account for the popularity of soaps among women, assuming the genre's universal appeal to the female audience. Modleski mentions the work of Marcia Kinder, who suggests that 'the open-ended, slow paced, multi-climaxed structure of soap-opera is in tune with patterns of female sexuality' (Modleski, 1984: 98). Mattelart contends that the time patterns of soaps, distinguished by repetition and eternity, are linked to the female timescale, 'a cycle that links it into cosmic time, the occasion for unparalleled ecstasy in unison with the rhythm of nature, and along with that infinite, womb-like dimension, the myth of permanence and duration' (1986: 15).

While these are not arguments I would endorse,[5] it is important to incorporate the thematic and narrative structures of soaps in order to account for the pleasures they invoke in women. The soap's focus on family life and personal relations is thought to be one of the factors explaining the genre's popularity among women. Even if the world of business and work enters the series, as happens in prime time soaps aimed at a general audience, the narratives remain concentrated on the personal relations and problems of business men, workers, secretaries etc. Some authors argue that the particular style in which these problems are addressed – endlessly talking about them rather than undertaking direct actions to solve them – is also appealing to women. Furthermore, in the context of the soap narrative, women express perfectly efficient and rational behaviour, a feature quite rare in other televised women. It is therefore alleged that soaps offer a 'feminine culture' of themes, values and styles that women know particularly well, and that is not otherwise very highly appreciated in contemporary society. Brown claims, for instance, that 'soap operas, like women's talk or gossip and women's ballads, are part of a women's culture that exists alongside dominant culture' (1990a: 205). Within the boundaries of women's culture 'it is acceptable behaviour to watch soaps. The boundaries establish for them a locus of empowerment for their own brand of pleasure.' Also, the specific treatment of personal themes and relationships is a source of pleasure. From Seiter's research it is evident that narratives in which traditional family values and structures are undermined are notably enjoyable: 'Women openly and enthusiastically admitted their delight in following soap operas as stories of female transgressions which destroy the ideological nucleus of the text – the sacredness of the family' (Seiter et al., 1989: 240). The vicious heroine is celebrated and the wife who opposes her hopeless marriage by beginning an affair can count on much support: 'O Bruce, my husband, gets so angry with me when I'm watching the show and they're married and I'm all for the affair. It's like [*voice changes to imitate Bruce*]: "I don't like this, I don't know about you." And I say: "Dump him!"' (p. 240). Christine Geraghty's (1990) textual analysis of shows provides an interesting clarification to these saboteur qualities of soaps. She contends that American soaps, like *Dallas* and *Dynasty*, turn around the problem that male 'patriarchs' have in keeping their family together. Their efforts are incessantly undermined by women, for instance ex-wives or adulterous daughters-in-law. Their presence and actions are a continual threat to the well-being of the family, always in danger of being torn apart. Apart from emotional tension, this narrative structure also produces the pleasurable knowledge that male power, embodied in the head of the family, is never complete and always under pressure. In British soaps like *Coronation Street* and *Eastenders*, women – often older characters – often function as head of the family. The pleasures derived from the female protagonist do not stem from their subversive qualities towards the patriarchal family as in American soaps, but from their positions of power.

To sum up: the particular gendered pleasures of soaps are thus seen to originate in the centrality of themes and values associated with the private sphere. The focus on women as protagonists, on their rational and calculated actions and the mischievous attitude towards male power form some of the sources of pleasure for the female audience. Further pleasures stem from the ability of soaps to evoke a mode of reception that is simultaneously critical and involved. The particular scheduling of daytime soaps ensures that the audience will consist of housewives and others working outside of the 9 to 5 labour market.

Technologies of gender?

In comparison with earlier feminist studies of the media, reception analysis has several advantages. The understanding of audiences as producers of meaning has directed researchers to the day-to-day experiences of audiences and has produced a steadily increasing body of material about the tastes, preferences and pleasures of women. As such reception analysis is clearly a useful contribution to the larger feminist project to rescue women's experiences from marginalization and invisibility. The studies discussed here indicate the existence of separate women's cultures organized around popular fiction and television drama. Radway (1984), for instance, argues that the romance experience constructs a female community of authors and readers that provides the affective support formerly offered by real social and kinship networks. Likewise, Brown (1990a: 205) contends the women's culture of which soaps are a part supply women with means of temporary escape from the pressures of patriarchy. However, despite the wealth of interview material and theoretical reflection in this area, fundamental issues in feminist media research – in particular the question of how media function as technologies of gender – have not yet been adequately addressed. The research carried out so far takes the concepts 'woman' and 'femininity' for granted rather than analysing them. For instance, the focus on female audiences of soaps seems inspired mostly by the quantitative fact that women are the most avid viewers of soaps. Concealed, but straightforward causal models are employed, assuming that the identification enabled by the female characters of soaps is an important reason for their popularity among women. Furthermore, it is thought that the thematic emphasis of soaps on problems and values from the private sphere must appeal to women in particular, 'belonging' as they do to the private sphere. Some authors modify the implicit essentialism of such arguments by explaining women's viewing styles and preferences by the conflation of gender and social position in the domestic context (among others, Hobson, 1980; Morley, 1986). Such moves, however, avoid the problem rather than addressing it. For what we then seem to know about gender and reception is how housewives – a particular social group which happens to consist of women mainly – relate to popular culture. Within contemporary patriarchal arrangements, this is valid knowledge surely, relevant to the experiences of numerous women. Given the increasing rarity of the nuclear family and the 'traditional housewife', however, it is rather disturbing that we hardly know anything about other groups of women, especially since in much research the tendency to equate 'housewife' with 'woman' appears hard to suppress (for example, Fiske, 1988, Brown, 1990a). Furthermore, the distinction addressed by most research is that between women and men, elevating gender to the overriding dimension of human identity, ignoring the possible intervention of other dimensions such as sexuality and ethnicity (to mention only the obvious). As a result, reception analysis as currently conducted tends to reconstruct dominant gender discourse rather than analyse its dynamics. Morley's (1986) innovative research into television and the family, discussed above, is probably a good example. Charlotte Brunsdon commented on this project that 'his findings conform so tightly to what might be guessed to be stereotypical masculine and feminine behaviour as to be almost unbelievable' (1986: 103). She proposed that additional research was needed among groups with different demographic profiles, particularly those living outside the heterosexual family unit. Unfortunately, such projects have not been widely carried out to date, and the housewife of the traditional nuclear family continues to exert an irresistible attraction to researchers.

The problem, however, is not merely a methodological one of incorporating different subgroups into the research design; it is more fundamentally the absence of comprehensive theorization about the way gender and the reception of popular culture are related. According to Ien Ang and Joke Hermes (1991) this is one of the most undertheorized questions in mass media research. In most reception analysis, gender – regardless of its conceptualization as a social category – is assumed to precede cultural preference and behaviour. First, you are a woman (that is, heterosexual housewife) or a man (that is, heterosexual breadwinner), and then you like soaps and romances or sport and documentaries. Such a notion of gender, as was discussed extensively in Chapter 3, construes the concept as a relatively constant and consistent feature of human identity, established early in life. However, in contemporary society (and in many earlier societies for that matter) being a 'woman' or a 'man' does not come easily and requires continuous work. So many distinct and contradictory subject positions are offered that it seems as if in each social situation an appropriate gender identity has to be established and expressed anew. A particular genre preference, such as women express for romance and soaps can thus be seen not only as a result of gender, but as a means to express something about themselves as well. Gender should thus be conceived not as a fixed property of individuals but as part of an ongoing process by which subjects are constituted often in paradoxical ways. For reception analysis, the relevant issue therefore becomes how gender is articulated in media consumption, in other words how 'gender identities – feminine and masculine subjectivities – are constructed in the practices of everyday life in which media consumption is subsumed' (Ang and Hermes, 1991: 308). Morley's suspicions referred to earlier in this chapter, that his respondents were more concerned with keeping up their appropriate gender identity in front of the other members of the family, would serve as a clear example of such processes. However, whereas Morley seemed to assume some 'true' identity hidden behind 'misleading' answers, the point here is that identity is always in process, never finished, stable or true. Media reception is one of the practices in which the construction of (gender) identity takes place. Ien Ang's essay about the 'feminine' pleasures of soaps can serve as an illustration. She argues that the female fictional characters of soaps and other series function as 'textual constructions of possible modes of femininity: as embodying versions of gendered subjectivity endowed with specific forms of psychical and emotional satisfaction and dissatisfaction, and specific ways of dealings with conflicts and dilemmas' (1990: 83). In the never-ending process of feminization – constructing the appropriate feminine identity – such fantasy modes of femininity offer opportunities to try out different subjectivities without the risks involved in real life. 'In fantasy and fiction, however, there is no punishment for whatever identity one takes up, no matter how headstrong or destructive; there will be no redistribution, no defeat will ensue' (1990: 86). Another interesting example drawn from empirical data comes from Sherry Turkle's research on women and computers. She wonders why women express such reticence about new information technologies and observes that 'women use their rejection of computers . . . to assert something about themselves as women. . . . It is a way to say that it is not appropriate to have a close relationship with a machine' (1988: 50).

Aside from the limited conceptualizations of gender, reception analysis also suffers from a bias in its research concerns, reflecting the gender politics of academic work. Overlooking the developments in reception analysis, one unmistakably observes an increasing 'gendering' of the field. Corner (1991), Curran (1990) and others have distinguished two critical projects in cultural studies: one is concerned primarily with public knowledge, interested in genres like news and current affairs and addressing the audience as citizens. The other focuses on popular culture and examines the implications of entertainment on social consciousness and values, analysing, for instance, soaps. This chapter has made clear that feminist work on the audience is carried out mainly within the popular culture project. Research about the public sphere of news has been seriously neglected by feminist researchers and some scholars working in this area see no problem in focusing their work on men only, in order not to 'contaminate' their findings with gender (Jensen, 1986). In spite of the theoretical recognition that gender construction involves both women and men, most research has focused on constructions of femininity in the media and genres that are read and appreciated predominantly by women; soap operas, romance novels and women's magazines. In addition, attention has been limited to female audiences of those genres, more often than not drawn from traditional family situations. The knowledge by now accumulated concerns a very particular group of media and genres consumed by a very particular group of women. To be sure this is a focus born from necessity, since these are precisely the genres and audiences that have been neglected by mainstream research. An academic community preoccupied with such prestigious issues as new communication technologies, the future of public broadcasting or the effects of political communication, does not come down very easily to the more mundane level of media use in the daily lives of 'ordinary women'. But consider the implicit message of this research focus: is gender really only constructed in 'women's media'? How about the constructions of masculinity found in sports programmes, war movies, *Playboy* and *Penthouse* to ventilate just a few stereotypes of men? How do men use those media to construct their gender identity, to express that they are not women? And to cut through the dichotomy of 'women's' and 'men's' media, how do men's 'feminine' activities such as reading a women's magazine or enjoying a soap opera relate to dominant constructions of masculinity, and how do women's readings of the news relate to their functioning as citizens? The focus on the reception of soaps, romances and women's magazines seriously narrows the potential for articulating a comprehensive cultural critique, for whole areas of social and cultural practice tend to be ignored: at the level of institutional negotiation, or of the production of actual texts, there is little research that goes beyond the observation that women work in a male dominated field; at the level of textual negotiation there are many genres we do not yet know much about, for example, news and current affairs, quality and popular press, sport, quizzes etc. And as far as reception analysis is concerned, the public knowledge project tends to become a new male preserve, concerned with ostensibly gender-neutral issues such as citizenship, but actually neglecting the problematic relation of non-white, non-male citizens to the public sphere, whereas the popular culture project seems to have become restricted to the pleasures of women in their domestic roles.

Having reviewed the main results of reception analysis, it turns out that many of the questions paramount to the theoretical concerns of this book have not yet been adequately answered. Although we have increasingly detailed insight in the use and interpretation of 'women's' genres by female audiences, we know next to nothing about the use and interpretation of 'men's' genres by male audiences. Thus, the question of how gendered audiences make sense of gendered media, how genre and gender are articulated in daily life, has only been partially answered. Although the research carried out so far does tell something about women, its theoretical flaws have prevented extensive ventures into issues such as the construction of gender discourse, the intersection of gender with other discourses, and the disciplining and regulatory effects of gender discourse on various levels. The latter question brings us back to the issue of whether consuming popular culture can be reconciled with feminist claims. The 'politics of pleasure' will be taken up in the final chapter.

Notes

1. Soap operas: Ang, 1985; Hobson, 1989, 1990; Seiter et al., 1989; Press, 1991. Romances: Radway, 1984. Women's magazines: Hermes, 1993. Video: Gray, 1992. Computers: Turkle, 1988. Telephone: Moyal, 1992.

2. There are a small number of lesbian romances too, published by feminist publishers (Hermes, 1992).

3. In Chapter 8 the 'authenticity' of audience reaction will be addressed when discussing the status of people's talk.

4. See, for example, Brown, 1990a.

5. See Chapter 3.

8

Research Methods

Research questions in the field of gender, culture and media can be approached with a variety of research methods and a range of data gathering and analysis techniques. A number of these have been mentioned in the previous chapters: quantitative content analysis has often been used to establish numbers, roles and other characteristics of the portrayal of women and men in the various media; the question of media effects, for instance of pornography and violence in the media, is frequently tackled by using experimental designs inspired by (social) psychological research; in cultivation and agenda setting research that attempts to assess long-term influences of mass media, large-scale surveys are common; the position and experiences of women working in the communication industries have been studied by conducting in-depth interviews and surveys; in assessing the visual and narrative qualities of single texts and genres, semiotic and structural analysis are often used; ethnography has recently come to influence audience research focusing on the uses and interpretations of media and texts.

Far from being exhaustive, this list is only an indication of the range of methods being employed to study issues in gender, culture and media. The variety is almost endless, since both communication and gender are discursive and social phenomena at the same time, to be studied through an array of methods that find their origins in the humanities and the social sciences (and in the case of gender studies in other disciplines as well). Therefore, in principle – although not always in practice – the study of gender, culture and media is interdisciplinary, in its theories and methods alike. In many cases, the methodological input for such research also comes from a body of ideas and procedures that can be loosely labelled as 'feminist' methods. Most authors agree that studying gender or women is by no means the same as doing feminist research. However, the issue of what exactly constitutes feminist research has been a subject of debate since the late 1970s, centring on questions such as: is there a feminist research method, if so, what does it actually consist of? Should there be a feminist research method and what is the relation between feminist research methods and other methods (cf. Reinharz, 1992: 4)? This debate has not taken a very particular form in communication studies, as I shall elaborate in the first section of this chapter. Feminist communication scholars' studies have discussed these questions very much in the framework of the more general dispute on feminist epistemology and methodology. My own position in this debate is that – in principle – all ordinary scientific methods can be employed in feminist research on gender, culture and communication, although the field often does require the development of new and creative methods of data gathering. Moreover some 'traditional' methodologies lend themselves particularly well to research fields and questions that are inspired by and related to feminist concerns. The specific themes, theories and approaches of this book, summarized briefly as 'the social construction of gender in cultural and media practices', suggest an interpretative research strategy, employing qualitative methods of data gathering and analysis. This strategy will be discussed in the second part of this chapter.

Feminist methods

Feminist scholarship is not a unified practice, but inevitably contains dilemmas and controversies, as the previous chapters have shown for the area of media and cultural studies. As concerns particular methods for doing research, feminists have engaged in developing appropriate 'tools' for doing feminist research since the mid-1970s. One of the early participants in this project is the German scholar Maria Mies (1978), whose work has inspired many feminist scholars on the European continent to rethink the premisses of their research. According to Mies, a feminist science should take issue with the following questions: the relation between the women's movement and women's studies (politics and science); the aims of science; research methodologies; the relation between activism and research; the relation between researcher and researched. Mies herself takes up a radical position by arguing that feminist scholarship should be an integral part of the women's movement. This implies, according to Mies, not only that the traditional requirements of value-freeness, neutrality and indifference towards research objects should be replaced by conscientious partisanship, but also that the contemplative, detached style of research should be substituted by the integration of research in emancipatory activities and that the choice of research themes should be determined by the strategic and tactical requirements of the women's movement. Whereas Mies' radical view on feminist scholarship as directly integrated in the women's movement is not widely supported, the relation between politics and science, the issue of how research should contribute to women's liberation, is central to the debate on feminist scholarship and evidently is handled in different ways.

Brenda Dervin claims that the political value of feminist scholarship lies in its desire to give women a voice in a world that defines them as voiceless: 'It is transformative in that it is concerned with helping the silent speak and is involved in consciousness raising' (1987: 109). Much of the work discussed in Chapter 7 on gender and reception is concerned with precisely that, demonstrating the invisible experiences of women with popular culture. However, the discussion in that chapter also showed that 'helping the silent speak' is not as unproblematic as it seems for it may easily lead to a celebratory and uncritical account of popular culture and pleasure (cf. Modleski, 1991). Within communication and cultural studies, this is an element of the specific form that the debate about the political and feminist relevance of research has taken. It will be taken up in more detail in the concluding chapter of this book.

Nina Gregg emphasizes another element of the question about the relevance of research for women's liberation in pointing to the availability and intelligibility of research results to women outside the academic world. She quotes Michelle Russell: 'As teachers, scholars, and students, how available will you make your knowledge to others as tools of their own liberation?' (Gregg, 1987: 14). It is interesting to note that 'making available' is a quite different requirement from Mies' postulate that feminist research is by definition available and intelligible to the women's movement.

Another central element in the debate about feminist research concerns the politics of doing research itself, the power relations a researcher herself is immersed in while conducting the research. Mies (1978) claims that feminist researchers should integrate a 'double consciousness' into the research process, that is, a consciousness of their own oppression as women and their privileged position as researchers. As a result new inequalities and exploitations would be prevented, namely those between the authoritative, well-paid, academic expert and the research subjects, women who often do not have much to gain from being the subject of research and who are positioned as merely delivering information and experiences for the professional benefit of others. A double consciousness would also permit a partial identification of the researcher with the research subject, in the sense that they both can recognize their *Betroffenheit* (a German term without adequate English translation), that is, their position as victims, their outrage, analysis, criticism and motivation for acting. Mies' identification – if not her solution – of an unequal power relation between researchers and researched is similar to the problems analysed by ethnographers recognizing that the interaction between an 'informant' and a researcher is a profoundly unequal one (Radway, 1989). Especially for feminist scholars, concerned with evening out the inequalities between women, this is a disturbing feature of any kind of research methodology: 'To the extent that part of the ideology of feminism is to transform the competitive and exploitative relations among women into bonds of solidarity and mutuality, we expect assistance and reciprocated understanding to be part of the research/subject relation' (Reinharz, 1992: 265).

Feminist researchers have found ways around the inequalities involved in the research encounters, for instance by studying their own direct experiences, preferences and surroundings. In her study of the American soap opera *Dallas*, for instance, Ien Ang (1985: 10) placed a small advertisement in a Dutch women's magazine to find her informants. The ad reads as follows: 'I like watching the TV serial *Dallas*, but often get odd reactions to it. Would anyone like to write and tell me why you like watching it too, or dislike it? I should like to assimilate these reactions in my university thesis. Please write to . . .'. Others have studied their own communities or peer groups. Partly, of course, the inherent tension between the researcher and the researched is then transformed into an internal conflict of the researcher, between, in Ien Ang's case, being a fan and being an academic analyst, and more in general between being both an insider and an outsider at the same time. Other researchers have tried to 'pay their debts' to their informants by giving them help and assistance when needed. For instance, Lilian Rubin, a researcher and a psycho-therapist, made herself available for free counselling when her respondents felt a need to talk further about the issues she had raised (Zaat, 1982).

The inequalities between the feminist researcher and her research subjects are not only particularly acute in the actual observations of and encounters with the women participating in the research, but also in the phase of conjuring up and writing down their experiences into a story about the research results. Notwithstanding the precautions and services offered in return, the relation between researcher and researched will remain a problematic one in feminist research, also because in the end the authority and responsibility for writing down the story lies with the researcher. Inevitably and inherently at odds with feminist assumptions and aims, she must speak for other women, telling their stories in her voice. For some researchers, the burden of authorship, as Morley (1991) has called it, weighs so heavily that they tend to get stuck in contemplation and reflexivity rather than actually doing research (Ang, 1989).

Feminist research then, is characterized by a radical politicization of the research process, internally as well as externally. Internally, by interrogating the power relations inherent in doing research, externally by aiming at producing results that are relevant to the feminist endeavour. This is the backdrop against which to understand the specific epistemological and methodological requirements of feminist research *vis-à-vis* the respective elements of the research cycle: concepts, design and operationalization, data gathering and analysis, quality control and reporting.

Interpretative research strategies

Feminist research has been conducted with all kinds of research strategies and methods, implying the absence of a 'politically correct' feminist method (cf. Reinharz, 1992). As in mainstream research, the choice of methods depends on the particular conceptualizations and research questions involved. A (if not the) key concept in feminist research is 'gender', the meaning of which has seriously changed in the past decade. As discussed at length in Chapter 3, our understanding of gender has moved away from it being a consistent feature of human life that precedes society and culture, to a conceptualization of gender as unstable and constructed in social and cultural practices. In research terms this means that gender used to be operationalized as an independent variable: 'Gender has been operationalized as a pregiven category that can account for measurable differences in women's and men's speech, interaction, and mass communication behavior' (Rakow, 1986: 11). The poststructuralist understanding of gender, requires an operationalization as a 'dependent variable' (a discourse) constructed out of a mixture of continually shifting, interacting and contradictory structural and cultural arrangements enacted and articulated in daily life. As suggested at the end of Chapter 3, the questions arising from this perspective pertinent to media research are: how is gender discourse constructed in the various 'moments' of mediated meaning production? How is gender discourse encoded in media texts? Which meanings are available in media texts and from which discourses do they draw? How do audiences construct 'gender' out of the socially situated interaction with media texts, and the related social practices? Traversing all these questions are the mechanisms of power, both as an oppressive and a productive force (see Chapter 3). Such a conceptualization of gender, and the particular research questions, necessitates research designs in which the construction of gender as a process and a product of social interaction and power relations can be analysed, thus requiring an interpretative research strategy that is sensitive to human interactions as well as to the structures of meaning arising from it.

'Interpretative' is a label that covers rather diverse research traditions that all start from the way human beings experience, define, organize and appropriate reality. More and more the differences between these traditions have become a matter of emphasis rather than of principle (Denzin, 1970; Douglas, 1970). 'Ethnography', for instance, has come to be almost synonymous with doing interpretative research, while originally the concept referred to a particular type of anthropological inquiry aimed at the reconstruction of everyday life in specific (sub)cultures by using the terms, concepts, definitions and understandings of the members of these cultures themselves. In communication and cultural studies 'ethnographic' studies of media audiences are currently passionately propagated to the extent that some complain that 'ethnography has become an abused buzzword in our field' (Lull, 1988: 242). Wester and Jankowski argue that as far as such studies are conducted – which is far less than they are propagated – they do not live up to the original requirements of ethnography: 'It is unclear what the studies have in common with either the research tradition or its methodology' (1991: 55). One of the problems of ethnographic audience studies, concerns the absence of (sub)cultural aspects in studying social groups like working or middle class women; their (lack of) cultural coherence is hardly ever problematized. Another traditional anthropological element missing from many ethnographic audience studies is participant observation as a means of data gathering. Without intense and protracted contacts with informants it seems hard to arrive at the intended holistic understanding of their particular cultural practices. Seiter et al. therefore conclude that 'television audience studies, even when they use ethnographic or qualitative methods, have not satisfied the requirements of ethnography proper and our own study is no exception' (1989: 227).

Methodological purism, however, does not stand much chance in a field that is increasingly distinguished by commonalities rather than differences. Lull (1990: 8), for instance, speaks of 'variations of ethnography' to describe all kinds of research that start from the interpretations and definitions of the people under study, and Gray (1992: 32) describes her study of the way women use and make sense of their video recorder as having 'ethnographic intentions'. For historical rather than programmatical reasons then, I shall briefly discuss the differences between traditions of interpretative research – symbolic interactionism, ethnography, ethnomethodology and phenomenology – that have proved to be relevant to mass communication research.[1]

Symbolic interactionism assumes that reality is the product of the interpretations of human beings which are formed in interaction between the self and others. People ground their actions on the basis of the meanings they arrive at in interaction with others. Central questions thus concern how human beings negotiate about definitions of situations and how such definitions guide their acts and experiences. In mass communication research this process of 'reality construction' has been studied with respect to media institutions as well as to media audiences. Several authors have shown that the work of journalists can be seen as a routinized, professional form of reality construction, that is, the reality of the news (for example, Altheide, 1976; Gans, 1979). Many of the recent audience studies discussed in Chapter 7 can be said to fall within a symbolic interactionist research paradigm, some elements of which were formulated quite early by one of its founding fathers, Herbert Blumer, in 1969. According to Blumer, audience research should be guided by five principles: audience studies should be carried out in the direct empirical context of media use; the reception of media should be understood against the background of individual and collective life histories which render current events and meanings intelligible; mass media use and effects should be seen in contingency with other influences, not as isolated phenomena; the process of interpretation of meanings by audiences precedes and modifies any possible media effect; media use should be seen as related to the use of other communication technologies. Such principles have now become accepted as common sense in reception analysis.

Ethnomethodologists focus on a particular aspect of the interactions between human beings, namely the implicit and explicit rules people employ to make sense of their everyday surroundings and experiences. Tuchman (1978b) has analysed the methods and procedures journalists use to understand and describe the daily flow of news events, distinguishing among other things between typifications of time and space. Lull (1990) has focused on the rules that families employ to regulate their experiences with television. He distinguishes between habitual rules, 'represented in patterns of routine human interaction' (1990: 68), parametric rules which allow for modification of the habitual rules within certain parameters, and tactical rules, 'attempts to achieve some personal or interpersonal objective that exists beyond the immediate context of media consumption' (1990: 69). Such rules can also be seen to exist on the macro level of societal rituals, and within the media industries in the form of historically developed, implicit rules about, for instance, good scripts, professional journalism and aesthetic excellence (cf. Cantor and Cantor, 1991).

In its pure sense, ethnographic mass communication research would focus on subcultures of communicators and media audiences. As said before, many interpretative studies of audiences go under the label of ethnography although it is often unclear what precisely the (sub)cultural coherence of the audience group involved is. In Radway's research on romance readers, the cultural connection between audience members was provided by their common preference for and understanding of romance novels, and their mutual relation to bookseller Dot. Media use and interpretation itself can thus construct a subculture, or an 'interpretative community' as Lindloff (1987) has called it. Other, more traditionally anthropological notions of subculture are present in the work of Hobson (1989, 1990) who studied the role of television in the day-to-day conversations of female telephone sales managers sharing the same office, and female local civil servants, and in a study of Wallace (1978) on television reception of convicted criminals in prison. Ethnographic studies of communicators are rare, although several products of journalists themselves would come close to such a qualification. Timothy Crouse's *The Boys on the Bus* (1972), on the norms, values, behaviour, rituals, pecking order etc. of journalists covering a presidential campaign could qualify as an ethnography of a particular subculture in journalism, particularly since his analysis is based on his travelling with journalists on the campaign trail. Whereas some feminist studies of the position of women in the media professions have focused on the masculine features of these professional subcultures (see Chapter 4), none of these studies has employed the kind of data gathering that would characterize them as ethnographic research.

Finally, phenomenology has provided an important input to interpretative research strategies. Whereas there are some obvious overlaps with symbolic interactionism, both analysing the social construction of reality, the main differences lie in the phenomenological emphasis on meaning structures and the organization of everyday knowledge. Moreover, phenomenology assigns less importance to empirical methods and relies on philosophical procedures to disentangle knowledge structures as well. Ervin Goffman's work *Frame Analysis* (1974) has inspired many communication scholars. In it he claims that events, occurrences, thoughts, feelings, and the like only become meaningful and transformed into 'experience' when they are

connected and integrated into a interpretative cognitive framework. He
has applied his theory in *Gender Advertisements* (1976), analysing the
organizational principles that underlie the portrayal of women and men in
advertisements and the way they are linked to everyday knowledge about
gender. Although there is no historical connection between phenomenology and semiology or structuralism, there is an analytical affinity in the
sense that both try to uncover the structural organization of meaning
(Denzin, 1987). Frame analysis has been extremely influential in the study
of ideological and thematic structures of news. Gitlin (1980), for instance,
has examined the way the student movement was 'framed' by news media
as a single-issue movement fragmented by internal conflict. In my own
research about the Dutch women's movement, inspired by Gitlin's work, I
found that media coverage was organized around three recurring issues
that defined feminism in opposition to women's emancipation as too
radical, directed against men and not representative of 'ordinary' women
(van Zoonen, 1992b, 1994).

What these different research traditions have in common is the emphasis
on the everyday interpretative and signifying practices of human beings,
the meanings that people give to their actions, and the way these meanings
direct their actions. It is the researcher's task to reconstruct those meanings
and understand the processes behind them and the processes that arise
from them. It is precisely this element which makes an interpretative
research design such a 'natural' choice for feminist scholars who have
among their many aims to save women's experiences from oblivion by
making their lives visible and their voices heard. What feminist research
has to add to interpretative research strategies is a notion of power, an
acknowledgement of the structural inequalities involved in and coming out
of the process of making meaning. The power to define situations and
identities, to frame issues and problems, to legitimize interpretations and
experiences is unequally distributed along lines of gender, ethnicity, class
and a range of other social and discursive formations and (re)produces
such inequalities at the same time (see also Chapter 3).

Aims of interpretative inquiries

The aims of interpretative research can vary widely. Often interpretative
research is equated with doing qualitative research, which is defined by
Strauss and Corbin as 'any kind of research that produces findings not
arrived at by means of statistical procedures or other means of quantifica-
tion' (1990: 17). As such, qualitative research can be conducted to provide
illustrations for quantitative data or to explore and define categories to be
used in quantitative research. Increasingly, qualitative procedures are used
by market researchers interested in probing beyond the social demographic
categories of the market and examining the nature and appeal of particular
lifestyles. Such uses of qualitative research differ fundamentally from the
interpretative aim to understand the everyday meanings and interpre-

tations people ascribe to their surroundings and the acts that arise from these interpretations. The empirical world, reality as constructed by human beings, forms the starting point of the research effort that aims at the development of a substantial theory based in the concrete and everyday experiences of the informants. Interpretative research is thus an inductive procedure to arrive at empirically grounded understandings and explanations of social phenomena (Glaser and Strauss, 1967).

Although the concepts 'interpretative' and 'qualitative' are often used interchangeably, I prefer to think of 'interpretative' as referring to a particular inductive research strategy and design, whereas 'qualitative' concerns a particular, non-quantitative way of gathering and analysing data. This distinction is necessary to credit the differences of purpose between the 'qualitative' research carried out by market researchers and the 'qualitative' research conducted by feminist and other critical scholars. Usually, interpretative research will use qualitative methods of data gathering and data analysis, although this is not by definition the case. Wester and Jankowski (1991) mention the Iowa School of symbolic interactionism which has employed surveys and standardized observation techniques in its research projects. Several aspects of the feminist research agenda suggest the use of qualitative techniques of data gathering and data analysis. To begin with it seems that the desire to avoid new inequalities between the researcher and the researched presumes that data gathering follows the definitions, categories, terms of the people under scrutiny and does not impose the researcher's own schemes. Secondly, the areas that feminist media researchers are interested in – the mundane, day-to-day, (un)conscious construction of meaning by media producers and audiences – are situated in the realm of the ordinary and taken for granted, only to be 'exposed' by methods sensitive to the cues of common behaviour, speech and experiences. Qualitative techniques of data gathering such as in-depth interviewing, participant observation and a range of other, less traditional and ad hoc data collection procedures are most adequate to gain insight into the meanings of everyday life.

Methods of data gathering

In interpretative research, the phases of data gathering and data analysis are not strictly separated, as data analysis often informs a new round of data gathering. Collecting and analysing data are thus conducted in a cyclical way until all possible information about the research field has been obtained and the theoretical concepts derived have been saturated. Nevertheless, data collection and analysis are discussed separately here for reasons of clarity. Participant observation, in-depth interviews and group interviews are the qualitative methods of collecting data most often used in (feminist) media research. Participant observation has been conducted mainly where the study of media organizations, news rooms in particular, is concerned. Only occasionally, participant observation is employed in audience studies (for example, Morley and Silverstone, 1991). It requires firsthand involvement in the phenomenon chosen for study which can range from merely observing on the site without taking part in the activities to full participation acting as a member of the community or setting concerned (cf. Tuchman, 1991). Other dimensions along which participant observation studies can differ are the degree of openness about the researcher's role and the amount of time spent at the research setting (Patton, 1980).

Reinharz (1992: 58–9) and Warren (1988) have registered the difficulties women encounter in doing participant observation in a mixed gender setting. Sexual harassment, physical danger and gender stereotyping, are but some of the many problems women have to cope with while making observations. In all cases women have to decide whether to go along with sexist treatment for the benefit of research results, or to oppose them with the risk of 'blowing their cover' as unobtrusive participants: 'At issue is the trade-off between accepting sexism on the one hand and the acquisition of knowledge . . . on the other' (Warren, 1988: 36). For feminist researchers these dilemmas are particularly pressing given the desire to make research contribute to the demise of sexism and oppression. The inevitable gender politics of participant observation may only partly explain why this particular method has hardly been used in feminist media research. Gaye Tuchman (1978b), for instance, observing male and female journalists at work and focusing among other things on the coverage of the women's movement, does not report to have been confronted with gender problems. Also, some questions for feminist media research concerning, for instance, the production of feminist media or the gendered reception of mass media, could be addressed by observing an all-female setting not directly burdened by gender politics. Apart from reasons having to do with institutional and financial impediments, it is quite unclear why participant observation has rarely been employed in feminist media research, even though some questions – particularly those concerning women's positions in the media workplace – would definitely benefit from this method of data collection.

In-depth interviewing is the most popular method in feminist media studies and cultural studies, particularly in research on audiences. Most of the studies discussed in Chapter 7 were carried out by conducting in-depth interviews. It involves relatively unstructured conversations with inform- ants about the subject of inquiry. These conversations can be held just once with each informant or consist of a series of talks. Lilian Rubin, the feminist researcher and psychotherapist who is famous for her research on working class women (1976), on women in their mid-life years (1979) and on intimacy in marriage (1983), held conversations which lasted between three and ten hours, necessitating repeated visits to her informants. In- depth interviews are open-ended, in the sense that the researcher only decides on a conversation theme. The particular interpretation of this theme and the direction of the conversation depend entirely on the informant. This has as an advantage that the informant can talk and associate on her own terms without being directed or hindered by the researcher. In a way the respondents participate in the research project by raising issues that they find important to the subject. Moreover, they are enabled to express their experiences as interrelated and not as isolated and relevant to the research phenomenon only. In her research about women's use of VCRs, Ann Gray recounts: 'Many of the women eagerly told me many stories about their family histories and their present lives, enjoying the opportunity to talk about themselves to an interested listener. Many of the conversations were fun and certainly transgressed all notions of the "ideal" research interview' (1992: 33). At the same time, the completely open-ended format of an in-depth interview has disadvantages, among other things a lack of comparability and an abundance of information of which the relevance to the research subject may be unclear.

Balancing the advantages and disadvantages of open-ended interviews many researchers decide in favour of a semi-structured interview using a questionnaire in which not only the topics to be discussed are decided on beforehand, but also the preferable sequence and the formulation of the initial, 'grand-tour' questions that allow participants to tell their story in their own terms. Within the specification of the semi-structured interview, there are also 'floating' prompts intended to elicit more information about the conversation topic, and 'planned' prompts aimed at discovering the participant's ideas about topics that are relevant to the research subject but which she herself does not spontaneously raise (McCracken, 1988). The planned nature of the semi-structured interview is to be taken quite loosely, however, since the final aim remains to reconstruct people's experiences and interpretations on their own terms. Therefore, in the actual interview the planned sequence can be completely overturned if participants 'decide' differently.

In the conversations of researcher and participants the establishment of 'rapport', that is, a relation of trust and respect that stimulates and facilitates the participant's articulation of her experience, is crucial to the quality of the interview. This can be frustrated by a range of difficulties such as a lack of experience or capacity of the researcher to listen empathetically and to prompt without being intrusive, the participant's desire to be a 'good respondent' and give correct answers, or by differences in status between interviewer and participant. Since many of the subjects feminist and interpretative researchers are interested in involve everyday topics and experiences or emotional predicaments that people are sensitive about, some have argued that in-depth interviewing is an instrument that is best handled by women. Reinharz quotes feminist researchers who claim that 'asking people what they think and feel is an activity females are socialized to perform, at least in contemporary Western society' (1992: 20). Whereas such an observation reconstructs existing definitions of femininity and (by omission) masculinity, it is important to realize that many tensions, facilitations and other processes, such as interruptions or supportive clues, involved in ordinary conversations are gender-specific and will play a role in in-depth interviews as well (Houston and Kramarae, 1991).

Gender patterns in conversation are especially important in the context of (mixed-gender) group interviews. Group interviews and discussion are the third method of data collection important to mass communication research, not so much for their quantitative presence but because some key research projects in the area of audience studies have been conducted by holding group interviews. The common procedure can involve a pre-arranged viewing of a television programme or movie by a usually already existing social group, although in marketing research in which 'focus group interviews' have become tremendously popular, it is more common to work with groups of people that are randomly selected (Krueger, 1988). David Morley (1980) showed an episode of the British current affairs programme *Nationwide* to twenty-nine groups selected on the basis of a shared educational, union and management background. In their study of the cross-cultural variations in the reception of *Dallas*, Katz and Liebes (1990) showed an episode of the soap to groups of befriended couples and neighbours from different ethnic backgrounds. After having viewed the episode together, the moderator initiates the discussion with an introductory 'grand tour' question that enables the participants to recount their viewing experiences. Similar to the format of in-depth interviews, the degree of structuring of the group discussion beforehand may vary according to the aims of the researchers. Katz and Liebes (1990: 159) started their group discussions with the question: 'What happened in the episode we have just been watching? How will you tell it tomorrow morning to someone who has not seen it?' Whereas this initial question is formulated quite vaguely, leaving possibilities for many types of discussion among participants (focusing on storylines, setting, characters etc.) the remainder of their interview guideline is heavily organized, including instructions as to how long each subject can be lingered on (for example, three to five minutes). Just as with in-depth interviewing, such a structure facilitates comparisons between groups but hinders the development of a discussion on the group's own terms, since the moderator is not allowed to go with the 'flow' of the group.

Doing group interviews has as an advantage that ordinary, everyday interpretative practices are reconstructed in a more 'realistic' way than is the case with individual interviews. Making meaning is a social process arising out of interaction with others. For feminist research there may be an additional advantage in that the group interview enables women to exchange experiences, build on each other's ideas and enhance awareness of their situation in a way similar to the processes of consciousness-raising groups (Callahan, quoted in Reinharz, 1992: 223). There are of course some evident disadvantages too. Discussions with existing groups may be burdened by previously existing formal or informal (power) relations which will inhibit some participants from expressing their opinions (Krueger, 1988: 97). Discussions with groups brought together for the purpose of the research may not yield valuable information if the participants do not feel comfortable in each other's presence or try to yield a favourable image. In her research about readers and readings of women's magazines, Joke Hermes evaluates her group interviews as follows:

> The respondents, used to marketing focus group interviews for product testing, were very enthusiastic about the interviews, which were more personal and asked more of their own interpretative skills than they were used to. For me, however, compared to the individual depth interviews of the first stage, the group interview was not a very productive method. . . . They refrained from giving views they thought would be radically different from the views of the others and . . . they sometimes overdid statements they thought would make a favourable impression. (1993: 93)

Such problems of 'image management', or power relations within a group may be exacerbated in mixed-gender groups which will quite likely bear the general characteristics of mixed-gender conversations in which women tend to be interrupted more frequently if not silenced completely by male participants disclaiming their contributions as idle chatter, nagging and whining, or 'besides the point' (Houston and Kramarae, 1991). Talking to married couples or groups of married couples, as did Katz and Liebes (1990) and Morley and Silverstone (1991), requires extra attention to the additional complications of husbands and wives (dis)communicating with each other (Leto Defranscisco, 1991; Tannen, 1990).

Ideally, interpretative research does not rely on a single type of data but takes advantage of triangulation, 'the act of bringing more than one source of data to bear on a single point' (Marshall and Rossman, 1989: 146). Multiple methods of data collection (and of data analysis for that matter) resulting from the triangulation principle will modify the weaknesses of each individual method and thus greatly enhance the quality and value of interpretative research projects. Although McCracken comments that 'as it now stands, many qualitative researchers are disinclined to use quantitative methods' (1988: 29), no particular method is excluded from triangulation. In her research on romance readers, Radway (1984) used structured questionnaires, open-ended group discussions, in-depth interviews and a protracted 'expert' interview with bookseller Dot to disentangle the meanings of romance reading for ordinary readers. Hermes (1993) employs in-depth interviews, group discussions and survey results to examine the variety in meaningful interpretative repertoires women draw from to interpret their reading of women's magazines. In their extensive ethnography of the uses and meanings of domestic communication technologies such as television, VCR, telephone and home computers, Morley and Silverstone employ participant observation, time-use diaries, 'proxemics', that is, the use of domestic space by household members, family discussions and individual interviews: 'Ethnography is a multifaceted process in which the requirements of detail and richness, rigor and systematicity, have to be carefully balanced, and where there is no single adequate methodological procedure' (1991: 160).

Data analysis

The analysis of qualitative data is a neglected area in interpretative research. According to McCracken it is 'the most demanding and least examined aspect of qualitative research' (1988: 41). As Miles argued in 1979, methods of analysing qualitative data are not well formulated and very few generally applicable guidelines exist. Whereas it is rare to find satisfactory sections on research designs in the recent upsurge of qualitative projects and 'ethnography', reports on data analysis are completely absent, although it must be said that the editorial policy of many publishers discourages the inclusion of 'tedious' methodological sections. However, even in publications entirely committed to qualitative methodologies in mass communication research detailed considerations of data analysis are missing (for example, Jensen and Jankowski, 1991). This is particularly troubling because sometimes side-line comments suggest that the data were not self-evident to begin with. In an otherwise inspiring study about class and gender difference in the appreciation of soaps, Andrea Press (1990) gives away that: 'many interviews I did yielded little information of value for the study, unfortunately, in part because of the open ended format'. Although Press did produce an interesting account of women's soap opera preferences, one cannot but wonder how she managed to draw conclusions from interviews that 'yielded little information'.

Fortunately, several authors have begun to address the problems involved in qualitative data analysis (Miles and Huberman, 1984; Strauss and Corbin, 1990). Qualitative methods of data analysis use words, texts and language as primary units, as opposed to the numbers of quantitative analysis. Analysing interviews, documents, field notes etc. therefore actually consists of analysing texts and language. Thus Jensen (1991) argues that textual criticism and discourse analysis are key constituents of the examination of interview material. Evident as this may seem, the methods of textual and linguistic analysis have as yet not often been applied in interpretative research.

A first issue to resolve then, concerns the status of language and people's talk. According to Potter and Wetherell (1987) one can approach language as a more or less accurate and more or less complete reflection of people's mental, cognitive and emotional states, attitudes, beliefs etc., assuming the existence of an 'inner' mental world that is referred to by 'outer' expressions such as verbal utterances. In a strongly worded comment, Potter and Wetherell claim that this view of language is not very relevant: 'The problem is construed at entirely the wrong level . . . Much of our vocabulary of mentalistic terms has no "inner" referent at all: instead of merely being descriptions of mental states these words are themselves an autonomous part of particular social practices' (1987: 178–9). Language should thus not be conceived as reflective, but as constructive and functional. The 'inner' world is not distinct from its 'expression', on the contrary, the distinction collapses by considering both the world 'out there' and the world 'in there' as constructed in language.[2]

The respective informative values of viewing language as reflection and language as construction can be illustrated by comparing the different emphases and results of two current research projects on women's use of mass media which both relied heavily on in-depth interviews. Ann Gray (1992) talked to women about their use of the television and the VCR and analysed the statements of her informants as an indication of the class-specific nature of gender differences in viewing preferences and styles (together with, among other things, an examination of the impact of education on viewing patterns). Class and gender are thus implicitly conceptualized as factors preceding and informing women's experiences with television. Joke Hermes (1993) on the other hand, asking women about their reading of women's magazines, organized her material by focusing on the different 'repertoires' or interpretative frameworks women employed to make sense of their reading. Her analysis of women's utterances on reading centred on the particular subjectivities women constructed for themselves by using different repertoires. Theoretically, this position was coined earlier in an article with Ien Ang (Ang and Hermes, 1991) and underlies the poststructuralist understanding of gender advanced in this book as well. The methodological implications of this position can best be clarified by discussing the analysis of in-depth interviewing in more detail.

The analysis of in-depth interviews can take a rather straightforward form. Rubin (1976), for instance, simply organized and summarized the statements of her informants along the lines of her conversation topics. The range of answers thus showed the variety of interpretations on each of her topics such as friendship, intimacy and sexuality. Strauss and Corbin (1990) have proposed a more grounded 'coding' procedure that starts from the concepts present in each single utterance of participants and combines them into more encompassing categories (open coding). The next step involves developing the relations between those categories – inductively on the basis of participants' conversations as well as deductively on the basis of the researcher's theoretical and interpretative capacities – in the form of a tentative 'paradigmatic' model (axial coding). In the final phase of selective coding, the model is elaborated and saturated until a grounded theory of the subject involved has been developed.

It is interesting to see the overlap between this procedure developed by social scientists and the examination of textual structures by discourse analysts. Van Dijk (1991), for instance, has observed that important elements in the semantic or thematic structure of texts are propositions (the conceptual meaning structure of a clause), the direct coherence between these propositions (local coherence) and the overall semantic unity of a text (global coherence). Whereas van Dijk discussed news texts mainly, the three coding phases suggested by Strauss and Corbin for the analysis of in-depth interviews coincide with the semantic structures as

	Category 1	**Category 2**	**... Category *N***
Participant 1			
Participant 2			
.			
.			
.			
Participant *N*			

Figure 8.1 *A fictional data matrix*

discerned by van Dijk and others. Open coding can be said to imply the identifications of concepts and propositions, axial coding trying to reveal the connections between categories could be considered an examination of local coherence, while selective coding would finally involve the analysis of global coherence.

The issue here is not so much to what extent Strauss and Corbin's analytic instruments precisely match semantic patterns, but the recognition of similar perspectives on the composition of texts. The analytic procedure moves from a focus on the smallest units present in texts (words, concepts, propositions) to the examination of relations between these concepts and the overall meaning they can be thought to be part of. It involves a process of continuous data reduction and analysis that is grounded in the empirical material. Miles and Huberman (1984) call for the use of 'data matrices' instead of pieces of narrative to facilitate this process. For instance, a simple data matrix to organize interview material may be concocted as shown in Figure 8.1 from the concepts and categories identified. The cells of this matrix would be filled with quotes, keywords, summaries etc. taken from the in-depth interviews displaying the inconsistencies, commonalities, patterns and configurations in the data in an immediately accessible form. Such a matrix enables the researcher to assess the relative value of the categories as well as examine the range of meanings articulated by individual participants.

Whereas most procedures for qualitative text analysis developed by social scientists such as the ones discussed above focus primarily on what has been said, discourse analysis provides the additional advantage of taking up the *style* of talk as well, examining paradigmatic (which words are chosen) and syntagmatic (how they are combined) choices of the participants. Paraphrasing van Dijk 'such stylistic choices also have clear social and ideological implications, because they often signal the opinions of the participants about the conversation topic as well as properties of the social and communicative situation . . . and the group membership of the speakers' (1991: 116). Moreover, discourse analysis would be sensitive to the pragmatic elements of language as present, for instance, in what has been referred to as 'speech acts'. Through language people not only describe their experience, feelings, opinions of others, situations etc., but they also engage in a form of social action. Austin (1976) captured this element of language quite succinctly in saying that people do things with words, thus directing textual analysis to the question of what is achieved by language rather than what is expressed by it.

We have now come back to the issue raised at the beginning of this section on the status of interview texts as reflecting or constructing some inner experience, opinion or state of mind of the participants. Taking the view that language operates both ways implies that the analysis of interviews should focus on what has been said, how it has been said and what is achieved by saying it in that particular manner. Especially the latter element is relevant in the context of questions concerning the construction of gender in discursive practices. Conceiving gender as a product rather than a precedent of language – the theoretical position developed in Chapter 3 – necessitates the analysis of the pragmatic elements of language, the acts and subjectivity constructed by speech. Although not yet fully established as a methodological tool for the analysis of in-depth interviews, discourse analysis provides the most promising instrumentarium for examining exactly how the construction of gender takes place in everyday speech (van Dijk, 1985).

A final comment needs to be made concerning data analysis. No matter how refined and systematic the analytic procedure used to extract information from qualitative data, making sense of language is an interpretative activity, whether conducted intuitively on a day-to-day basis by ordinary human beings or systematically by scientists who earn their living with it. Ien Ang (1989: 105) argues that

> because interpretations always inevitably involve the construction of certain representations of reality (and not others), they can never be 'neutral' and merely 'descriptive'. After all, the 'empirical' captured in either quantitative or qualitative form, does not yield self-evident meanings: it is only through the interpretative framework constructed by the researcher that understandings of the 'empirical' come about. . . . Here then the thoroughly political nature of any research manifests itself. What is at stake is a politics of interpretation. (1989: 105)

All too often, this is taken to mean a politically informed approach to research resulting sometimes in a disregard of methodical issues. As may have become clear in this chapter, the politics of interpretation involves much broader issues, present in the articulation of the research question, the choice of methods and the foci of data analysis. 'Data', whether quantitative or qualitative, do not speak for themselves but are constructed in the research process and the answers to be derived from them are the result of interpretative procedures followed by researchers rather than self-evident, natural knowledge encapsulated in them and waiting to be caught with the appropriate instruments.

This does not imply that academic interpretations and knowledge are of the same order as everyday knowledge and meanings. Whereas both can be seen as constructions, be it with a completely different status, the academic researcher has the moral and political obligation to reconstruct different perspectives and allow for an examination and an evaluation of her interpretative activities and procedures. Every choice made along the way of the interpretative research process needs to be explained and justified, thus enabling a discussion about the nature of the interpretations, the status of the results and the 'politics' of the project as a whole. How this can be achieved is the subject of the last section of this chapter.

Quality control

Several features of interpretative research are said to endanger its claim to scientific value and relevance. To begin with, interpretative research is often conducted by one researcher who formulates the research question, decides on sampling, designs instruments for data collection and analysis, then actually collects and analyses empirical material and finally conjures up the research report. Miles and Huberman (1984: 230) therefore say that the researcher has a vertical monopoly in the research process. In addition, a stable 'canon' of generally agreed upon procedures, techniques and rules for making inferences is not likely to develop for it is contradictory to the nature of interpretative research, linked as it is to the variable nature of social reality. Replicability, for instance, an ordinary quality criterion in quantitative inquiries which is usually taken to mean that different researchers will come up with the same result when conducting any given study anew, is not a very useful measure of quality in interpretative research. It assumes an unchanging research area whereas interpretative researchers focus on the processes involved in constructing meaning, thus assuming change rather than stability (Marshall and Rossman, 1989; Strauss and Corbin, 1990).

As a result interpretative researchers are often confronted with concerns about subjective and biased interpretations. Miles and Huberman mention as particular dangers the 'holistic fallacy' of perceiving too many patterns and too much coherence in data, 'elite bias' or overreliance on the statements of articulate and enthusiastic informants, and 'going native', 'being co-opted into the perceptions and explanations of local informants' (1984: 230). Some scholars counter such concerns by construing interpretative research as the preserve of a talented, creative and erudite intellectual elite. Billig (1988: 189), for instance, seems to yearn for a return of 'the traditional scholar' whose work is 'anti-methodological in that hunches and specialist knowledge are more important than formally defined procedures'. Billig presents nearly a caricature of an ordinary researcher who faithfully but mechanically follows the rules and prescriptions of the handbooks, as opposed to the traditional scholar, an ideal intellectual who has a broad general knowledge, who creatively discerns patterns and coherence and who finally produces a wise and sustained argument. The suggestion thus emerges that doing interpretative research is an option not available to just anybody. McCracken strongly opposes such a mystification and claims that some interpretative researchers conceive themselves as 'the secret elite of this world for it is only they who can grasp and use the magical methods of the qualitative tradition' (1988: 13).

Increasin ly, however, the 'magic' of interpretative research is being captured and contained in requirements, prescriptions and other procedures to validate research results. Wester (1987: 45) mentions three criteria to assess the quality of interpretative inquiries: theoretical compatibility and comprehension (do the results match the orientations of the participants); analytical relevance; and functionality. Likewise, Potter and Wetherell (1987: 169) mention coherence and fruitfulness and McCracken (1988: 50) suggests the adoption of criteria from the humanities, 'symptoms of truth' – such as exactness, internal and external consistence, unity, power and fertility. Reviewing the work of other interpretative methodologists would produce additional lists of quality criteria (for example, Kirk and Miller, 1984; Lincoln and Guba, 1985; Miles and Huberman, 1984). Common to these suggestions are the requirements that the research results match the meaning and interpretations of the participants (fit); that the theory developed should have some explanatory value for other comparable settings as well (generality); and that the research process and report consist of explicit procedures and choices. Reflecting on the latter, Glaser and Strauss (1967: 232) argue that the researcher and the reader share a joint responsibility: 'The researcher ought to provide sufficiently clear statements of theory and description so that readers can carefully assess the credibility of the theoretical framework he offers.' Keeping the cautions formulated by Ang (1989) about the politics of interpretation and the overall goals of feminist research in mind, an additional criterion may involve some reflection on the intervention of the research in existing social formations: 'to advance an interpretation is to insert it into a network of power relations' (Pratt, quoted in Ang, 1989: 105).

Whereas some of the criteria themselves seem to border on the obvious, the means to realize them are much less self-evident. The design of the study itself may contain elements enhancing fit and generality. As said earlier, triangulating data sources and methods tends to even out the flaws of individual research methods and augments the likelihood that a variety of perspectives have been brought into the examination and analysis. The inclusion of comparative elements in the research design – comparing different groups of people, different sites, different cases – is a means to expand the generality of the results. Yin, for instance, claims that 'the evidence from multiple cases is often considered more compelling, and the overall study is therefore regarded as being more robust' (1989: 52). Comparison is also a useful instrument in analysing data and testing conclusions. Miles and Huberman mention that the exceptions to basic findings, the 'outliers' and extreme cases, are particularly helpful in this respect: 'The outlier is your friend' (1984: 237), whether it is an exceptional person, site, setting or event, and should not be smoothed away or ignored. Outliers tell something about the generality of the study and can function as protective devices against the holistic fallacy of perceiving too much coherence in data. Marshall and Rossman (1989) recommend for the researcher to play the devil's advocate by distrusting and undermining her own conclusions, checking out negative instances and developing rival explanations.

All these are means to enhance the internal quality of the study, the issue of whether a researcher has made the most but not too much of her data. They are also relevant for another quality criterion that has to do with the degree of 'fit' as Glaser and Strauss (1967) call it, between the grounded theory developed by the researcher and the preconstructed world it tries to capture. In other words, the issue is whether the results of a study as constructed by the researcher match the experiences and the interpretations of the research participants. Triangulation, comparison and other methods aside, an important test here lies in the outcomes of participant feedback. Apart from the ethical aspect of letting informants know what has been concluded about them and their worlds, feedback provides insight in the quality and relevance of inferences and makes sure that they are not completely off the wall. This is not to say that participant feedback will and must always result in informants agreeing completely with the researcher's interpretations. On the contrary, some rejection seems likely for a range of reasons, such as intrinsic variations of perception between informants, results conflicting with informants' self-image and interest, results presented in incomprehensible academic jargon etc. Therefore, Miles and Huberman (1984) conclude that participant feedback is a means to learn more about the site, as well as about the relevance of inferences. Moreover, it is important to emphasize again that there is not one single truth about the research site, a truth that is known to informants and is waiting to be adequately mapped by the researcher to be confirmed again by participants. Every analysis is an act of interpretation, and interpretations – including those of researchers – are by definition contested. For the researcher, the task is to find a balance between faithfully reconstructing the meanings, definitions and interpretations of individual participants and producing a grounded theory, an analytic and encompassing picture of the whole collective process of making meaning.

In this chapter I have argued that an interpretative research strategy, employing qualitative methods of data gathering and analysis, is most appropriate in the context of feminist media theory and research. This is not to say that other designs and methods are inherently at odds with the feminist project. On the contrary, in many contexts quantitative methods make perfect sense.[3] However, given the theoretical understanding of gender, culture and media developed in earlier chapters, the research perspective developed in this chapter is the most adequate one. It is characterized by a radical politicization of the research process which is expressed internally by problematizing the interaction between participants and researchers and by foregrounding the moral and political responsibilities of the researcher, and externally by the desire to make research contribute in one way or another to the feminist project. Many feminist researchers define the latter as saving women's experiences and achievements from oblivion and giving women a voice. An interpretative research strategy that starts from the meanings and interpretations human beings themselves employ in their activities therefore provides an adequate instrumentarium for feminist media research. Moreover, the theoretical position preceding an interpretative research strategy of reality as con- structed out of the symbolic interactions between human beings agrees with the views on media and gender advanced in this book, focusing on the construction of gender in production, texts and reception of mass media. Translated into research terms, the interpretative feminist research cycle is characterized by the following elements: its key concept is gender, 'operationalized' as a dependent 'variable', produced by rather than preceding social and discursive practices; the interpretative design is inductive in that it builds a substantive theory from empirical observations; it uses qualitative means of data collection such as in-depth and group interviews and participant observation; its data analysis techniques are also qualitative using words, sentences and language as units of analysis, focusing on what is achieved by the linguistic operations of respondents rather than what is reflected by them; it tries to enhance its scientific quality by triangulation, comparison, explicit reporting of choices and procedures and participant feedback. Finally, it is self-reflexive in the sense that it acknowledges its own constructed nature, its own politics of interpretation and its own intervention in the construction of gender.

Notes

1. This section draws from an article by Frissen and Wester (1990).

2. The distinction between language as reflection and language as construction is similar to the discussion engaged in in Chapter 5, on the status of media content as a set of symbols of reality providing a 'mirror' of the world, or as a set of symbols for reality involving the (re)construction of the symbolic environment.

3. Quantitative methods can make sense for inventory purposes and often in contexts of research used to prepare policy measures. Policy makers often request hard data to substantiate their proposals.

9

Conclusion

Arriving at a conclusion on the various aspects of feminist media studies discussed here seems somewhat contradictory to one of the aims of this book, to show the heterogeneity and richness of the field. Conclusions suggest and construct a degree of closure and consistency which is necessarily at odds with the diverse positions, concerns and debates within feminist media studies. The topics covered in this book range from stereotypes, pornography and ideology to journalism, advertising, film and television to masculinity, ethnicity, popular culture and methodology. Likewise, the scope of approaches discussed extends from critical theory and feminist studies, to psychoanalysis, poststructuralism and cultural studies; approaches that originate both in the social sciences and the humanities.[1]

In this diversity, some coherence was provided by locating existing theory and research within a cultural studies framework assuming the core problematic to be the struggle for the meaning of gender. The intention of this chapter is to recapture the main lines of argument without reducing the variety of the field to a more or less circumscribed position. Again, a summary or conclusion constructs a closure that does not distinguish the field. Next, I shall discuss how the approaches advanced in this book relate to the perennial concern of feminist studies: its relevance to a wider feminist politics.

If one definite standpoint was advanced in this book, it is that the relation between gender and communication is primarily – although not only – a cultural one, concerning a negotiation of meanings and values that informs whole ways of life and which is vice versa informed by existing ways of life, with configurations of power and economic inequities being a key element within them.[2] As such, media are part of feminism's cultural and – albeit to a lesser extent – its material struggle.

Mass media are central sites in which these negotiations take place, evidently at the level of media texts, but also at the level of the other 'moments' of the mass mediated production of meaning, encoding and decoding; both media producers and media audiences construct meaning. The various forces bearing on the construction of meaning differ considerably, not only between the institutional production of meaning and the audience's production of meaning, but also within each of these 'moments'. Research on media organizations has shown that the production structure is consistently gendered in terms of gender divisions in the workforce, in terms of organizational cultural and policy and in terms of the political economy of the media. However, it turned out to be infeasible to link the gendered production structure directly to the divergent features of media output. The ever returning question whether an increase of women communicators would imply an improvement of the representation of women and femininity – a question that is often defined in similar terms when it concerns communicators of colour – ignores that gender itself is a contested discourse and cannot be assumed to be articulated consistently across the board of media organizations. As was claimed in Chapter 4, specific organizational policies, routines, job requirements etc. are traversed by gender, ethnicity, professionalism and other discourses to produce organizational identities incorporating both the individual preferences and styles of communicators and the productional culture of the specific media organization. Whereas this organizational identity will often accord with traditional social arrangements, how exactly the gendered structure of production affects the encoding process and ultimately the construction of gender in media texts, depends on the particular coupling of these organizational identities with organizational goals and demands.

As a result of the complexities and the contradictions in the production process, media texts themselves cannot be characterized in terms of single meanings. Stereotypical, degrading, humiliating and violating representations of women and feminity abound in mass media content much to the annoyance of ordinary women and feminists alike. Notwithstanding the overload of traditional constructions of femininity and masculinity, gender as encoded in media texts does not carry univocal interpretations and may signify a variety of concepts and myths. The codes that confer meaning on to the signs of femininity are culturally and historically specific and will never be completely unambiguous or consistent. It is especially in the fissures opened up by the tensions in the production process and by the inherent multi-accentuality of signs that gender as a meaningful distinction in itself can be undermined and that possibilities for negotiated or oppositional readings are located. In analysing the gender of the gaze, for instance, the emphasis of many feminist researchers has shifted from examining the way women in patriarchy are constructed as visual objects for the male spectator to an inquiry into the possibilities for visual pleasures which dominant culture, cinema in particular, offers to women. In identifying the niches in dominant culture, feminist film scholars have shown how mainstream cinema allows – be it often against the grain – female spectator positions, with women as well as men functioning as objects of the female gaze.

The turn to audience research, which characterizes most feminist media studies at present, can be seen as the inevitable corollary of the recognition of the multiplicity of meanings in media texts and of the resulting demise of the text as a privileged site of meaning. Audiences are no longer seen as positioned or interpellated by media texts, subjected to the vicious intentions of patriarchal power and ideology, but are considered to be active producers of meaning, interpreting and accommodating media texts to their own daily lives and culture. As the emerging pile of research on women's reception of popular culture – white housewives in particular – seems to show, soap operas and romances are part of a culture in which themes and values from the private sphere are validated, in which women are considered to be rational beings and in which the ridiculization and attenuatation of traditional patriarchal attitudes and morals is a source of pleasure. In the reception of popular culture, gender identities are continually reconstructed in unforeseeable ways. The pleasures popular culture offers to women may be seen as a potential source of subversion, as is Radway's view (1984), but one may also have to respect – as Joke Hermes (1993) suggests – the fact that popular culture 'may be used to realign oneself with dominant identities' (1993: 209).

The emphasis on the unstable character of gender and the continuous negotiation taking place at various dimensions of mass media, may suggest that it is a volatile, almost meaningless category that can be filled with meaning according to individual preferences, social conditions, cultural peculiarities or historical contingencies. It may obscure the power relations in which gender is embedded and the very terminology of 'gender' may conceal that 'masculinity' often implies a discourse of power and centrality, whereas 'femininity' is more commonly related to powerlessness and marginality. To put it differently: the theoretical observation that gender is a constructed and shifting subject position unstably constituted by the points of intersection of an array of radically heterogeneous discourses should not lead to the conclusion that conventional forms of oppression and inequality have disappeared. On the contrary, several authors argue that women's gains in the social arena and the increased instability of gender definitions have resulted in a backlash which expresses itself in mass media and in increased violence against women (for example, Faludi, 1991). The poststructuralist movement within feminism does imply, however, that the struggle for social and cultural transformation cannot be seen as a struggle against a single configuration of power, nor can it be expected to take on a ubiquitous and perdurable form. The definition of that struggle too is a contested terrain without fixed solutions and strategies (and even without a firm existence, as the 'waves' of feminism show). This is apparent, for instance, when we consider how differently feminist media scholars have estimated the contribution of their work to broader feminist concerns.

Unmistakably, feminist politics of some sort is relevant to all research discussed here, as we can read in many introductory statements. Seiter et al. hope that an understanding of the various kinds of pleasures that television offers, will produce new perspectives on the relation between ideology and television (1989: 2). 'Politics' is thus implicitly defined in a discurisve realm as having to do with ideology. Barrett (1982), Radway (1984) and Modleski (1991) find audience pleasures legitimate but hope to make them productive for feminist issues and movements. Radway, for instance, raises questions about 'specific modes of intervention, about how romance writers and readers as well as feminist intellectuals, might contribute to the rewriting of the romance in an effort to articulate its founding fantasy to a more relevant politics' (1984: 17). 'Politics' thus implicitly refers to mobilization for the ideas of the women's movement. Brown (1990a) and Fiske (1988) talk of audience empowerment. Thus Brown hopes to find a 'feminine way of speaking that acknowledges subordination and yet empowers women, not necessarily to change the world, but to develop an image of ourselves as powerful' (1990a: 22). Politics in their work is about a revaluation of feminity and has the almost therapeutic connotation of making women feel powerful. Hermes (1993: 205) hopes to contribute to increased respect for women and 'to do battle with the insulting stereotypes surrounding women's media use'. Likewise Hobson (1989, 1990) aims at making visible the active interpretations of audiences in order to counteract the downgrading comments that usually fall on them.

This list could easily be extended, but the diversity is clear. Although most of these goals are a common part of the femininist academic project to save women's experiences from oblivion and make them an accepted part of history and culture, the recognition of the existence of such a women's culture is not without its problems as the proclamations of authors like Barret, Radway and Modleski testify. Their concern is the question of whether and how popular culture functions in favour of feminist issues and movements. Their fear is that the vicarious pleasures offered by popular culture, the compensatory experience, the fantasies that make life at present acceptable, as Ien Ang (1985) has phrased it, reconcile women with patriarchy and keep them from converting to the ideas of the women's movement. Thus the articulation of politics and pleasure is framed as a problem of the mobilization of women for feminist politics. However, if mobilization is the issue – for ideas as well as for participation within a movement – one wonders why the point of departure is popular culture? Memories, essays and research about how women became aware of the women's movement mention articles in newspapers, notes on bulletin boards and personal contacts. An interest in women's issues and participation in the women's movement originate from direct personal experiences informed and circumscribed by social relations and hardly ever from an encounter with popular culture (van Zoonen, 1991c, 1992b) Furthermore, as is evidenced by the recent 'comings out' of feminists enjoying popular culture, pleasure in romances, soaps and the like by no means precludes a feminist consciousness nor a feminist activism. In this particular definition of politics as mobilization for feminism, one might therefore conclude that popular culture is a separate realm of fantasy that has little to do with political or feminist attitudes (Ang, 1985).

It would be my assertion when assessing the relevance of (studying) media and popular culture for feminist concerns, that one should distinguish at least between the different struggles feminism is involved in. As a social movement it has the double edge of being an interest group lobbying and struggling for social and legal changes beneficial to women and of challenging cultural preoccupations and routines concerning femininity and gender.[3] Undeniably, both struggles are political and inform each other, nevertheless, they are of a different kind resulting in different interactions with the media and different requirements of media performance. Considering feminism's presence in the traditional political arenas of governments, unions, political parties etc., and its presence as a movement able to mobilize women in demonstrations, sit-ins and other extraparliamentary politics, news media are of foremost relevance for feminism. It is the representation of concrete feminist demands, activities, politics and politicians which is at stake, raising the question of how media perform as an 'agency of public knowledge' and how they enable people to function as citizens (Corner, 1991). One would expect that feminist concerns about the role of the media in the mobilization and support for feminist ideas and activities would be discussed predominantly with respect to the performance of media as agents of public knowledge. Unfortunately, this is a severely neglected area in feminist media studies which have made relatively little impact on the study of news and current affairs or political communication. Despite the undesirable gendering of media studies itself resulting from it, I would suggest that the current focus on the feminist value of popular culture obscures the differential considerations feminism needs to develop when thinking about the media. For several reasons it is completely justified to expect a decent, ethical and more or less accurate representation of feminist politics and politicians in news media. Not only do news media claim for themselves a rather unambiguous relation with 'truth' and 'the world out there' – a claim legitimized in democratic societies by numerous social and legal privileges for news media and journalists – also, people as citizens rely on and believe in the capacity of news media to present them with a true picture of reality. In such a context it is extremely troubling that feminism is represented in limited and often hostile ways (Hollingsworth, 1986, van Zoonen, 1992b).

Such considerations do not hold for popular culture, however. As said in Chapter 3, much media output – popular culture in particular – is not about reality but about collective dreams, fantasies and fears. The abundance of research on the reception of popular culture seems to show that audiences may be perfectly able to recognize these fantasies as such and to distinguish them from the realm of information or confirmation on social affairs or even personal life. Hermes (1993), for instance, concludes after numerous interviews with readers of women's magazines that the magazines' abundant messages on femininity (fashion, make-up, dieting) leave little impression.

This is not to deny any possible political or social implications of popular culture. Curran and Sparks (1991: 231), for instance, suggest that 'entertainment features promote social integration within a "model" of society in which the existence of fundamental differences of interest is tacitly denied and commonality of interest and identity is regularly affirmed'. Whereas this may be true for some audiences, the recollections of black feminist critic bell hooks quoted in Chapter 7 show that dominant white TV entertainment also functions to reconstruct the social experiences of blacks being excluded and marginalized. How popular culture is articulated with a concrete political or social awareness thus seems to depend much more on particular cultural and historical experiences of audiences than on the features of popular culture itself.

The relevance (or lack of it) of popular culture for feminism, however, should therefore be looked for on a different plane. The poststructuralist shift in feminist media studies, often accused of undermining the relevance of theory and research for feminist politics, would lead the debate to the ways in which gender is articulated in popular culture. Throughout this book it was emphasized that gender discourse as it is negotiated in media production, text and reception is unstable and dynamic, including and excluding certain versions of femininity in an often contradictory way. Nevertheless, this instability could be much bigger to the extent that it would become impossible to speak of 'gender' at all. That would possibly qualify as a poststructuralist utopia in which 'freedom lies in our capacity to discover the historical links between certain modes of self-understanding and modes of domination, and to resist the ways in which we have already been classified and identified by dominant discourses' (Sawicki, 1991: 43). Whereas such an attempt at continual fluctuation, at insecurity and indetermination would be hard to justify and apply in the area of concrete social policy making, it would be perfectly feasible and desirable as a form of cultural politics preventing the emergence of any tenacious and adamant definition of femininity and masculinity with its devastating consequences. The absence of such fixed identities and the resulting ongoing articulation of difference would not undermine solidarities and politics in the traditional sense, as is often feared, but would instead enable a variety of alliances against the many configurations of power.

That such an abstract notion of cultural politics can inform concrete projects is clear when looking at a case in the German alternative and feminist publishing house Argument Verlag in Hamburg. This publisher translates and distributes feminist detective novels in a separate series called the *Ariadne-Frauenkrimireihe*. The editors of the series have set up a variety of accompanying activities such as public lectures, workshops and the publication of a special magazine on the series, *Ariadne Forum*. This magazine is meant to provide building blocks for a feminist culture and fans of the Ariadne series are invited to send in their ideas, opinions, reading tips etc. Readers are thus given the opportunity to take possession of the series which is in the eyes of the editors a prerequisite for an alternative cultural politics:

> People should have the opportunity to take possession of such things, in the sense of an identification that does not only enable recognition but also self reflection and the development of utopian criteria. Then people would become

the producers of their own social and cultural order, . . . of their own lives and cultural identities resulting in a variety that would encourage even larger variety. (Laudan, 1992)[4]

Thus the Ariadne project animates the construction of meaning ordinarily taking place in the reception of media products. The readers of the series are not only provided with new books which they will read according to their own social and cultural location, but they are also invited to extend their interpretative activities. Being offered the editors' considerations in prefaces to the detective novels and in *Ariadne Forum*, getting to know authors in interviews, getting to meet other readers through letters to the editors, the Ariadne fans are thus enabled to indeed make the novels and the series their own. In a way, the project resembles the community of romance readers Radway (1984) wrote about held together by bookstore owner Dot and her newsletter on the best buys. Although that community emerged as a result of reader activities, the implications are similar to the Ariadne project: an interpretative community is being constructed in which the traditional relations of producer and consumer of mass culture are undermined and reversed and in which audiences are empowered to construct their own meanings out of what is offered to them.

Thus the poststructuralist turn in feminist media studies can be seen to open up new possibilities for feminist media politics rather than jeopardizing its political relevance as is often feared. In addition to the numerous institutional policies feminism has engaged in, such as equal opportunities programmes, feminist petitions to deny and portray regulations,[5] the poststructuralist turn suggests that the utopian instability and destruction of gender may result from an encouragement of the interpretative activities of audiences as well as from an intervention in the institutional production of diverse media texts.

Notes

1. Nevertheless, a number of issues have received little attention, notably those having to do with gender and communication in non-western cultures, whether these cultures are located in geographically separate areas or within the contested boundaries of Western Europe and the United States. In relation, the articulation of gender and ethnicity – although addressed in Chapters 2 and 6 – has not been discussed in great detail. In this sense, feminist media studies regrettably reflects rather than subverts the prevailing configurations of power within the academic world. Most theory and research takes place in first world countries and is carried out by white male scientists. Women's or feminist studies may differ from the overall picture in terms of gender politics, as was expounded in Chapter 2, but only partly escape white and first world patterns of dominance. Feminist media studies are no exception; in one of the first overviews of research, Gallagher (1980) noted a dearth of material from third world and communist countries. Overlooking contemporary research on media production, texts and reception, the absence of research on these areas and the exiguous attention for the articulation of gender and ethnicity indicates the endurance of first world and white dominance.

2. As said in earlier chapters, this is not to deny the material aspect of women's relation to the media which expresses itself for instance in the unequal access of women to the media, as producers as well as consumers.

3. In theory and research on new social movements this distinction between politics in the traditional sense of lobbying and negotiating and politics that is concerned with alternative modes of living and values, is recognized as constitutive of *new* social movements like the peace, environmental, student and women's movements. Dahlerup (1986), for instance refers to women's rights and women's liberation to distinguish the two elements of the movement; others speak of institutional and autonomous politics respectively.

4. My translation.

5. It is quite hard to find an up-to-date overview of all these different attempts at changing media institutions. However, a good monitor is provided by the newsletter 'Gender Roles and Mass Media', edited by Madeleine Kleberg and Ulla Abrahamsson, Department of Journalism, Media and Communication, Stockholm University, PO Box 12850, S-11297 Stockholm, Sweden.

References

Abrahamson, U. (1990) '"Are we nearing the top of the hill?" Notes from a Decade of Working toward Equality in Swedish Broadcasting'. Paper presented to the 17th Conference of the International Association of Mass Communication Research, Bled.

d'Acci, J. (1987) 'The case of *Cagney and Lacey*', in H. Baehr and G. Dyer (eds), *Boxed In: Women and Television*, London: Pandora, pp. 203–26.

Altheide, D. (1976) *Creating Reality: How TV News Distorts Events*. Beverly Hills, CA: Sage.

Ang, I. (1983) 'Mannen op zicht. Marges van het vrouwelijk voyeurisme', *Tijdschrift voor Vrouwenstudies [Journal of Women's Studies]*, 4(3): 418–35.

Ang, I. (1985) *Watching Dallas: Soap Opera and the Melodramatic Imagination*, London: Methuen.

Ang, I. (1988) 'Feminist desire and female pleasure', *Camera Obscura*, 16, 179–91.

Ang, I. (1989) 'Wanted Audiences. On the politics of empirical audience research', in E. Seiter, H. Borchers, G. Kreutzner and E. Warth (eds), *Remote Control: Television, Audiences and Cultural Power*. London: Routledge, pp. 96–115.

Ang, I. (1990) 'Melodramatic identifications: television and women's fantasy', in M.E. Brown (ed.), *Television and Women's Culture: The Politics of the Popular*. London: Sage, pp. 75–88.

Ang, I. (1991) *Desperately Seeking the Audience*. London: Routledge.

Ang, I. and Hermes, J. (1991) 'Gender and/in media consumption', in J. Curran and M. Gurevitch (eds), *Mass Media and Society*. London: Edward Arnold, pp. 307–29.

Arbuthnot, L. and Seneca, G. (1982) 'Pretext and text in *Gentlemen Prefer Blondes*, *Film Reader 5*. Reprinted in P. Erens (ed.), *Issues in Feminist Film Criticism*. Bloomington, IN: Indiana University Press, pp. 112–26.

Austin, J. (1976) *How To Do Things With Words*. 2nd edn. Oxford: Oxford University Press.

Baehr, H. (1980) 'The impact of feminism on media studies – just another commercial break?', in D. Spender (ed.), *Men's Studies Modified. The Impact of Feminism on the Academic Disciplines*. Oxford: Pergamon Press, pp. 141–53.

Baehr, H. (1981) 'Women's employment in British television', *Media, Culture and Society*, 3(2): 125–34.

Barrett, M. (1982) 'Feminism and the definition of cultural politics', in R. Brunt and C. Rowan (eds), *Feminism, Culture and Politics*. London: Lawrence and Wishart.

Barrett, M. (1992) 'Words and things: materialism and method in contemporary feminist analysis', in M. Barret and A. Philips (eds), *Destabilizing Theory: Contemporary Feminist Debates*. Cambridge: Polity Press, pp. 201–19.

Barrett, M. and Philips, A. (1992) 'Introduction', in M. Barrett and A. Philips (eds), *Destabilizing Theory: Contemporary Feminist Debates*. Cambridge: Polity Press, pp. 1–9.

Barthes, R. (1957) *Mythologies*. Paris: Editions de Seuil. (English translation, Paladin Books, 1973).

Bausinger, H. (1984) 'Media, technology and daily life', *Media, Culture and Society*, 6: 343–51.

Beasly, M. (1989) 'Newspapers: is there a new majority defining the news?', in P. Creedon (ed.), *Women in Mass Communication: Challenging Gender Values*. London: Sage, pp. 180–94.

Becker, E., Citron, M., Lesage, J. and Ruby Rich, B. (1981) 'Lesbians and film: introduction to special section', *Jump Cut*. 29: 45–57.

Berelson, B. (1952) *Content Analysis in Communication Research*. Glencoe, IL.: Free Press.

Berger, A. (1982) *Media Analysis Techniques*. Beverly Hills, CA: Sage.

Berger, J. (1972) *Ways of Seeing*. London: BBC and Penguin Books.

Berger, P. and Luckman, T. (1966) *The Social Construction of Reality: A Treatise in the Sociology of Knowledge*. Harmondsworth: Penguin Books.

Billig, M. (1988) 'Methodology and scholarship in understanding ideological explanation', in C. Antaki (ed.), *Analysing Everyday Explanation*, Beverly Hills, CA: Sage.

Blumer, H. (1969) *Symbolic Interactionism. Perspective and Method*, Englewood Cliffs, NJ: Prentice Hall.

Braidotti, R. (ed.) (1993) *Een beeld van een vrouw; de visualisering van het vrouwelijke in een postmoderne cultuur* [*The Visualization of Femininity in a Postmodern Culture*]. Kampen: Kok.

Brennan, T. (ed.) (1989) *Between Psychoanalysis and Feminism*. London: Routledge.

Brown, M.E. (ed.) (1990a) *Television and Women's Culture: The Politics of the Popular*, London: Sage.

Brown, M. E. (1990b) 'Motley moments: soap opera, carnival, gossip and the power of utterance', in M. Brown (ed.), *Television and Women's Culture: The Politics of the Popular*, London: Sage, pp. 183-200.

Brunsdon, C. (1986) 'Women watching television', *MedienKultur*, 4: 100-12.

Brunsdon, C. (1988) 'Feminism and soap opera', in K. Davies, J. Dickey and T. Stratford (eds), *Out of Focus: Writing on Women and the Media*. London: The Women's Press.

Brunsdon, C. (1993) 'Identity in feminist television criticism', *Media, Culture and Society*, 15(2): 309-20.

Burstyn, V. (ed.) (1985) *Women against Censorship*. Vancouver: Douglas and MacIntyre.

Busby, L. (1975) 'Sex-role research on the mass media', *Journal of Communication*, Autumn, pp. 107-31.

Bush, C. (1983) 'Women and the assessment of technology: to think, to be, to unthink, to free', in J. Rothschild (ed.), *Machina ex dea. Feminist Perspectives on Technology*, New York: Pergamon Press, pp. 151-70.

Butler, J. (1992) 'Contingent foundations: feminism and the question of "postmodernism" ', in J. Butler and J. Scott (eds), *Feminists Theorize the Political*, London: Routledge, pp. 3-21.

Butler, M. and Paisley, W. (1980) *Women and Mass Media: Resourcebook for Research and Action*. New York: Hasting House.

Byars, J. (1991) *All that Hollywood Allows. Re-reading Gender in 1950s Melodrama*, Chapell Hill, NC: University of North Carolina Press.

Cagan, E. (1978) 'The selling of the women's movement', *Social Policy*, 8 (May/June): 4-12.

Camargo, N. de (1987) 'Women in media management and decision making: a study of radio in Ecuador', in *Women and Decision Making: The Invisible Barriers*. Paris: Unesco, pp. 44-62.

Cantor, M. (1978) 'Where are the women in public broadcasting?', in G. Tuchman (ed.), *Hearth and Home: Images of Women in the Media*, New York: Oxford University Press, pp. 78-90.

Cantor, M. (1980) *Prime Time Television: Content and Control*, Beverly Hills, CA: Sage,

Cantor, M. (1988) 'Feminism and the media', *Society*, July/August, pp. 76-81.

Cantor, M. and Cantor, J. (1991) *Prime Time Television: Content and Control*, 2nd edn. Beverly Hills, CA: Sage.

Cantor, M. and Pingree, S. (1983) *The Soap Opera*. Beverly Hills, CA: Sage.

Carey, J. (1989) *Communication as Culture: Essays on Media and Society*, Boston, MA: Unwin Hyman.

Carragee, K. (1990) 'Interpretative media study and interpretative social science', *Critical Studies in Mass Communication*. 7(2): 81-96.

Castro, J. (1988) 'Women in television: an uphill battle', *Channels*, January, pp. 42-52.

Certeau, M. de (1984) *The Practices of Everyday Life*, Berkeley, CA: University of California Press.

Ceulemans, M. and Fauconnier, G. (1979) *Mass Media: the Image, Role and Social Conditions of Women*. Paris: Unesco.

Chapkis, W. (1986) *Beauty Secrets: Women and the Politics of Appearance*. Dutch translation: Schoonheidsgeheimen, Amsterdam: SARA.

Commission of the European Communities (1987) *Gelijke Kansen in de Europese Omroep: Een Praktijkgids [Equal Opportunities in European Broadcasting]*. Brussels: Commission of the European Communities.

Communication (1986) 'Feminist critiques of popular culture', Special Issue, 9(1).

Corner, J. (1991) 'Meaning, genre and context: the problematics of "Public Knowledge" in the new audience studies', in J. Curran and M. Gurevitch (eds), *Mass Media and Society*, London: Edward Arnold, pp. 267–306.

Courtney, A. and Whipple, T. (1983) *Sex Stereotyping in Advertising*, Lexington, MA: Lexington Books.

Coward, R. (1982) 'Sexual violence and sexuality', *Feminist Review*. 11 (Summer), pp. 9–22.

Coward, R. (1984) *Female Desire: Women's Sexuality Today*. London: Paladin Books.

Craen, S. (1987) 'Women in broadcast management: a case study of the Canadian Broadcasting Corporation's Programme of Equal Opportunity', in *Women and Decision Making: The Invisible Barriers*. Paris: Unesco, pp. 95–118.

Creedon, P. (ed.) (1989) *Women in Mass Communication: Challenging Gender Values*. Beverly Hills, CA: Sage.

Crouse, T. (1972) *The Boys on the Bus*. New York: Random House.

Cummings, M. (1988) 'The changing image of the black family on television', *Journal of Popular Culture*, 22(2): 75–87.

Curran, J. (1991) 'The new revisionism in mass communication research: a reappraisal', *European Journal of Communication*, 5(2–3): 135–64.

Curran, J. and Sparks (1991) 'Press and popular culture', *Media, Culture & Society*, 13(2): 215–37.

Dahlerup, D. (ed.) (1986) *The New Women's Movement. Feminism and Political Power in Europe and the USA*. London: Sage.

Davies, K., Dickey, J. and Stratford, T. (eds) (1987) *Out of Focus: Writing on Women and the Media*. London: The Women's Press.

Denzin, N. (1970) *Sociological Methods: A Sourcebook*. Chicago: Aldine.

Denzin, N. (1987) 'On semiotics and symbolic interaction', in *Symbolic Interaction*. 10(1): 1–19.

Dervin, B. (1987) 'The potential contribution of feminist scholarship to the field of communication', *Journal of Communication*, Autumn, pp. 107–20.

Diekerhof, E., Elias, M. and Sax, M. (1985) *Voor zover Plaats aan de Perstafel*. Amsterdam: Meulenhoff Educatief.

Dijk, T. van (ed.) (1985) *Handbook of Discourse Analysis*. (vols 1·4). London: Academic Press.

Dijk, T. van (1991) *News as Discourse*. Hillsdale, NJ: Erlbaum.

Dimmick, J. and Coit, P. (1982) 'Levels of analysis in mass media decision making', *Communication Research*, 9(1): 3–32.

Doane, M. (1982) 'Film and the masquerade; theorizing the female spectator', *Screen*, 23(3–4), Reprinted in P. Erens (ed.) (1990) *Issues in Feminist Film Criticism*, Bloomington, IN: Indiana University Press, p. 41–58.

Doane, M. (1991) *Femmes Fatales: Feminism, Film Theory, Psychoanalysis*. London: Routledge.

Dominick, J. and Rauch, G. (1972) 'The image of women in network TV commercials', *Journal of Broadcasting*. 16: 259–65.

Douglas, J. (ed.) (1970) *Understanding Everyday Life: Toward the Reconstruction of Everyday Knowledge*, Chicago: Aldine.

Dworkin, A. (1980) 'Pornography and grief', in L. Lederer (ed.), (1980) *Take Back the Night: Women on Pornography*, New York: Morrow.

Dworkin, A. (1981) *Pornography: Men Possessing Women*. New York: Perigee.

Dyer, R. (1982) 'Don't look now', *Screen*, 23(4): 61–74.

Easthope, A. (1986) *What a Man's Gotta Do: The Masculine Myth in Popular Culture*, London: Paladin Books.

Edelman, M. (1964) *The Symbolic Uses of Politics*. Urbana, IL.: University of Illinois Press.

Eisenstein, Z, (1981) *The Radical Future of Liberal Feminism*. New York: Longman.

Elliott, P. (1977) 'Media organizations and occupations – an overview', in J. Curran, M. Gurevitch and J. Woollacott (eds), *Mass Communication and Society*. London: Edward Arnold, pp. 142–73.

Ellsworth, E. (1986) 'Illicit pleasures: feminist spectators and personal best', in P. Erens (ed.) (1990), *Issues in Feminist Film Criticism*. Bloomington, IN: Indiana University Press, pp. 183–97.

Erens, P. (ed.) (1990) *Issues in Feminist Film Criticism*. Bloomington, IN: Indiana University Press.

Ettema, J. (1982) 'The organizational context of creativity: a case study from public television', in J. Ettema and D. Whitney (eds), *Individuals in Mass Media Organizations: Creativity and Constraint*, Beverly Hills, CA: Sage, pp. 91–106.

European Journal of Communication (1990) Communication research in Europe: the state of the art, special issue, 5(2–3): 131–379.

Fahim, F. (1987) 'Professional women in Egyptian radio and television', in *Women and Decision Making: The Invisible Barriers*, Paris: Unesco.

Faludi, S. (1991) *Backlash: The Undeclared War against American Women*. New York: Crown.

Ferguson, M. (1983) *Forever Feminine; Women's Magazines and the Cult of Femininity*. London: Heinemann.

Fiske, J. (1988) *Television Culture*. London: Methuen.

Fiske, J. (1980 [1982]) *Introduction to Communication Studies*. London: Routledge.

Fiske, J. and Hartley, J. (1978) *Reading Television*, London: Methuen.

Flitterman, S. (1985) 'Thighs and whiskers: the fascination of Magnum PI', *Screen*, 26(2): 42–58.

Flitterman-Lewis, S. (1992) 'Psychoanalysis, film and television', in R. Allen (ed.), *Channels of Discourse, Reassembled*. London: Routledge, pp. 203–47.

Foucault, M. (1976) *La Volonté de Savoir*. Paris: Gallimard.

Franklin, S., Lury, C. and Stacey, J. (eds) (1991) *Off Centre: Feminism and Cultural Studies*. New York: Harper Collins Academic.

Franzwa, H. (1978) 'The image of women in television: an annotated bibliography', in G. Tuchman (ed.), *Hearth and Home: Images of Women in the Media*, New York: Oxford University Press.

Frazer, E. (1987) 'Teenage girls reading *Jackie*', *Media. Culture and Society*, 9(4): 407–25.

Friedan, B, (1963) *The Feminine Mystique*. London: Penguin Books.

Frissen, V. and Meier, U. (1988) 'Zwijmelen tussen de schuifdeuren', in L. van Zoonen (ed.), *Tussen Plezier en Politiek: Feminisme en de media*, Amsterdam: SUA (Socialistische Uitgeverij Amsterdam).

Frissen, V. and Wester, F. (1990) 'Recente Toepassingen van de Interpretatieve Onderzoeksbenadering in de Communicatiewetenschap', *Massacommunicatie*, 18(2): 153–75.

Gaines, J. (1987) 'Women and representation; can we enjoy alternative pleasure?', in D. Lazere (ed.), *American Media and Mass Culture*, Berkeley, CA: University of California Press, pp. 357–72.

Gaines, J. (1988) 'White privilege and looking relations: race and gender in feminist film theory', *Screen*, 29(4): 12–27.

Gallagher, M. (1977) 'Negotiation of control in media organizations and occupations', in T. Bennet, J. Curran and J. Woollacott (eds), *Culture, Society and the Media*. London: Methuen, pp. 151–73.

Gallagher, M. (1980) *Unequal Opportunities: The Case of Women and the Media*. Paris: Unesco.

Gallagher, M. (1984) *Employment and Positive Action for Women in the Television Organizations of the EEC Member States*, Brussels: Commission of the European Communities.

Gallagher, M. (1985) *Unequal Opportunities: Update*. Paris: Unesco.

Gallagher, M. (1992) 'Women and men in the media', *Communication Research Trends*, special issue 12(1): 1–36.

Gamman, L. and Marshment, M. (1988) *The Female Gaze*. Seattle: Real Comet Press.

Gans, H. (1979) *Deciding What's News*, New York: Vintage Books.

Geraghty, C. (1990) *Women and Soap Opera*. Cambridge: Polity Press.

Gerbner, G., Gross, L., Morgan, M. and Signorelli, N. (1980) 'Aging with television: images on television drama and conceptions of social reality'. *Journal of Communication*, 32(2): 100–27.

Gitlin, T. (1980) *The Whole World is Watching: Media in the Making and the Unmaking of the New Left*. Berkeley, CA: University of California Press.

Gitlin, T. (1983) *Inside Prime Time*. New York: Pantheon.

Glaser, B. and Strauss, A. (1967) *The Discovery of Grounded Theory*. Chicago: Aldine.

Gledhill, C, (1988) 'Pleasurable negotiations', in E.D. Pribram (ed.), *Female Spectators: Looking at Film and Television*. London: Verso, pp. 64–79.

Goffman, E. (1974) *Frame Analysis*. New York: Harper and Row.

Goffman, E. (1976) *Gender Advertisements*. London: The Society for the Study of Visual Communication.

Gray, A. (1987) 'Behind closed doors: videorecorders in the home', in H. Baehr and G. Dyer (eds), *Boxed in: Women and Television*. London: Pandora.

Gray, A. (1992) *Video Playtime: The Gendering of a Leisure Technology*. London: Routledge.

Greer, G. (1971) *The Female Eunuch*. London: Paladin.

Gregg, N, (1987) 'Reflections on the feminist critique of objectivity', *Journal of Communication Inquiry*, 11(1): 8–18.

Gripsrud, J. (1990) 'Toward a flexible methodology for studying media meaning: *Dynasty* in Norway', *Critical Studies in Mass Communication*, June: 117–28.

Grossberg, L., Nelson, C. and Treichler, P. (eds) (1992) *Cultural Studies*. London: Routledge.

Hall, S. (1973) 'Encoding/decoding', reprinted in S. Hall, D. Hobson, A. Lowe and P. Willis (eds) (1980) *Culture, Media, Language*. London: Hutchinson.

Hansen, M. (1986) 'Pleasure, ambivalence, identification: Valentino and female spectatorship', *Cinema Journal*, 1, 6–32.

Harding, S. (1987) *The Science Question in Feminism*. London: Cornell University Press.

Hartley, J. (1982) *Understanding News*. London: Methuen.

Haskell, M. (1987) *From Reverence to Rape: The Treatment of Women in Movies*, 2nd edn. Chicago: University of Chicago Press.

Hermes, J. (1992) 'Sexuality in lesbian romance fiction', *Feminist Review*, 42: 49–67.

Hermes, J. (1993) *Easily Put Down: Women's Magazines, Readers, Repertoires and Everyday Life*. PhD thesis, University of Amsterdam. (To be published by Polity Press, Cambridge, 1994/95.)

Hermes, J. and van Zoonen, L. (1988) 'Fun or serious business? Feminist television programmes in the Netherlands'. Paper presented to the Third International Interdisciplinary Congress of Women's Studies, Dublin.

Hermsen, J. and van Lenning, A. (eds) (1991) *Sharing the Difference. Feminist Debates in Holland*. London: Routledge.

Hirsch, P. (1973) 'Processing fads and fashions: an organization-set analysis of culture industry systems', *American Journal of Sociology*, 77: 639–59.

Hirsch, P. (1977) 'Occupational, organisational and institutional models in mass communication', in P. Hirsch, P. Miller and F. Kleine (eds), *Strategies for Communication Research*, Beverly Hills, CA: Sage, pp. 13–42.

Hobson, D. (1980) 'Housewives and the mass media', in S. Hall, D. Hobson, A. Lowe and P. Willis (eds), *Culture, Media, Language*. London: Hutchinson, pp. 105–14.

Hobson, D. (1989) 'Soap operas at work', in E. Seiter, H. Borchers, G. Kreutzner and E. Warth (eds), *Remote Control: Television, Audiences and Cultural Power*. London: Routledge, pp. 150–67.

Hobson, D. (1990) 'Women, audiences and the workplace', in M.E. Brown (ed.), *Television and Women's Culture: The Politics of the Popular*, London: Sage, pp. 61–74.

Hole, J. and Levine, E. (1971) *Rebirth of Feminism*. New York: Quadrangle.

Holland, P. (1987) 'When a woman reads the news', in H. Baehr and G. Dyer (eds), *Boxed In: Women and Television*. London: Pandora, pp. 133–50.

Hollingsworth, M. (1986) *The Press and Political Dissent*. London: Pluto.

Holsti, O. (1969) *Content Analysis for the Social Sciences and the Humanities*, Reading, MA: Addison Wesley.

hooks, bell (1989) *Feminist Theory: From Margin to Center*, Boston, MA: South End Press.

hooks, bell (1990) *Yearning: Race, Gender and Cultural Politics*, Boston, MA: South End Press.

Houston, M. and Kramarae, C. (1991) 'Women speaking from silence', *Discourse and Society*, special issue, 2(4): 387–502.

Irukwu, E. (1987) 'Women in Nigerian broadcasting: a study of their access to decision making positions', in *Women and Decision Making: The Invisible Barriers*. Paris: Unesco, pp. 63–80.

Jaggar, A. (1983) *Feminist Politics and Human Nature*. Totowa, NJ: Rowman and Allanheld.

Janus, N. (1977) 'Research on sex-roles in the mass media: toward a critical approach', *Insurgent Sociologist*, 7(3): 19–32.

Jensen, E. (1982) 'Television newscasts in a woman's perspective'. Paper presented at the 14th Conference of the International Association for Mass Communication Research, Prague.

Jensen, K. (1986) *Making Sense of the News*. Arhus: University of Arhus Press.

Jensen, K. (1991) 'Humanistic scholarship as qualitative science; contributions to mass communication research', in K. Jensen and N. Jankowski (ed.), *Handbook of Qualitative Methodologies for Mass Communication Research*. London: Routledge, pp. 17–44.

Jensen, K. and Jankowski, N. (1991) *Handbook of Qualitative Methodologies in Mass Communication Research*. London: Routledge.

Jhally, S. (1987) *The Codes of Advertising*. London: Frances Pinter.

Johnson, S. (1989) 'Magazines: women's employment and status in the magazine industry', in P. Creedon (ed.), *Women in Mass Communication: Challenging Gender Values*. Beverly Hills, CA: Sage, pp. 195–213.

Johnstone, J., Slawski, E. and Bowman, W. (1976) *The Newspeople*. Urbana, IL.: University of Illinois Press.

Joshi, S. (1987) 'Invisible barriers: women at senior levels in Indian television', in *Women and Decision Making: The Invisible Barriers*, Paris: Unesco, pp. 17–43.

Journal of Communication Inquiry (1987) 'The Feminist Issue', Special Issue, 11(1).

Kabbani, R. (1986) *Europe's Myths of the Orient*. London: Pandora Press.

Kaplan, E.A. (1987) 'Feminist criticism and television', in R. Allen (ed.), *Channels of Discourse*, University of Carolina Press. (Second edition, London: Routledge, 1992.

Katz, E. and Lazarsfeld, P. (1955) *Personal Influence*, Glencoe, IL,: Free Press.

Katz, E. and Liebes, T. (1990) *The Export of Meaning: Cross-Cultural Readings of Dallas*. Oxford: Oxford University Press.

King, S.B. (1990) '"Sonny's virtues": the gender negotiations of *Miami Vice*', *Screen*, 31: 281–95.

Kirk, J. and Miller, M. (1987) *Reliability and Validity in Qualitative Research*, Beverly Hills, CA: Sage.

Köcher, R. (1986) 'Bloodhounds or missionaries; role definitions of German and British journalists', *European Journal of Communication*, 1(2): 43–64.

Kodama, M. (1991) *Women in Modern Journalism*. (Originally published as *Jaanarizumu no joseikan*.) Tokyo: Gakubunsha.

Komter, A. (1985) *De Macht van de Vanzelfsprekendheid*, The Hague: VUGA.

Krippendorf, K. (1980) *Content Analysis: An Introduction to Its Methodology*. Beverly Hills, CA: Sage.

Krueger, R.A. (1988) *Focus Groups: A Practical Guide for Applied Research*. Beverly Hills, CA: Sage.

Lafky, S. (1989) 'Economic equity and the journalistic work force', in P. Creedon (ed.), *Women in Mass Communication: Challenging Gender Values*. Beverly Hills, CA: Sage, pp. 164–79.

Lafky, S. (1990) 'Gender and the professional values and orientation of journalists: a cross cultural comparison'. Paper presented to the Association for Education in Journalism and Mass Communication, Minneapolis.

Larkin, A.S. (1988) 'Black women film makers defining ourselves: feminism in our own voice', in E. Pribram (ed.), *Female Spectators: Looking at Film and Television*. London: Verso, pp. 157–74.

Laudan, E. (1992) 'Unsere Krimiheldinnen: reiten sie für die Wirklichkeit?', *Ariadne Forum*, 1. Hamburg: Argument Verlag.

Lauretis, T. de (1984) *Alice Doesn't: Feminism, Semiotics, Cinema*, Bloomington, IN: Indiana University Press.

Lauretis, T. de (1987) *Technologies of Gender: Essays on Theory, Film and Fiction*. London: Macmillan.

Lazier-Smith, L. (1989) 'A new "genderation" of images to women', in P. Creedon (ed.), *Women in Mass Communication: Challenging Gender Values*. London: Sage, pp. 247–60.

Lederer, L. (ed.), (1980) *Take Back the Night: Women on Pornography*, New York: Morrow.

Leiss, W., Kline, S. and Jhally, S. (1986) *Social Communication in Advertisements*. London: Nelson/Routledge.

Leman, J. (1987) 'Programmes for women in 1950s British television', in H. Baehr and G. Dyer (eds), *Boxed in: Women and Television*. London: Pandora Press, pp. 73–96.

Leto Defrancisco, V.(1991) 'The sounds of silence: how men silence women in marital relations', *Discourse and Society*, 2(4): 413–24.

Leong, W.T.(1991) 'The pornography "Problem": disciplining women and young girls', *Media, Culture and Society*, 13(1): 91–118.

Lévi–Strauss, C. (1962) *La Pensée Sauvage*, Librairi Plon, Paris.

Lewis, J. (1991) *Ideological Octopus: an Exploration of TV and Its Audience*. London: Routledge.

Lincoln, Y. and Guba, E. (1985) *Naturalistic Inquiry*. Beverly Hills, CA: Sage.

Lindloff, T. (1987) 'Media audiences as interpretive communities', *Communication Yearbook*, 11: 81–107.

Livingstone, S. (1991) 'Audience reception: the role of the viewer in retelling romantic drama', in J. Curran and M. Gurevitch (eds), *Mass Media and Society*. London: Edward Arnold, pp. 285–306.

Lull, J. (1988), 'The audience as nuisance', *Critical Studies in Mass Communication*, 5(3): 239–42.

Lull, J. (1990) *The Social Uses of Television*. Beverly Hills, CA: Sage.

Mannoni, D.(1950) *Psychology de la colonisation*. Paris: Editions de Seuil.

Manuel, P. (1985) 'Blacks in British television drama: the underlying tensions', *Media Development*. 4: 41–3.

Marshall, C. and Rossman, G. (1989) *Designing Qualitative Research*. Beverly Hills, CA: Sage.

Mattelart, M. (1986) *Women, Media, Crisis: Femininity and Disorder*. London: Comedia.

McCormack, T. (1978) 'Machismo in media research: a critical review of research on violence and pornography', *Social Problems*, 25(5): 544–55.

McCracken, G. (1988) *The Long Interview*, Beverly Hills, CA: Sage.

McQuail, D. (1987 [1983]) *Introduction to Mass Communication Theory*, 2nd edn. London: Sage.

McRobbie, A. (1982) '*Jackie*: an ideology of adolescent femininity', in B. Waites, T. Bennet and G. Martin (eds), *Popular Culture: Past and Present*, London: Croom Helm, pp. 263–83.

McRobbie, A. (1991) *Feminism and Youth Culture: From Jackie to Just Seventeen*, Basingstoke: Macmillan.

Media, Culture & Society (1990) The Other Europe? Special Issue, 12(2).

Melucci, A. (1988) *Nomads of the Present. Social Movements and Individual Needs*. London: Hutchinson Radius.

Merrit, S. and Gross, H. (1978) 'Women's page/life style editors: does sex make a difference?', *Journalism Quarterly*, 55(3): 508–14.

Mies, M. (1978) 'Frauenforschung oder feministische Forschung. Die Debatte um feministische Wissenschaft und Methodologie', in *Beiträge zur feministische Theorie und Praxis*, (Munich) no. 1. English translation in G. Bowles and R. Duelli Klein (eds), (1981), *Theories of Women's Studies*. Berkeley, CA: University of California Press.

Miles, M. (1979) 'Qualitative data as an attractive nuisance', *Administrative Science Quarterly*, 24, 590–601.

Miles, M. and Huberman, K. (1984) *Qualitative Data Analysis: A Sourcebook of New Methods*. London: Sage.

Modleski, T. (1984) *Loving with a Vengeance: Mass Produced Fantasies for Women*. London: Methuen.

Modleski, T. (1986) 'Introduction', in T. Modleski (ed.), *Studies in Entertainment: Critical Approaches to Mass Culture*. Bloomington, IN: Indiana University Press, pp. ix–xix.

Modleski, T. (1990) 'Hitchcock, feminism, and the patriarchal unconscious', in P. Erens (ed.), *Issues in Feminist Film Criticism*, Bloomington, IN: Indiana University Press, pp. 41–58.

Modleski, T. (1991) *Feminism without Women*, London: Routledge.

Montgomery, K.C. (1989) *Target Prime Time*. New York: Oxford University Press.

Moores, S. (1990) 'Texts, readers and contexts of reading: developments in the study of media audiences', *Media, Culture and Society*, 12(1), 9–30.

Moritz, M. (1989) 'American television discovering gay women: the changing context of programming decisions at the networks', *Journal of Communication Inquiry*, 13(2): 62–79.

Morley, D. (1980) *The Nationwide Audience*, London: British Film Institute.

Morley, D. (1986) *Family Television: Cultural Power and Domestic Leisure*, London: Comedia.

Morley, D. (1989) 'Changing paradigm in audience studies', in E. Seiter, H.Borchers, G. Kreutzner and E. Warth (eds), *Remote Control: Television, Audiences and Cultural Power*. London: Routledge.

Morley, D. (1991) *Television, Audiences and Cultural Studies*. London: Routledge.

Morley, D. and Silverstone, R. (1991) 'Communication and context: ethnographic perspectives on the media audience', in K. Jensen and N. Jankowski (eds), *A Handbook of Qualitative Methodologies for Mass Communication Research*. London: Routledge, pp. 149–62.

Mouffe, C. (1992) 'Feminism, citizenship, and radical democratic politics', in J. Butler and J.W. Scott (eds), *Feminists Theorize the Political*. London: Routledge, pp. 369–85.

Moyal, A. (1992) 'The gendered use of the telephone: an Australian case study', *Media, Culture and Society*, 14(1): 51–72.

Muir, A.R. (1987) *A Woman's Guide to Jobs in Film and Television*. London: Pandora Books.

Mulvey, L. (1975) 'Visual pleasure and narrative cinema' *Screen*, 16(3): 6–18. Reprinted in P. Erens (ed.), (1990), *Issues in Feminist Film Criticism*, Bloomington, IN: Indiana University Press, pp. 28–71.

Mulvey, L. (1979) 'Afterthoughts on "visual pleasure and narrative cinema" inspired by *Duel in the Sun*', *Framework*, 10 (Spring): 3–10.

Muramatsu, Y. (1990) 'Of women, by women, for women? Toward new hopes for television in Japan'. Paper presented to the 17th Conference of the International Association of Mass Communication Research, Bled.

Murdock, G. (1980) 'Fabricating fictions: approaches to the study of television drama production', *Communication*, 6: 17–32.

Neale, S. (1983) 'Masculinity as spectacle', *Screen*, 24(6): 2–16.

Nederveen Pieterse, J. (1990) *Wit over zwart: Beelden van Afrika en zwarten in de westerse populaire cultuur [Images of Africa and Blacks in Western Popular Culture]*. Amsterdam: Tropenmuseum.

Neverla, I. (1986) 'Balanceakte zwischen Angleichung und Abweichung im Journalism. Aspekte beruflicher Sozialisation von Journalistinnen', *Publizistik*, 31(1/2): 129–38.

Neverla, I. and Kanzleiter, G. (1984) *Journalistinnen*, Frankfurt: Campus Verlag.

Nicholson, L. (1990) (ed.) *Feminism/postmodernism*. London: Routledge.

O'Sullivan, T., Hartley, J., Saunders, D. and Fiske, J. (eds) (1989 [1983]) *Key Concepts in Communication*, London: Routledge.

Paglia, C. (1990) *Sexual Persona*. New Haven, NJ: Yale University Press.

Patton, M. (1980) *Qualitative Evaluation Methods*. London: Sage.

Potter, J. and Wetherell, M. (1987) *Discourse and Social Psychology*. London: Sage.

Press, A. (1991) *Women Watching Television: Gender, Class and Generation in the American Television Experience*, Philadelphia: University of Pennsylvania Press.

Press, A. (1992) 'Class, gender and the female viewer', in M.E. Brown (ed.), *Television and Women's Culture: The Politics of the Popular*. London: Sage.

Pribram, E. (ed.) (1988) *Female Spectators: Looking at Film and Television*. London: Verso.

Propp, V. (1923) *Morphology of the Folktale*. Austin: University of Texas Press. (Second edition, 1968.)

Radway, J. (1984) *Reading the Romance: Women, Patriarchy and Popular Literature*. Chapel Hill, NC: University of North Carolina Press.

Radway, J. (1989) 'Ethnography among elites; comparing discourses of power', *Journal of Communication Inquiry*, 13(2), 3–12.

Rakow, L. (1986) 'Rethinking gender research in communication', *Journal of Communication*, Winter, pp. 11–26.

Rao, L. (1992) 'The new woman image on Indian television – marketing strategies for selling products and ideas'. Paper presented at the 18th Conference and General Assembly of IAMCR, Guaraja Brazil.

Reinharz, S. (1992) *Feminist Methods in Social Research*. New York: Oxford University Press.

Roach, J. and Felix, P. (1988) 'Black looks', in L. Gamman and M. Marshment (eds), *The Female Gaze: Women as Viewers of Popular Culture*. London: Women's Press, pp. 130–9.

Rogge, J.-U. (1989) 'The media in everyday family life: some biographical and typological aspects', in E. Seiter, H. Borchers, G. Kreutzner and E. Warth (eds), *Remote Control: Television, Audiences and Cultural Power*. London: Routledge, pp. 168–79.

Rosen, M. (1973) *Popcorn Venus: Women, Movies and the American Dream*. New York: Coward, McCann. Geoghegan.

Rubin, G. (1975) 'The traffic in women: notes on the "political economy" of sex', in R. Reiter (ed.), *Toward an Anthropology of Women*, New York: Monthly Review Press.

Rubin, L. (1976) *Life in the Working Class Family*, New York: Basic Books.

Rubin, L. (1979) *Women of a Certain Age*. New York: Harper and Row.

Rubin, L. (1983) *Intimate Strangers*. New York: Harper and Row.

Saferstein, B. (1991) 'Collective cognition and collaborative work: the effects of cognitive and communicative processes on the organization of television production', *Discourse and Society*, 3(1): 61–87.

Saucier, K. (1986) 'Healers and heartbreakers; images of women and men in country music', *Journal of Popular Culture*, 20(3): 147–67.

Sawicki, J. (1991) *Disciplining Foucault: Feminism, Power and the Body*. London: Routledge.

Schamber, L. (1989) 'Women in mass communication education: who is teaching tomorrow's communicators?', in P.J. Creedon (ed.), *Women in Mass Communication: Challenging Gender Values*. London: Sage, pp. 148–62.

Schröder, K. (1988) 'The pleasure of *Dynasty*: the weekly reconstruction of self-confidence', in Ph. Drummond and R. Paterson (eds), *Television and its Audience*, London: British Film Institute, pp. 61–82.

Seiter, E. (1992) 'Semiotics, structuralism and television', in R. Allen (ed.), *Channels of Discourse, Reassembled*. London: Routledge, pp. 31–66.

Seiter, E., Borchers, E., Kreutzner, G. and Warth. E. (1989) 'Don't treat us like we're so stupid and naive: towards an ethnography of soap opera viewers', in E. Seiter, H. Borchers, G. Kreutzner and E. Warth (eds), *Remote Control: Television, Audiences and Cultural Power*. London: Routledge, pp. 223–47.

Short, C. (1991) *Dear Clare . . . this is what women feel about Page Three*. London: Hutchinson Radius.

Showalter, E. (ed.) (1989) *Speaking of Gender*. New York: Routledge.

Silverstone, R. (1988) 'Television myth and culture', in J. Carey (ed.), *Media, Myths and Narratives: Television and the Press*. London: Sage, pp. 20–47.

Smith, C., Fredin, E. and Nardone, C. (1989) 'Television: sex discrimination in the TV newsroom – perception and reality', in P. Creedon (ed.), *Women in Mass Communication: Challenging Gender Values*, Beverly Hills, CA: Sage, pp. 227–46.

Smith, R. (1976) 'Sex and occupational roles in Fleet Street', in D.L. Barker and S. Allen (eds), *Dependence and Exploitation in Work and Marriage*. London: Longman.

Smith, R. (1980) 'Images and equality: women and the national press', in H. Christian (ed.), *The Sociology of Journalism and the Press*. London: Routledge and Kegan Paul, pp. 239–59.

Stacey, J. (1987) 'Desperately seeking difference', in P. Ehrens (ed.) (1990) *Issues in Feminist Film Criticism*. Bloomington, IN: Indiana University Press, pp. 365–80.

Stacey, J. and Thorne, B. (1985) 'The missing feminist revolution in sociology', *Social Problems*, 32(4): 301–16.

Steeves, L. (1987) 'Feminist theories and media studies', *Critical Studies in Mass Communication*, 4(2), 95–135.

Stone, V.A. (1988) 'Trends in the status of minorities and women in broadcast news', *Journalism Quarterly*, 65: 288–93.

Strauss, A. and Corbin, J. (1990) *Qualitative Data Analysis*, Beverly Hills, CA: Sage.

Stuart, A. (1990) 'Feminism: dead or alive?' in J. Rutherford (ed.), *Identity, Community, Culture, Difference*. London: Lawrence and Wishart, pp. 98–113.

Tannen, D. (1990) *You Just Don't Understand*. New York: Ballantine Books.

Thomas, W.I. (1928) *The Child in America*. New York: Knopf.

Thoveron, G. (1986) 'European televised women', *European Journal of Communication*, 1(3), 289–301.

Tong, R. (1989) *Feminist Thought*. Cambridge: Polity Press.

Tuchman, G. (1978a) *Hearth and Home: Images of Women and the Media*. New York: Oxford University Press.

Tuchman, G. (1978b) *Making News*. New York: Free Press.

Tuchman, G. (1991) 'Qualitative methods in the study of news', in K. Jensen and N. Jankowski (eds), *A Handbook of Qualitative Methodologies for Mass Communication Research*, London: Routledge, pp. 72–92.

Turkle, S. (1988) 'Computational reticence: why women fear the intimate machine', in C. Kramarae (ed.), *Technology and Women's Voices: Keeping in Touch*. London: Routledge, pp. 41–61.

Turow, J. (1982) 'Unconventional programs on commercial television: an organizational perspective', in J.S. Ettema and D.C. Whitney (eds), *Individuals in Mass Media Organizations*. Beverly Hills, CA: Sage, pp. 107–29.

Unesco (1987) *Women and Decision Making: The Invisible Barriers*, Paris: Unesco.

Vance, C. (ed.) (1984) *Pleasure and Danger: Exploring Female Sexuality*. Boston, MA: Routledge and Kegan Paul.

Wallace, D. (1978) 'Television crime shows and conflictual socialization'. Paper presented at the ASA World Congress of Sociology, Uppsala.

Wallace, M. (1975) 'Anger in isolation: a black feminist's search for sisterhood'. Reprinted in M. Wallace (1990), *Invisibility Blues: from Pop to Theory*. London: Verso.

Warner, M. (1985) *Monuments and Maidens: The Allegory of the Female Form*. London: Picador.

Warren, C. (1988) *Gender Issues in Field Research*. Beverly Hills, CA: Sage.

Wassenaar, I. (1975) *Vrouwenbladen: Spiegels van een Mannenmaatschappij [Women's Magazines: Mirrors of Male Society]*. Amsterdam: Wetenschappelijke Uitgeverij.

Wernick, A. (1991) *Promotional Culture: Advertising, Ideology and Symbolic Expression*. London: Sage.

Wester, F. (1987) *Strategieën voor Kwalitatief Onderzoek [Strategies for Qualitative Research]*. Muiden: Coutinho.

Wester, F, and Jankowski, N. (1991) 'The qualitative tradition in social science inquiry: contributions to mass communication research', in K. Jensen and N. Jankowski (eds), *A Handbook of Qualitative Methodologies for Mass Communication Research*, London: Routledge, pp. 44–74.

Whitlow, S. (1977) 'How male and female gatekeepers respond to news stories of women', *Journalism Quarterly*, 54(3): 573–9.

Wijngaard, R. van der (1990) 'Le fait d'être femme, d'être journaliste, c'est pas evident'. MA Thesis, Department of Communication, University of Amsterdam.

Williams, L. (1984) '"Something else besides a mother": *Stella Dallas* and the maternal melodrama', in P. Ehrens (ed.) (1990) *Issues in Feminist Film Criticism*. Bloomington, IN: Indiana University Press, pp. 137–63.

Williamson, J. (1978) *Decoding Advertisements*. London: Marion Boyars.

Williamson, J. (1986) 'Woman is an island: femininity and colonization', in T. Modleski (ed.), *Studies in Entertainment: Critical Approaches to Mass Culture*. Bloomington, IN: Indiana University Press, pp. 99–118.

Winship, J. (1987) *Inside Women's Magazines*. London: Pandora Press.

Wolff, N. (1990) *The Beauty Myth*. London: Chatto and Windus.

Women Take Issue (1978) Women's Studies Group, Centre for Contemporary Cultural Studies. London: Hutchinson.

Yin, R. (1989) *Case Study Research: Design and Methods*. Beverly Hills, CA: Sage.

Zaat, M. (1982) 'De door Lilian Rubin gevolgde methode van onderzoek [Lilian Rubin's research method]', *Tijdschrift voor Vrouwenstudies*, 3(1): 74–91.

Zoonen, L. van (1988) 'Rethinking women and the news', *European Journal of Communication*, 3(1): 35–54.

Zoonen, L. van (1989) 'Professional socialization of feminist journalists in the Netherlands', *Women's Studies in Communication*, 12(3): 1–23.

Zoonen, L. van (1991a) 'Feminist perspectives on the media', in J. Curran and M. Gurevitch (eds), *Mass Media & Society*. London: Edward Arnold, pp. 33–54.

Zoonen, L. van (1991b) 'A tyranny of intimacy? women, femininity and television news', in P. Dahlgren and C. Sparks (eds), *Communication and Citizenship: Journalism and the Public Sphere in the New Media Age*. London: Routledge, pp. 217–35.

Zoonen, L. van (1991c) *'Moeten Strijdende Vrouwen zo Grof Zijn?': De Vrouwenbeweging en de Media [The Women's Movement and the Media]*. Amsterdam: SUA.

Zoonen, L. van (1992a) 'Feminist theory and information technology', *Media, Culture & Society*, 14(1): 9–30.

Zoonen, L. van (1992b) 'The women's movement and the media: constructing a public identity', *European Journal of Communication*, 7(4): 453–76.

Zoonen, L. van (1992c) 'Gender and film', *Journal of Communication*, Autumn, 42(4): 180–5.

Zoonen, L. van (1994) 'A dance of death? new social movements and mass media', in D. Paletz (ed.), *Political Communication Research in Action: States, Institutions, Movements, Audiences*. Cresskill, NJ: Hampton Press.

Zoonen, L. van and Donsbach, W. (1988) 'Professional values and gender in British and German journalism'. Paper presented at the 38th Annual Conference of the International Communication Association, New Orleans.

Index